TEXAS

HOME LANDSCAPING

Including Oklahoma

Other titles available in the *Home Landscaping* series:

CALIFORNIA

MID-ATLANTIC

MIDWEST
including Southern Canada

NORTHEAST
including Southeast Canada

NORTHWEST
including Western British Columbia

SOUTHERN COASTAL

SOUTHEAST

WESTERN

TEXAS

HOME LANDSCAPING

Including Oklahoma

Greg Grant

Roger Holmes

CREATIVE HOMEOWNER®

TEXAS HOME LANDSCAPING
WORDWORKS

EDITORS	Roger Holmes, Greg Grant
EDITORIAL CONSULTANT	Rita Buchanan
CREATIVE HOMEOWNER EDITOR	Neil Soderstrom
COPY EDITORS	Sarah Disbrow
INTERIOR DESIGN	Deborah Fillion
ILLUSTRATORS	Steve Buchanan (Portfolio of Designs); Michelle Angle Farrar, Lee Hov, Robert LaPointe, Rick Daskam, Teresa Nicole Green (Guide to Installation)

Manufactured in China

Current Printing (last digit)
10 9 8 7 6 5

Texas Home Landscaping, Third Edition
ISBN: 978-1-58011-513-1

Creative Homeowner®, *www.CreativeHomeowner.com,*
is distributed exclusively in North America by
Fox Chapel Publishing Company, Inc., 800-457-9112,
903 Square Street, Mount Joy, PA 17552,
and in the United Kingdom by Grantham Book Service,
Trent Road, Grantham, Lincolnshire, NG31 7XQ.

We are always looking for talented authors. To submit an idea, please send a brief inquiry to acquisitions@foxchapelpublishing.com.

About the Authors

Greg Grant is a horticulturist with the Stephen F. Austin State University Pineywoods Native Plant Center in Nacogdoches. He previously held positions with the Texas Agricultural Extension Service, Louisiana State University, Lone Star Growers, San Antonio Botanical Garden, and Mercer Arboretum. He is a regular contributor to *Texas Gardener, Neil Sperry's Gardens,* and *Ornamental Outlook* magazines and co-author of *The Southern Heirloom Garden.*

Roger Holmes is the founding editor of *Fine Gardening* magazine. He co-edited the monumental Taylor's *Master Guide to Gardening* and other highly regarded gardening books, and produced the landscaping series of which this book is part. He also co-wrote Creative Homeowner's *Creating Good Gardens.*

Safety First

Though all concepts and methods in this book have been reviewed for safety, it is not possible to overstate the importance of using the safest working methods possible. What follows are reminders—do's and don'ts for yard work and landscaping. They are not substitutes for your own common sense.

- *Always* use caution, care, and good judgment when following the procedures described in this book.

- *Always* determine locations of underground utility lines before you dig, and then avoid them by a safe distance. Buried lines may be for gas, electricity, communications, or water. Start research by contacting your local building officials. Also contact local utility companies; they will often send a representative free of charge to help you map their lines. In addition, there are private utility locator firms that may be listed in your Yellow Pages. Note: previous owners may have installed underground drainage, sprinkler, and lighting lines without mapping them.

- *Always* read and heed the manufacturer's instructions for using a tool, especially the warnings.

- *Always* ensure that the electrical setup is safe; be sure that no circuit is overloaded and that all power tools and electrical outlets are properly grounded and protected by a ground-fault circuit interrupter (GFCI). Do not use power tools in wet locations.

- *Always* wear eye protection when using chemicals, sawing wood, pruning trees and shrubs, using power tools, and striking metal onto metal or concrete.

- *Always* read labels on chemicals, solvents, and other products; provide ventilation; heed warnings.

- *Always* wear heavy rubber gloves rated for chemicals, not mere household rubber gloves, when handling toxins.

- *Always* wear appropriate gloves in situations in which your hands could be injured by rough surfaces, sharp edges, thorns, or poisonous plants.

- *Always* wear a disposable face mask or a special filtering respirator when creating sawdust or working with toxic gardening substances.

- *Always* keep your hands and other body parts away from the business ends of blades, cutters, and bits.

- *Always* obtain approval from local building officials before undertaking construction of permanent structures.

- *Never* work with power tools when you are tired or under the influence of alcohol or drugs.

- *Never* carry sharp or pointed tools, such as knives or saws, in your pockets. If you carry such tools, use special-purpose tool scabbards.

The Landscape Designers

John Ahrens, with Barry Landry, RLA, and Nena Scott, King's Creek Landscape Management, Austin, Texas. Their designs appear on pp. 36–39, 60–63, 70–73, and 88–91.

Mark Bowen, Living Art Landscapes, Houston, Texas. His designs appear on pp. 30–33, 80–83, and 84–87.

Michael Buccino, Michael Buccino Associates, Palm Desert, California. His designs appear on pp. 34–35 and 64–65.

Rosa Finsley, with Cheryl Bryant, King's Creek Gardens, Cedar Hill, Texas. Their designs appear on pp. 52–55, 94–97, and 112–115.

Michael Parkey, Dallas, Texas. His designs appear on pp. 20–23, 56–59, and 100–103.

Susan Romiti and Ross Holmquist, Mike Parker Landscape, Laguna Beach, California. Their design appears on pp. 28–29.

Carolyn Singer owns Foothill Cottage Gardens, Grass Valley, California. Her design appears on pp. 78–79.

John S. Troy, with Anne Solsbery, John S. Troy Landscape, San Antonio, Texas. Their designs appear on pp. 40–43, 48–51, and 66–69.

John Valentino and Bob Truxell, Truxell and Valentino Landscape Development, Inc., Clovis, California. Their designs appear on pp. 98–99, and 110–111.

Jenny Webber, Oakland, California. Her design appears on pp. 92–93.

Mary Wilhite and Sharon Lee Smith, Blue Moon Gardens, Tyler, Texas. Their designs appear on pp. 24–27, 44–47, 74–77, and 106–109.

Richard William Wogisch, Oasis Gardens, San Francisco, California. His design appears on pp. 104–105.

Contents

About This Book

Of all the home-improvement projects homeowners tackle, few offer greater rewards than landscaping. At the main entrance, an attractive brick walkway flanked by eye-catching shrubs and perennials provides a cheerful welcome. A carefully placed grouping of small trees, shrubs, and fence panels creates privacy on the patio or screens a nearby eyesore from view. An island bed divides the backyard into several areas for a variety of activities.

Planting and caring for shrubs, perennials, and other plants can afford years of enjoyment. For those who like to build things, outdoor construction projects can be especially satisfying.

While the installation and maintenance of plants and outdoor structures are within the means and abilities of most people, few of us are as comfortable determining exactly which plants or structures to use and how best to combine them. It's one thing to decide to dress up the front entrance or patio, another to come up with a design for doing so.

That's where this book comes in. Here, in the Portfolio of Designs, you'll find designs for more than 28 common home-landscaping situations, created by landscape professionals. Drawing on years of experience, these designers balance functional requirements and aesthetic possibilities, choosing the right plant or structure for the task, confident of its proven performance in similar landscaping situations.

The second section, Plant Profiles, gives information on all the plants used in the book. Complementing the Portfolio of Designs and Plant Profiles is the Guide to Installation, the book's third section, which will help you install and maintain the plants and structures called for in the designs. The discussions that follow take a closer look at each section; we've also printed representative pages of the sections on pp. 9 and 10 and pointed out their features.

Portfolio of Designs

This section is the heart of the book, providing examples of landscaping situations and solutions that are at once inspiring and accessible. Some are simple, others more complex, but each one can be installed in a few weekends by homeowners with no special training or experience.

For most situations, we present two designs, the second a variation of the first. As the sample pages on the facing page show, the first design is displayed on a two-page spread. A perspective illustration (called a "rendering") depicts what the design will look like several years after installation, when the perennials and many of the shrubs have reached mature size. To see how a landscape

changes within a single year, see "Seasons in Your Landscape," pp. 12-15. For more on how plantings change as they age, refer to "As Your Landscape Grows," pp. 16-17. The rendering also shows the planting as it will appear at a particular time of year. A site plan indicates the positions of the plants and structures on a scaled grid. Text introduces the situation and the design and describes the plants and projects used.

The second design, presented on the second two-page spread, addresses the same situation as the first but differs in one or more important aspects. It might show a planting suited for a shady rather than a sunny site, or it might incorporate different structures or kinds of plants to create a different look. As in the first design, we present a rendering, site plan, and written information, but in briefer form. The second spread also includes photographs of a selection of the plants featured in the two designs. The photos showcase noteworthy qualities—lovely flowers, handsome foliage, or striking form—that these plants contribute to the designs.

Install plants exactly as shown here or rearrange groupings and substitute favorite ones to suit your taste.

The Texas State Flower

Although the wildflower called "Bluebonnet" (*Lupinus subcarnosus*) is the state flower, we did not include it in this book because it is not easy to grow. A winter annual, it does best in the middle of the state. If you want to replace any annuals in the Portfolio of Designs section with Bluebonnet, it is widely available as seed. However, it is rarely successful, and because Bluebonnet is a spring bloomer, it is typically not available for fall or winter transplanting.

PORTFOLIO OF DESIGNS

FIRST DESIGN OPTION

Plants & Projects
Noteworthy qualities of the plants and structures and their contributions to the design.

Concept Box
Summarizes an important aspect of the design; tells whether the site is sunny or shady and what season is depicted in the rendering.

Site Plan
Positions all plants and structures on a scaled grid.

Summary
An overview of the situation and the design.

Rendering
Shows how the design will look when plants are well established.

Summary
Addressing the same situation as the first design, this variation may differ in design concept, site conditions, or plant selection.

Variations on a Theme
Photos of inspiring designs in similar situations.

SECOND DESIGN OPTION

Site Plan
Plants and structures on a scaled grid.

Concept Box
Site, season, and design summary.

Rendering
Depicts the design when plants are well established.

PLANT PROFILES

Choices
Selections here help you choose from the many varieties of certain popular plants.

Detailed Plant Information
Descriptions of each plant's noteworthy qualities and requirements for planting and care.

Plant Portraits
Photos of selected plants.

GUIDE TO INSTALLATION

Sidebars
Detailed information on special topics, set within ruled boxes.

Step-by-Step
Illustrations show process; steps are keyed by number to discussion in the main text.

ABOUT THIS BOOK **11**

Plant Profiles

This section of the book includes a description of each of the plants featured in the Portfolio. These profiles outline the plants' basic preferences for environmental conditions—such as soil, moisture, and sun or shade—and provide advice about planting and ongoing care.

Working with plant experts in Texas, we selected plants carefully, following a few simple guidelines: every plant should be a proven performer in the state; once established, it should thrive without pampering. All plants should be available from a major local nursery or garden center. If they're not in stock, they could be ordered, or you could ask the nursery staff to recommend suitable substitutes.

In the Portfolio section, you'll note that plants are referred to by their common name but are cross-referenced to the Plant Profiles section by their Latinized scientific name. While common names are familiar to many people, they can be confusing. Distinctly different plants can share the same common name, or one plant can have several different common names. Scientific names, therefore, ensure greater accuracy and are more appropriate for a reference section such as this. Although you can confidently purchase most of the plants in this book from local nurseries using the common name, knowing the scientific name allows you to ensure that the plant you're ordering is the same one shown in our design.

Guide to Installation

In this section you'll find detailed instructions and illustrations covering all the techniques you'll need to install any design from start to finish. Here we explain how to think your way through a landscaping project and anticipate the various steps. Then you'll learn how to do each part of the job: readying the site; laying out the design; choosing materials; addressing basic irrigation needs; building paths, trellises, or other structures; preparing the soil for planting; buying the recommended plants and putting them in place; and caring for the plants to keep

them healthy and attractive year after year.

We've taken care to make installation of built elements simple and straightforward. The paths, trellises, and arbors all use basic, readily available materials, and they can be assembled by people who have no special skills or tools beyond those commonly used for home maintenance. The designs can be adapted easily to meet specific needs or to fit with the style of your house or other landscaping features.

Installing different designs requires different techniques. You can find the techniques that you need by following the cross-references in the Portfolio to

pages in the Guide to Installation, or by skimming the Guide. You'll find that many basic techniques are reused from one project to the next. You might want to start with one of the smaller, simpler designs. Gradually you'll develop the skills and confidence to do any project you choose.

Most of the designs in this book can be installed in several weekends; some will take a little longer. Digging planting beds and erecting fences and arbors can be strenuous work. If you lack energy for such tasks, consider hiring a neighborhood teenager to help out; local landscaping services can provide more comprehensive help.

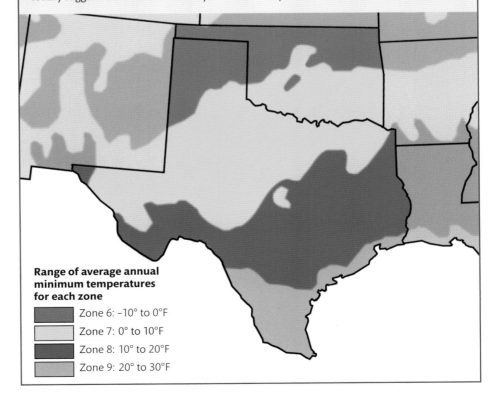

TEXAS AND OKLAHOMA HARDINESS ZONES

This map is based on one developed by the U.S. Department of Agriculture. It divides Texas and its neighbors into "hardiness zones" based on minimum winter temperatures. While most of the plants in this book will survive the lowest temperatures in Zone 7, a few may not. These few are noted in the Plant Profiles descriptions, where we have usually suggested alternatives. When you

buy plants, most will have "hardiness" designations corresponding to a USDA hardiness zone on the map. A Zone 7 plant, for example, can be expected to survive winter temperatures as low as 0°F, and it can be used with confidence in Zones 7 and 8, but not in the colder Zone 6. It is useful to know your zone and the zone designation of any plants that you wish to add to those in this book.

Range of average annual minimum temperatures for each zone

- Zone 6: –10° to 0°F
- Zone 7: 0° to 10°F
- Zone 8: 10° to 20°F
- Zone 9: 20° to 30°F

Seasons in Your Landscape

One of the rewards of landscaping is watching how plants change through the seasons. During the winter months, you look forward to the bright, fresh flowers of spring. Then the lush green foliage of summer is transformed into the blazing colors of fall. Perennials that rest underground in winter can grow chest-high by midsummer, and hence a flower bed that looks flat and bare in December becomes a jungle in July.

To illustrate typical seasonal changes, we've chosen one of the designs from this book (see pp. 74–75) and shown here how it would look in spring, summer, fall, and winter. As you can see, this planting looks different from one season to the next, but it always remains interesting. Try to remember this example of transformation as you look at the other designs in this book. There we show how the planting will appear in one season and call attention to any plants that will stand out at other times of year.

The task of tending a landscape also changes with the seasons. So we've noted the most important seasonal jobs in the annual work cycle.

Gaura

Dwarf pampas grass

SPRING

Gaura

Dwarf pampas grass

Chaste tree

Soft-tip yucca

Trailing rosemary

Trailing rosemary

SUMMER

Chaste tree

Soft-tip yucca

Autumn sage

Gray santolina

Red yucca

Russian sage

Spring

The spring flower season begins in March in much of Texas and peaks in April when the lawns turn green and the trees leaf out. In this garden, spring offers a refreshing display of new growth. Grasses and perennials are greening up, and a thick profusion of new shoots sprout from the cut-back crown of the chaste tree. A sprinkling of miniature blue flowers on the rosemary and the gaura's pinkish white flower buds garnish the greenery. Do a thorough cleanup in early spring. Remove last year's perennial flower stalks and foliage, cut ornamental grasses to the ground, prune shrubs and trees, renew the mulch, lightly fertilize, and neaten the edges between flower beds and lawn.

Summer

The summer garden is an explosion of color. Nearly every plant is in bloom. The nodding lily-like flowers of the soft-tip yucca, the purple spikes of the chaste tree, and the coral red spikes of the red yucca make a big show. The diminutive blue, white, and yellow flowers of the Russian sage, gaura, and santolina shout less for attention but are no less pleasing. Despite its name, autumn sage produces a fine show of tubular red flowers. White plumes wave in the breeze above clumps of dwarf pampas grass. Water new plantings at least once a week during dry spells, and water older plants, too, if the soil gets so dry that they wilt. Pull any weeds that sprout up through the mulch; this is easiest when the soil is moist.

Fall

Fall brings changes in the garden as well as mercifully cooler temperatures. New for the season are the small lavender-purple flowers that almost smother the pale gray foliage of the fall aster. Dead-heading has produced a full second bloom on the chaste tree, while distinctive seedpods have replaced bright flowers on the soft-tip and red yuccas. Gaura and autumn sage continue to bloom, and the plumes of the pampas grass reflect some weathering. The Russian sage has lost most of its tiny blossoms, but its foliage is an attractive, wispy presence. The santolina has been sheared to keep it tidy. You can leave grasses and perennial stalks standing all winter, if you choose, or clear them away whenever hard frosts turn them brown or knock them down. Toss the stems on the compost pile, along with any leaves that you rake up.

FALL

Gaura

Dwarf pampas grass

Autumn sage

WINTER

Trailing rosemary

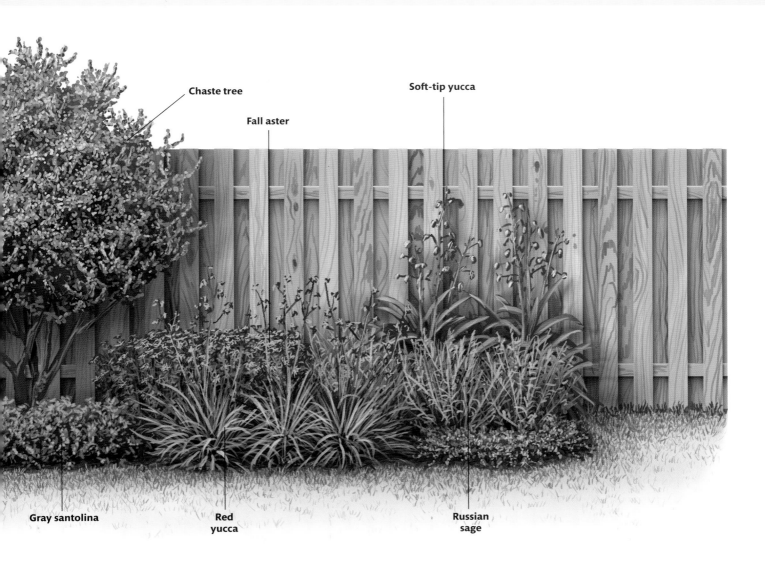

Chaste tree

Soft-tip yucca

Fall aster

Gray santolina

Red yucca

Russian sage

Trailing rosemary

Winter

In winter, when much of the landscape turns tan and brown, you'll appreciate evergreen plants such as the red and soft-tip yuccas, trailing rosemary, and santolina. After a hard frost, the Russian sage, fall aster, and gaura have been cut back to ground-hugging crowns. The narrow leaves and plumes of the dwarf pampas grass remain a pleasing sight throughout the winter, as do the branching forms of the chaste tree and autumn sage. In late winter, cut back these two plants in preparation for vigorous new growth in the spring.

As Your Landscape Grows

Landscapes change over the years. As plants grow, the overall look evolves from sparse to lush. Trees cast cool shade where the sun used to shine. Shrubs and hedges grow tall and dense enough to provide privacy. Perennials and ground covers spread to form colorful patches of foliage and flowers. Meanwhile, paths, arbors, fences, and other structures gain the comfortable patina of age.

Continuing change over the years—sometimes rapid and dramatic, sometimes slow and subtle—is one of the joys of landscaping. It is also one of the challenges. Anticipating how fast plants will grow and how big they will eventually become is difficult, even for professional designers, and it was a major concern in formulating the designs for this book.

To illustrate the kinds of changes to expect in a planting, these pages show one of the designs at three different "ages." Even though a new planting may look sparse at first, it will soon fill in. And because of careful spacing, the planting will look as good in ten to fifteen years as it does after three to five. It will, of course, look different, but that's part of the fun.

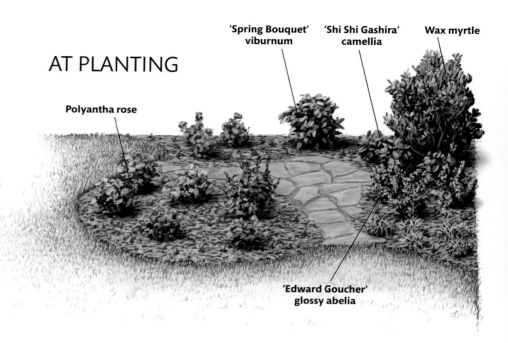

AT PLANTING

'Spring Bouquet' viburnum

'Shi Shi Gashira' camellia

Wax myrtle

Polyantha rose

'Edward Goucher' glossy abelia

THREE TO FIVE YEARS

Tropical plumbago

'Shi Shi Gashira' camellia

'Edward Goucher' glossy abelia

'Bath's Pink' dianthus

'Blue Princess' verbena

'Indigo Spires' salvia

At Planting—Here's how the backyard hideaway (pp. 86–87) might appear immediately after a fall planting. The plants, of course, are small, though their size may vary from what we show here if you want to spend more for more mature trees and shrubs. The multitrunked wax myrtle looks like a bush rather than the small tree it will become. The viburnum, glossy abelia, and polyantha rose are several years from filling out their spaces or your expectations. With a good fall start and spring awakening, the perennials will make a creditable show next summer. The first year after planting, be sure to water during dry spells and to pull weeds that pop up through the mulch.

Three to Five Years—As shown here in fall, the planting has filled out nicely. Limbed up to about 5 ft., the wax myrtle provides shade for the bench, while the nearby shrubs have grown to make a comfy enclosure. The now well-established perennials join the shrubs in producing the blue and pink floral scene. Evergreen foliage of the wax myrtle, camellia, viburnum, and glossy abelia make this an attractive spot through the winter as well.

Ten to Fifteen Years—Shown again in fall, the planting has become even more of a hideaway with the passing years. The wax myrtle envelopes the site with its presence and its shade. The shrubs are fuller and larger, though kept in bounds by judicious pruning. The perennials have been divided several times since planting to keep them healthy and tidy looking. Their off-spring may feature in parts of the landscape elsewhere on the property.

TEN TO FIFTEEN YEARS

Wax myrtle

'Spring Bouquet' viburnum

Tropical plumbago

'Shi Shi Gashira' camellia

Polyantha rose

'Edward Goucher' glossy abelia

'Bath's Pink' dianthus

'Blue Princess' verbena

'Indigo Spires' salvia

Portfolio *of* Designs

As you peruse the following pages, you will find 48 home landscape designs by 19 notable landscape designers who have devised ways to enhance entrances, decks, and patios; create gardens of colorful perennials and shrubs as well as structures and plantings for shady hideaways; dress up nondescript walls; and even make a centerpiece of a lowly recycling area. Large color illustrations show what the designs will look like, and site plans delineate the layout and planting scheme. Each design is accompanied by text that describes the plants and projects appearing in them. Installed as shown or adapted to meet your site and personal preferences, these designs can make your property more attractive, more useful, and—most important— more enjoyable for you, your family, and your friends.

Up Front Informal

TURN A SMALL FRONT YARD INTO A WELCOMING GARDEN

With a little imagination and a host of pleasing plants, front yards can be transformed into inviting front gardens. Replacing the existing lawn and concrete walkways with colorful plantings and decorative paving will not only reduce mowing and watering, it will also provide a pleasant setting for welcoming guests or watching the world go by.

The transformation from yard to garden begins here with an oversized front walk that widens into a space for sitting. The front walk and patio are tightly laid flagstone to accommodate foot traffic and furniture. A more casual path to the drive is set with wide joints that are planted with a grasslike ground cover.

Bordering the seating area is an informal planting of trees and shrubs. The small red oak and two large hollies will create a cozy atmosphere around the entry, and the tree will provide shade as it matures. Beneath these taller plants are colorful shrubs, grasses, perennials, and a durable carpet of evergreen ground covers. While the ground covers won't stand up to much traffic, they will look good year-round with less water and maintenance than a turfgrass lawn.

The planting is illustrated here at its showiest—during the cooler months of fall—when the weather invites lingering outdoors. But each season holds attractions. An abundance of emerging foliage will give the garden a fresh look in spring, the Turk's cap blooms will invite hummingbirds in summer, and evergreen foliage and purple and red berries will keep color in the garden through winter.

Plants & Projects

Once established, the plants in this design are not particularly demanding. Prune trees and shrubs as needed to maintain size and shape. Seasonal cleanup will keep the planting tidy.

SITE: Sunny

SEASON: Fall

CONCEPT: Well-chosen plants and paving create an entry garden of comfortable informality.

Ⓐ Texas red oak (use 1 plant) Growing 30 ft. high and wide after many years, this red oak is a fitting shade tree for a small garden. It has silvery bark and lacy leaves that turn from green to red and orange in fall. See *Quercus buckleyi*, p. 140.

Ⓑ 'Warren's Red' possumhaw holly (use 2) These multitrunked deciduous hollies have small lustrous dark-green leaves. They bear countless showy red berries in fall that persist on bare silver-gray branches in the winter. See *Ilex decidua* 'Warren's Red', p. 132.

Ⓒ American beautyberry (use 1) Prized for its bright clusters of violet berries that hang on through winter, this deciduous shrub spreads into a loose thicket of green leaves under the red oak. See *Callicarpa americana*, p. 123.

Ⓓ Dwarf Burford holly (use 4) This durable shrub's glossy evergreen foliage and dense round shape create a handsome screen for the heavenly bamboo. Red berries peek through the foliage in winter. See *Ilex cornuta* 'Burfordii Nana', p. 132.

Ⓔ 'Gulf Stream' heavenly bamboo (use 9) An outstanding evergreen shrub. Fine-textured foliage turns from bronze to green to red. See *Nandina domestica* 'Gulf Stream', p. 137.

Ⓕ 'Strictus' porcupine grass (use 2) This ornamental grass forms a graceful vase of yellow-striped emerald green leaves. Silvery tan flower plumes wave above the plant in fall. The foliage and flowers stay showy even while the grass is dormant in winter. See *Miscanthus sinensis* 'Strictus', p. 136.

Ⓖ Inland sea oats (use 12) A clump-forming grass grown for long, dangling, oatlike seedheads that dance above the foliage in late summer, turning from light green to bronze and then to tan. See *Chasmanthium latifolium*, p. 125.

Ⓗ Turk's cap (use 8) Cousin to hibiscus, these bushy perennials make an attractive flowering hedge near the patio. Deep-green foliage is speckled from late spring to fall with red blossoms resembling small Turkish turbans. See *Malvaviscus arboreus drummondii*, p. 136.

Ⓘ Fall aster (use 16) These carefree perennials form a solid mass of fine-textured foliage completely covered in autumn with lavender-purple daisylike blossoms. See *Aster oblongifolius*, p. 120.

Ⓙ Mexican bush sage (use 7) From late summer to frost, this grayish green bushy perennial bristles with long spikes of purple and white flowers. See *Salvia leucantha*, p. 145.

Ⓚ Ground covers (as needed) Two low-growing evergreen perennials make durable "welcome mats" along the paths and around the patio. Asian jasmine (*Trachelospermum asiaticum*, p. 148) spreads to form a thick glossy carpet of small green leaves on both sides of the front walk. Mondo grass (*Ophiopogon japonicus*, p. 138) has fine dark-green foliage that adds grassy texture around the patio and between the flagstones on the narrow walk to the driveway.

Ⓛ Container Plant a patio pot with purple fountain grass for a fountain of foliage topped with foxtail-like flowers. See Annuals, p. 119.

Ⓜ Paving A wide front walk of flagstone handles heavy foot traffic and outdoor furniture. A more casual flagstone path to the drive has wide joints filled with prepared soil and planted with mondo grass. See p. 160.

SITE: Sunny

SEASON: Summer

CONCEPT: A front garden of elegant simplicity complements a home with a symmetrical facade.

1 square = 1 ft.

D 'Climbing Pinkie' polyantha rose

B Glossy abelia

A 'Natchez' crapemyrtle

E 'Tangerine Beauty' cross vine

L Fence

M Walkway

C Dwarf yaupon holly

F 'Morning Light' Japanese maiden grass

K Mexican heather

H 'Blue Princess' verbena

G 'Powis Castle' artemisia

J 'Bath's Pink' dianthus

I Variegated lilyturf

B Glossy abelia

Plants & Projects

A **'Natchez' crapemyrtle** (use 4 plants)
A small deciduous tree with mottled cinnamon-brown bark and shiny bright-green foliage with good fall color. The tips of the branches bear large clusters of crepe-papery white flowers in summer. See *Lagerstroemia* x *fauriei* 'Natchez', p. 133.

B **Glossy abelia** (use 2)
Chosen for its dense deep green foliage, this shrub is covered in summer with honeysuckle-like, pinkish-white flowers that attract butterflies. See *Abelia* x *grandiflora*, p. 118.

C **Dwarf yaupon holly** (use 26)
These evergreen shrubs form neat mounds of tiny, oval, olive-green leaves. They can be sheared into a low hedge for an even more formal appearance. See *Ilex vomitoria* 'Nana', p. 132.

D **'Climbing Pinkie' polyantha rose** (use 2)
A mannerly, thornless, climbing rose that bears loose clusters of pink, semidouble flowers from April through November. See *Rosa* x *polyantha* 'Climbing Pinkie', p. 142.

E **'Tangerine Beauty' cross vine** (use 3)
This twining vine will cover the fence with lustrous, dark green

Up front formal

Homes that have a symmetrical facade are especially suited for a formal garden makeover, one that complements and accents the geometry of the architecture. This design offers a simpler makeover than the first by retaining existing concrete walks. The symmetrical layout features a central oval of lawn flanked by almost mirror image plantings on each side of the main walk. A loose-surface path extends the cross walk to a garden bench, a perfect perch for enjoying the view.

Whether approaching from the street or the drive, visitors get an attractive welcome. Small flowering trees and a hedge of low-growing shrubs give the garden its structure. A variety of contrasting foliage textures and colors provide interest year-round. And there are flowers in spring and summer.

leaves all year. Bears orange or red trumpet-shaped flowers in late spring and again in fall. See *Bignonia capreolata* 'Tangerine Beauty', p. 121.

F **'Morning Light' Japanese maiden grass** (use 2)
This lovely grass has slender foliage and a fountainlike shape. See *Miscanthus sinensis* 'Morning Light', p. 136.

G **'Powis Castle' artemisia** (use 14)
Silvery mounds of lacy foliage make this evergreen perennial an outstanding choice next to the lavender-blue verbena and the pink-blooming climbing rose. See *Artemisia* x 'Powis Castle', p. 120.

H **'Blue Princess' verbena** (use 16)
This perennial forms a fine mat of deep-green leaves topped with masses of tiny lavender-blue flowers. Especially showy in spring. See *Verbena* x *hybrida* 'Blue Princess', p. 149.

I **Variegated lilyturf** (use 50)
This evergreen ground cover forms grassy clumps of slender leaves striped bright green and creamy yellow. Bears spikes of very small lavender flowers in June. See *Liriope muscari* 'Variegata', p. 137.

J **'Bath's Pink' dianthus** (use 44)
A fine-textured perennial that forms a mat of silver-gray foliage all year. Topped in spring with pretty pink flowers. See *Dianthus* 'Bath's Pink', p. 127.

K **Mexican heather** (use 12)
For texture as well as color, plant in the circular bed where the walks intersect. This tender perennial forms a low bush of tiny leaves in fernlike fans and delicate lavender-pink flowers. See *Cuphea hyssopifolia*, p. 126.

L **Fence**
Interlaced with flowering vines, the lattice-panel fence behind the bench creates a sense of privacy, as well as a focal point for the garden. See p. 183.

M **Walkway**
A loose surface of decomposed granite extends the existing walkway to the bench and provides a level surface beneath it. See p. 160.

PLANT PORTRAITS

These well-behaved plants require little care while garnering lots of attention.
● = First design, pp. 20–21
▲ = Second design, pp. 22–23

Variegated lilyturf
(*Liriope muscari* 'Variegata', p. 137) ▲

'Strictus' porcupine grass
(*Miscanthus sinensis*, p. 136) ●

'Natchez' crapemyrtle
(*Lagerstroemia* x *fauriei*, p. 133) ▲

'Climbing Pinkie' polyantha rose
(*Rosa* x *polyantha*, p. 142) ▲

Dwarf Burford holly
(*Ilex cornuta* 'Burfordii Nana', p. 132) ●

'Warren's Red' possumhaw holly
(*Ilex decidua*, p. 132) ●

A Foundation with Flair

FLOWERS AND FOLIAGE CREATE A FRONT GARDEN

Rare is the home without foundation plantings. These simple skirtings of greenery hide unattractive underpinnings and help integrate a house with its surroundings. Useful as these plantings are, they are too often monochromatic expanses of clipped evergreens, dull as dishwater. But as this design shows, a low-maintenance planting can be more varied, more colorful, and more fun.

By adding smaller plants in front of the taller shrubs near the house and including a small flowering tree, a mix of shrubs and perennials, and a flowering vine along the railing, the design transforms a foundation planting into a small garden. Here, there's something for everyone to enjoy, from porch sitters to passersby.

Starting in early spring with fragrant jasmine and rosemary and the eye-stopping flowers of the esperanza and verbena, the garden reaches full exuberance in summer, with bright flowers in yellows, purples, blues, and oranges. Foliage in a mixture of greens and grays and a variety of textures showcases the flowers, several of which attract butterflies and hummingbirds. And the evergreen leaves of many plants extend the planting's appeal through the winter.

SITE: Sunny

SEASON: Midsummer

CONCEPT: Mixing small trees, vines, shrubs, and perennials makes a colorful foundation planting.

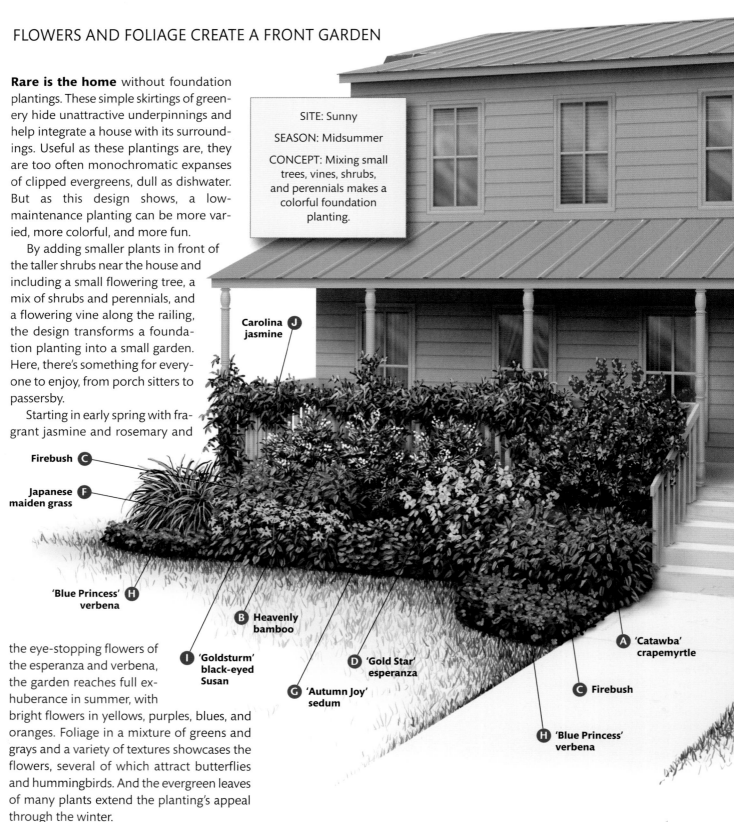

Carolina jasmine **J**

Firebush **C**

Japanese maiden grass **F**

'Blue Princess' verbena **H**

B Heavenly bamboo

I 'Goldsturm' black-eyed Susan

G 'Autumn Joy' sedum

D 'Gold Star' esperanza

A 'Catawba' crapemyrtle

C Firebush

H 'Blue Princess' verbena

Porch

Porch columns

Steps

Lawn

Walk

1 square = 1 ft.

Heavenly bamboo

Rosemary

Japanese maiden grass

Firebush

'Gold Star' esperanza

'Blue Princess' verbena

Plants & Projects

This is a low-care planting that offers a dazzling display of color in summer and fall. In addition to routine seasonal pruning, cut the firebush back in midsummer to keep it in check. If the verbena quits blooming, shear it back to about one-third to encourage new bloom. Train the jasmine up porch columns by attaching the vines to wires with twist ties. Add trellising if you want additional shade on the porch. For winter color in the beds, consider planting pansies or snapdragons when perennials fade.

A 'Catawba' crapemyrtle (use 1 plant)
Next to the steps, this small shrublike tree greets guests with showy purple flowers in summer and brilliant orange leaves in fall. See *Lagerstroemia indica* 'Catawba', p. 133.

B Heavenly bamboo (use 5)
The foliage of this evergreen shrub forms lacy layers that take on burgundy tones in fall. Clusters of tiny white flowers in summer produce bright-red berries that add interest in the winter. See *Nandina domestica*, p. 137.

C Firebush (use 6)
Small red-orange flowers light up this bushy tropical shrub in summer, attracting butterflies and hummingbirds as well as human admirers. See *Hamelia patens*, p. 129.

D 'Gold Star' esperanza (use 6)
Known also as Texas yellow bells, this shrub bears big bright clusters of yellow flowers from spring to fall, creating a colorful contrast with the crapemyrtle and firebush beside it. See *Tecoma stans* 'Gold Star', p. 148.

E Rosemary (use 2)
This shrubby perennial herb forms a tight bouquet of branches clad in small needle-like leaves and topped with small blue flowers in early spring. It makes a fragrant edging next to the steps, within easy reach to snip a few leaves for cooking. See *Rosmarinus officinalis*, p. 143.

F Japanese maiden grass (use 3)
A beautiful fine-textured grass that looks like a fountain. Flower plumes appear in late summer, and both leaves and flowers stay attractive through winter. See *Miscanthus sinensis*, p. 137.

G 'Autumn Joy' sedum (use 3)
This bold-textured perennial grows in neat mounds of grayish green succulent leaves. Dense clusters of tiny burnt-orange flowers appear in fall, turn pink, and gradually fade to tan. See *Sedum* 'Autumn Joy', p. 146.

H 'Blue Princess' verbena (use 8)
Butterflies can't resist this perennial's lavender-blue flowers, which bloom continuously from spring to fall in clusters the size of silver dollars. See *Verbena* x *hybrida* 'Blue Princess', p. 149.

I 'Goldsturm' black-eyed Susan (use 4)
In early summer golden dark-eyed daisylike flowers rise above this perennial's deep-green heart-shaped foliage. See *Rudbeckia fulgida* 'Goldsturm', p. 143.

J Carolina jasmine (use 3)
Shiny neat evergreen leaves and a show of fragrant yellow flowers in spring make this vigorous vine ideal for training up porch columns or along a railing. See *Gelsemium sempervirens*, p. 129.

PLANT PORTRAITS

This mix of shrubs and perennials will dress up the most nondescript foundation, while requiring little care.

● = First design, pp. 24–25

▲ = Second design, pp. 26–27

Heavenly Bamboo
(*Nandina domestica*, p. 137) ●

'Catawba' crapemyrtle
(*Lagerstroemia indica*, p. 133) ●

Sasanqua camellia
(*Camellia sasanqua*, p. 123) ▲

'Gumpo White' dwarf evergreen azalea
(*Rhododendron*, p. 141) ▲

'Wheeler's Dwarf' pittosporum
(*Pittosporum tobira*, p. 139) ▲

In a shady setting

This foundation planting graces a house with a shady entry. The mix of evergreen foliage and cool white flowers not only brightens up the shade, but also makes it even more welcome on a hot summer's day.

Foliage is the key here. The large jagged leaves of the fatsia and the more delicately cut fronds of the holly fern are striking accents. The less dramatic foliage of the evergreen and camellia azaleas is a highly effective backdrop for displaying the lovely flowers of these plants.

Lower-growing perennials and bulbs also contribute attractive foliage, and their flowers reinforce the planting's flowering color scheme of cool whites and pinks. With its mix of bold foliage and lovely flowers, this planting can be enjoyed from the windows as well as the street.

Plants & Projects

A Sasanqua camellia (use 1 plant)
Lovely flowers and glossy leaves on this small evergreen tree will accent and soften the corner of the house. Camellias come in many sizes and colors. For this design, choose a late-blooming and tall-growing, white-flowered cultivar. See *Camellia sasanqua*, p. 123.

B Fatsia (use 4)
This evergreen shrub hides its stems in layers of very large, shiny, bright green leaves. A handsome foundation plant, it also provides a bold contrast to the azaleas and ferns. See *Fatsia japonica*, p. 127.

C 'Gumpo White' dwarf evergreen azalea (use 8)
This attractive fine-leaved shrub blooms profusely in spring and is just the right size to tuck in under the windows. See *Rhododendron* x 'Gumpo White', p. 141.

Sasanqua camellia **A**

Purple heart **F**

F Snowflake

C 'Gumpo White' dwarf evergreen azalea

B Fatsia

D 'Wheeler's Dwarf' pittosporum

Holly fern **E**

Snowflake **G**

D 'Wheeler's Dwarf' pittosporum

B Fatsia

Holly fern **E**

Purple heart **F**

G Snowflake

See site plan for **H**.

Stoop

Steps

Walk

Lawn

1 square = 1 ft.

SITE: Shady

SEASON: Spring

CONCEPT: Handsome foliage and eye-catching flowers enhance a foundation on a shady site.

D **'Wheeler's Dwarf' pittosporum** (use 4)
Glossy bright-green leaves and a pleasing round shape make this a fine evergreen shrub for the middle of the garden bed. See *Pittosporum tobira* 'Wheeler's Dwarf', p. 139.

E **Holly fern** (use 6)
This evergreen fern forms a dense patch of shiny, serrated, dark-green leaflets and fuzzy brown leaf stems. See Ferns: *Cyrtomium falcatum*, p. 128.

F **Purple heart** (use 11)
Planted among the shrubs, this perennial will add handsome succulent purple leaves and showy pink flowers to the many greens of the summer garden. See *Setcreasea pallida* 'Purple Heart', p. 146.

G **Snowflake** (use 60)
Planted among the Mexican petunias, these spring bulbs produce grassy leaves and numerous flower stems topped with small clusters of tiny white flower bells. See Bulbs: *Leucojum aestivum*, p. 122.

H **Dwarf Mexican petunia** (use 20)
Picking up where the spring bulbs leave off, this perennial's elegant white blooms and dark leaves are on display from summer through fall. See *Ruellia brittoniana* 'Katie', p. 144.

Fancy Foundation

CREATE A STRIKING ENTRY GARDEN

There's something to enjoy in all four seasons in this foundation planting, which has been transformed into a small garden to welcome visitors. All the plants bear eye-catching flowers in pinks, purples, or blues for long seasons, some almost year-round. They are sure to attract hummingbirds and butterflies for your enjoyment. Foliage in a mixture of greens and grays and a variety of textures showcases the flowers and is handsome in its own right. In front of the bed, the airy chitalpa casts a light shade on the front windows and provides a measure of privacy without blocking the street entirely.

Mexican **D**
bush sage

Plants & Projects

This is a low-care, low-water-use planting. In addition to routine seasonal pruning, you can promote flowering of the butterfly bush by cutting older stems to 1 ft. long in late winter. Shear the sweet-pea shrub to maintain the variation in height with the neighboring Cape mallows and, if necessary, below window height, as shown here.

Ⓐ 'Pink Dawn' chitalpa (use 1 plant)
This small but fast-growing deciduous tree provides airy shade near the house. Spectacular clusters of ruffled, trumpet-shaped pink flowers bloom in early summer. See x *Chitalpa tashkentensis*, p. 125.

Ⓑ 'Nanho Blue' butterfly bush (use 1)
Anchoring the corner of the house is a dwarf form of a popular deciduous shrub. Spikes of fragrant blue flowers at the ends of its arching shoots attract butterflies from midsummer through fall. See *Buddleia davidii*, p. 121.

Ⓒ Blue hibiscus (use 1)
The coarse, deeply cut, dark evergreen leaves of this shrub are a bold accent by the steps. Large lavender-blue flowers heighten the effect off and on throughout the year. See *Alyogyne huegelii*, p. 119.

Ⓓ Mexican bush sage (use 1)
This shrubby perennial is prized for its long, arching purple-and-white flower spikes and attractive gray-green foliage. See *Salvia leucantha*, p. 145.

Ⓔ Cape mallow (use 2)
Pink, hollyhocklike flowers blanket this fast-growing evergreen shrub almost year-round. (Its bloom season is more restricted in cooler areas.) See *Anisodontea* x *hypomandarum*, p. 119.

Ⓕ Sweet-pea shrub (use 3)
This evergreen shrub's light-textured foliage is covered for months with small purple flowers. See *Polygala* x *dalmaisiana*, p. 140.

Ⓖ 'Goodwin Creek Gray' lavender (use 3)
Fragrant gray foliage and short spikes of blue flowers recommend this mounding evergreen shrub. Blooms in early summer and for much of the year where winters are mild. See *Lavandula*, p. 133.

Ⓗ Garden penstemon (use 3)
This perennial's striking flower spikes are right at the front of the planting. Blooms in late spring and summer. Choose one with pink or purple flowers. See *Penstemon gloxinioides*, p. 139.

Ⓘ Pincushion flower (use 3)
Showcased at the center of the planting, this perennial bears light-blue flowers above airy foliage for much of the summer. See *Scabiosa caucasica*, p. 146.

Ⓙ 'Peter Pan' agapanthus (use 7)
A dwarf variety of a perennial, its blue pom-pom-like flowers float above green foliage by the front steps in late spring and summer. See *Agapanthus*, p. 119.

G 'Goodwin Creek
Gray' lavender

H Garden
penstemon

A 'Pink Dawn' chitalpa

F Sweet-pea shrub

B 'Nanho Blue' butterfly bush

'Goodwin Creek Gray' lavender **G**

E Cape mallow

I Pincushion flower

Blue hibiscus **C**

G 'Goodwin Creek Gray' lavender

F Sweet-pea shrub

'Peter Pan' agapanthus **J**

SITE: Sunny

SEASON: Summer

CONCEPT: A mixture of shrubs and perennials makes a foundation planting with year-round color.

Stoop

Steps

Walk

Lawn

1 square = 1 ft.

First Impressions

MAKE A PLEASANT PASSAGE TO YOUR FRONT DOOR

Why wait until a visitor reaches the front door to extend a cordial greeting? An entryway landscape of well-chosen plants and a revamped walkway not only make the short journey a pleasant one, they can also enhance your home's most public face and help settle it comfortably in its surroundings.

In this design, a flagstone walkway curves gracefully to the front door, creating a roomy planting bed near the house. Extending along the driveway, the paving makes it easier for passengers to get in and out of a car. Where the paving widens out at the front stoop, there's room for a welcoming bench sheltered by a small tree. Fragrant flowers and eye-catching foliage make the stroll to the door inviting, while providing interest to viewers inside the house and on the street.

The plants here are selected for a shady entry, one that gets less than six hours of sun a day. Flowers and foliage will keep the entry colorful and fragrant throughout the year. Redbud blossoms will join the daffodils and dianthus in the early spring, followed by columbine, plumbago, Mexican petunia, and gardenia. All but the gardenia continue to bloom well into fall. White daffodils and red camellias arrive in November just in time for the winter holidays.

SITE: Shady

SEASON: Spring

CONCEPT: Easy-care plantings and a distinctive walkway enhance a home's main entrance.

1 square = 1 ft.

'Yuletide' sasanqua camellia — C

Tropical plumbago — H

Dwarf yaupon holly — D

Walkway — K

Holly fern — G

Plants & Projects

Preparing the planting beds and laying the flagstone walkway are the main tasks in this design. Once plants are established, only seasonal cleanup and pruning are required.

A Redbud (use 1 plant)
With a splurge of pink blossoms in early spring, this small deciduous tree is an eye-catching accent. Heart-shaped leaves are light green in summer and yellow in fall. See *Cercis canadensis*, p. 124.

B 'Daisy' gardenia (use 2)
This desirable shrub will scent the entry with sweet white blossoms in May and June. Foliage stays fresh and glossy all year. See *Gardenia jasminoides* 'Daisy', p. 128.

C 'Yuletide' sasanqua camellia (use 1)
This evergreen shrub or small tree grows 5 ft. tall and wears a thick coat of dark-green leaves. Fragrant red flowers bloom in time for Christmas. See *Camellia sasanqua* 'Yuletide', p. 123.

D Dwarf yaupon holly (use 5)
These shrubs form neat low mounds of tiny, oval, evergreen leaves in front of the windows. Clusters of red berries decorate the foliage in winter. See *Ilex vomitoria* 'Nana', p. 132.

E Dwarf Mexican petunia (use 22)
The large lush leaves of this low-growing perennial emerge just in time to cover fading spring bulbs. Purple flowers bloom from the center of each plant all season. See *Ruellia brittoniana* 'Katie', p. 144.

F Texas gold columbine (use 3)
This perennial forms neat mounds of lacy foliage. Slender stalks bear delicate golden flowers in spring and summer. See *Aquilegia chrysantha hinckleyana*, p. 119.

G Holly fern (use 16)
An unusual evergreen fern with leathery, rather than lacy, fronds. The dark-green glossy leaves add coarse-textured sheen under the redbud and along the walk. See Ferns: *Cyrtomium falcatum*, p. 128.

H Tropical plumbago (use 5)
Ideal as a ground cover beside the drive, this trouble-free perennial creates compact tufts of small, pointed, pale-green leaves. Its clear blue flowers look cool and inviting next to the pavement, especially in summer heat. See *Plumbago auriculata*, p. 139.

I 'Bath's Pink' dianthus (use 9)
This perennial creates a pretty border of fine-textured blue-green foliage topped in spring with masses of delicate and fragrant pink flowers. Leaves look fresh all year. See *Dianthus* 'Bath's Pink', p. 127.

J 'Ice Follies' daffodil (use 27)
Scatter these bulbs on both sides of the walk for white flowers in spring. The spiky leaves are a nice blue-green. See Bulbs: *Narcissus pseudonarcissus* 'Ice Follies', p. 122.

K Walkway
Flagstones of random size and shape are perfect for the curved walk and for the stepping-stones into the front lawn. See p. 160.

L Bench Extend your welcome beyond the front door with a comfortable bench next to the stoop.

B 'Daisy' gardenia

A Redbud

G Holly fern

L Bench

J 'Ice Follies' daffodil

F Texas gold columbine

I 'Bath's Pink' dianthus

J 'Ice Follies' daffodil

See site plan for E.

PLANT PORTRAITS

These perennials and shrubs enhance a blank wall and narrow entry walk with handsome foliage and pretty flowers all year.

● = First design, pp. 30–31
▲ = Second design, pp. 32–33

Althea
(*Hibiscus syriacus*, p. 131) ▲

'Daisy' gardenia (*Gardenia jasminoides*, p. 128) ●

'Yuletide' sasanqua camellia
(*Camellia sasanqua*, p. 123) ●

'Apple Blossom' yarrow
(*Achillea millefolium*, p. 118) ▲

A sunny welcome

If your entrance is sunny, consider this design. Here, flagstone walkways invite visitors to stroll from the driveway to the front door along a choice of paths lined with eye-catching flowers and equally attractive foliage.

Many of these perennials bloom nonstop from spring to frost. Viburnum's fragrant white bouquets arrive early in March, and the lavender blossoms of aster appear in the fall, extending an already long season of bloom well into November. Handsome foliage, much of it evergreen, ensures interest all year. Like the planting in the previous design, this one needs only seasonal care.

Plants & Projects

Ⓐ Althea (use 1 plant)
A lavish floral display greets visitors when this deciduous shrub blooms in summer and fall. A cultivar with large lavender flowers suits this design well. Trim up about 3 ft. to make room for nearby plants. See *Hibiscus syriacus*, p. 131.

Ⓑ 'Spring Bouquet' viburnum (use 2)
This compact shrub has deep-green foliage that stays attractive all year. Clusters of lightly scented white flowers open from pink buds in early spring. See *Viburnum tinus* 'Spring Bouquet', p. 150.

Ⓒ 'Belinda's Dream' rose (use 1)
This rose forms a lovely vase of glossy leaves and exquisite pink flowers. See *Rosa* x 'Belinda's Dream', p. 142.

Ⓓ 'Edward Goucher' glossy abelia (use 3)
Small sparkling leaves line the arching branches of this evergreen shrub, turning from dark green to purple-bronze in winter. From spring to fall, clusters of honeysuckle-like pink blossoms dangle from all of the branches. See *Abelia* x *grandiflora*, 'Edward Goucher', p. 118.

Ⓔ Rosemary (use 3)
This low-growing evergreen shrub produces tiny pungent gray-green leaves. Whorls of equally aromatic blue flowers dot the shrub in late winter and early spring. See *Rosmarinus officinalis*, p. 143.

Ⓕ Daylily (use 16)
This mounding perennial trims the walk with slender grassy leaves and large trumpet-shaped flowers. There are many flower colors from which to choose. We've shown a pale-coral pink with a yellow throat. A soft yellow variety would work as well. See *Hemerocallis* hybrids, p. 130.

Ⓖ Fall aster (use 1)
Just one of these perennials will fill the space near the walkway with a dense stand of gray-green leaves, blanketed all fall with small lavender daisylike flowers. See *Aster oblongifolius*, p. 120.

Ⓗ 'Apple Blossom' yarrow (use 7)
Fine feathery leaves and a lacework of tiny pink flowers that bloom for months makes this perennial an especially lovely companion for pink roses. See *Achillea millefolium* 'Apple Blossom', p. 118.

Ⓘ 'Homestead Purple' verbena (use 3)
This perennial forms a bright green mat of foliage that is covered from spring through fall with clusters of violet-purple flowers. See *Verbena* x *hybrida* 'Homestead Purple', p. 149.

Ⓙ 'Confetti' lantana (use 3)
A bushy perennial, it offers a festive mix of pink and yellow flowers throughout the growing season. Shear after bloom cycles. See *Lantana camara* 'Confetti', p. 134.

B 'Spring Bouquet' viburnum

A Althea

F Daylily

K Ox-eye daisy

G Fall aster

H 'Apple Blossom' yarrow

C 'Belinda's Dream' rose

F Daylily

D 'Edward Goucher' glossy abelia

Walkway **M**

I 'Homestead Purple' verbena

J 'Confetti' lantana

Rosemary **E**

L 'Powis Castle' artemisia

SITE: Sunny

SEASON: Summer

CONCEPT: Meandering paths create an enticing entry among colorful plants.

House

Stoop

Driveway

Lawn

1 square = 1 ft.

K **Ox-eye daisy** (use 5)
In spring, small white daisies with bright-yellow centers rise on tall stalks above this perennial's foliage. See *Chrysanthemum leucanthemum*, p. 125.

L **'Powis Castle' artemisia** (use 3)
This perennial forms a billowy mound of fragrant silver-white foliage that complements the other forms and colors in the planting. See *Artemisia* x 'Powis Castle', p. 120.

M **Walkway**
Paving of irregular flagstones curves around the planting beds and widen out gracefully to the stoop. See p. 160.

An Entry Oasis

EXTEND A FRIENDLY DESERT WELCOME

A trend in new suburban developments is to crowd larger homes onto smaller and smaller lots. As a consequence, homeowners enjoy spaciousness inside the house but not outside. Making the most of limited space for outdoor living requires expanding the uses of some traditional areas.

This design transforms the entrance of a desert home from a corridor linking the front door and the driveway into a courtyard garden that invites gathering or relaxing outdoors. Shaded by the canopy of a small tree, enclosed by a wall low enough to allow breezes in, and soothed by the trickle of a small fountain, the courtyard can be enjoyed by family and friends year-round.

The design celebrates the desert environment and low-maintenance, low-water use principles. Local materials such as gravel, granite, and boulders provide natural surfaces to showcase striking

desert plants. To fully integrate the design with the yard and house, you may want to cover the entire yard in gravel as we've shown here. It makes a water-efficient surface that is comfortable for both plants and people. Note the mounded undulating surface around the wall, indicated on the plan by broken lines.

The desert-loving plants featured here contribute distinctive forms, textures, and colors. Grouped together they create a dramatic composition. Spiky agave and ocotillo are boldly paired with the loosely arching bougainvillea and low-spreading lantana. The flowers in the planting bloom in spring, and they are a spectacular sight.

See site plan for Ⓔ Ⓘ Ⓚ Ⓝ.

Plants & Projects

Installing the paving, wall, and fountain are the biggest jobs here, though not beyond the means of a resourceful do-it-yourselfer. Once established, the plants will thrive with occasional watering and just seasonal care.

Ⓐ **Desert willow** (use 1)
From spring to fall this tree's willowy gray-green leaves are decorated with orchidlike flowers in shades of red, purple, pink, and white. The flowers are followed by long dangling seedpods. Leaves drop in win-

SITE: Sunny

SEASON: Spring

CONCEPT: A host of desert plants and a shady courtyard make an inviting entry to a desert home.

Ⓑ **Twin-flower agave**

Ⓗ **Ocotillo**

Ⓓ **'Rosenka' bougainvillea**

Ⓑ **Twin-flower agave**

Ⓓ **'Rosenka' bougainvillea**

Ⓜ **Stone wall**

ter, exposing attractive twisting branches. See *Chilopsis linearis*, p. 125.

B Twin-flower agave (use 4)
An unusually fine-textured agave, with narrow succulent leaves that form a perfect rosette 2 to 3 ft. in diameter. In spring, it sends up double spikes of large, pale-yellow, bell-shaped flowers. See *Agave geminiflora*, p. 119.

C 'New Gold' bougainvillea (use 1)
Trained on a trellis, this evergreen vine's lavish display of gold flowers will be eye-catching from the street or drive. Blooms spring and summer. See *Bougainvillea*, p. 121.

D 'Rosenka' bougainvillea (use 2)
This bougainvillea's arching branches are festooned with papery gold and pink flowers for a long time in spring and summer. It makes a lush green mound in winter. See *Bougainvillea*, p. 121.

E Damianita (use 2
Fragrant yellow daisies blanket this small shrub in spring and fall. Needlelike leaves have a pungent but pleasant aroma. Evergreen. See *Chrysactinia mexicana*, p. 125.

F Mexican grass tree (use 1)
This unusual shrub creates a fountain of succulent evergreen foliage. As it matures it forms a central trunk capable of reaching 10 ft. tall and produces long dense clusters of bell-shaped white flowers in summer. See *Dasylirion longissima*, p. 127.

G Euphorbia hybrid (use 2)
Euphorbias have been hybridized into dozens of varieties. Pick a compact one for this entry. Shown here is crown of thorns (*E. milii*), which has bright red flowers all year. See *Euphorbia* hybrids, p. 127.

H Ocotillo (use 1)
This desert shrub is noted for its burst of brilliant orange-red blossoms in spring. Leaves are small, gray-green, and deciduous in dry spells. See *Fouquieria splendens*, p. 128.

I Madagascar palm (use 1)
This exotic tree looks like a cross between a cactus and a palm; its plump, spiny trunk is crowned with straplike deep-green leaves. See *Pachypodium lamerei*, p. 138.

J Lantana (use 2)
Small lavender flowers brighten this low-spreading perennial's dark-green leaves. Evergreen and ever-blooming where winters are mild. See *Lantana montevidensis*, p. 134.

K Annuals (as needed)
A collection of colorful pansies and snapdragons adds a festive look to this desert entry.

L Paving
Flagstones in muted desert tones provide an attractive surface for the patio. See p. 161.

M Stone wall
Choose your favorite stone. Shown here is a colorfully veined granite.

N Water feature
Water is a wonderful focal point for a courtyard. Incorporate a small fountain or pool into the landscape. See p. 168.

O Gravel
Gravel emulates a desert surface. Shown here is desert tan bird's-eye gravel.

House

1 square = 1 ft.

A Desert willow

Dashed lines indicate mounded planting beds.

C 'New Gold' bougainvillea

G Euphorbia hybrid

O Gravel

F Mexican grass tree **L** Paving **B** Twin-flower agave **J** Lantana

A No-Mow Slope

A TERRACED GARDEN TRANSFORMS A STEEP SITE

SITE: Sunny

SEASON: Fall

CONCEPT: Retaining walls, steps, and plants tame this slope and enhance the home's public face.

F Russian sage

J Coreopsis

C Spineless prickly pear

H Copper canyon daisy

A Texas mountain laurel

B Turk's cap

F Russian sage

H Copper canyon daisy

Dwarf pampas grass **E**

Yucca **K**

Mealycup **D** sage

'Trailing Lavender' **G** lantana

Ox-eye daisy **I**

Yucca **K**

Retaining wall **L** and steps

F Russian sage

E Dwarf pampas grass

Steep slopes can be a landscaping headache. Planted with lawn grass, they're a chore to mow, and they can present problems of erosion and maintenance if you try to establish other ground covers or plantings. One solution to this dilemma is shown here—tame the slope by building a low retaining wall and steps. Then plant the resulting flat (or flatter) beds with an assortment of interesting low-care trees, shrubs, and perennials.

Steep slopes near the house are common in some areas of Texas. Here, a narrow steeply sloping front yard has been terraced and walled and the lawn replaced by plantings. The result transforms the home's public face and creates an enticing walk to the front door. You can extend the planting, or leave some lawn for kids to enjoy.

Visitors approaching from the sidewalk pass through colorful shrubs and perennials. A small landing on the steps, introduced at wall height, offers the opportunity to pause and enjoy nearby plants. The walk from the drive is no less pleasant. Visitors from both directions will be met with a profusion of blooms in nearly every season, and a few surprises as well: the sweet scent of Texas mountain laurel in spring, the spectacle of large white yucca blossoms in summer, and purple cactus fruit in fall.

Plants & Projects

Reshaping the slope and building the hardscape (retaining walls, steps, and walkways) is a big job. Even if you plan to do much of the work yourself, it is prudent to consult a landscape contractor for advice. Once the plants are established, this design requires little more than seasonal pruning and cleanup.

Ⓐ Texas mountain laurel (use 1 plant)
A Texas native evergreen tree with gnarly branches and attractive bark. Wisteria-like clusters of grape-scented flowers in spring are followed by fat bean pods that eventually reveal shiny red seeds. See *Sophora secundiflora*, p. 146.

Ⓑ Turk's cap (use 9)
This tough perennial makes a velvety patch of foliage that showcases small red flowers all season. See *Malvaviscus arboreus drummondii*, p. 136.

Ⓒ Spineless prickly pear (use 2)
A bold "sculpture" for the entry, this cactus forms an interesting patchwork of coarse succulent leaf pads. In some years, it may produce yellow flowers in summer and purple fruits in the fall. See *Opuntia lindheimeri*, p. 138.

Ⓓ Mealycup sage (use 11)
The fringe of bright-blue flowers borne on this perennial makes a pretty edge around plants and lawn. Shear a few times during the season to refresh their bloom. See *Salvia farinacea*, p. 146.

Ⓔ Dwarf pampas grass (use 11)
These fountains of fine-textured grass are topped in late summer with feathery creamy white flowers. Foliage is evergreen. See *Cortaderia selloana* 'Pumila', p. 126.

Ⓕ Russian sage (use 14)
This erect perennial forms an airy vase of slender, silver-leaved stems tipped with tiny pale-blue flowers. Blooms nonstop from midsummer to fall. Cut plant back after frost. See *Perovskia atriplicifolia*, p. 139.

Ⓖ 'Trailing Lavender' lantana (use 4)
This perennial spreads into a wide mound of fuzzy leaves covered with small domes of lavender-purple flowers. See *Lantana montevidensis* 'Trailing Lavender', p. 134.

Ⓗ Copper canyon daisy (use 8)
A pretty, lace-leafed perennial marigold bearing bright-gold flowers in autumn. See *Tagetes lemmonii*, p. 147.

Ⓘ Ox-eye daisy (use 8)
White daisies with yellow centers will cheer visitors in spring. The rest of the season this perennial offers a mound of curly green leaves. See *Chrysanthemum leucanthemum*, p. 125.

Ⓙ Coreopsis (use 15)
A mounding perennial with linear leaves and many slender stalks of single flower heads with sunlike rays. See *Coreopsis lanceolata*, p. 126.

Ⓚ Yucca (use 3)
These spiky evergreen shrubs make striking accents. Spectacular stalks of nodding white flowers rise as high as lampposts in late spring and last through midsummer. See *Yucca filamentosa*, p. 151.

Ⓛ Retaining wall and steps
The walls and steps are made with a precast concrete retaining-wall system available at garden centers. See p. 172.

House · Stoop · Walkway · Driveway · Lawn · Sidewalk · 1 square = 1 ft.

PLANT PORTRAITS

These durable, low-care plants will help transform difficult hillsides.

- ● = First design, pp. 36–37
- ▲ = Second design, pp. 38–39

'Petite Salmon' oleander
(*Nerium oleander*, p. 137) ▲

Periwinkle
(*Vinca major*, p. 150) ▲

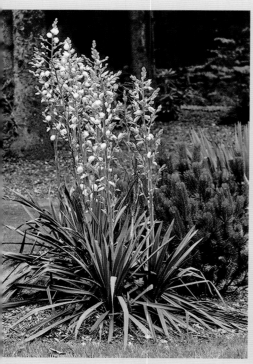

Yucca (*Yucca filamentosa*, p. 151) ●

'Evergreen Giant' lilyturf
(*Liriope muscari*, p. 135) ▲

'Trailing Lavender' lantana
(*Lantana montevidensis*, p. 134) ●

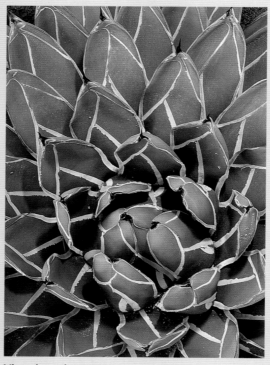

Victoria regina agave
(*Agave victoriae-reginae*, p. 119) ▲

Working with a hillside

If terracing a slope with retaining walls and steps does not appeal to you, or is beyond your budget, consider this design. Here we've worked with the existing hillside, replacing turfgrass with tough, easy-care ground covers. A small tree provides a colorful accent as well as a modest level of privacy from street and sidewalk traffic.

These plants thrive in the poor, dry soil and the heat often found on slopes. Their tenacious root systems, particularly those of periwinkle and lilyturf, will hold the soil in place. With no exception, these plants require infrequent watering once they're established.

The planting is as attractive as it is durable. There are flowers blooming nearly all season. And the varied textures and colors of the foliage are pleasing year-round.

Plants & Projects

Ⓐ Chaste tree (use 1 plant)
Well-suited to dry hillside conditions, this small deciduous tree produces showers of blue-purple flowers all season. See *Vitex agnus-castus*, p. 150.

Ⓑ 'Petite Salmon' oleander (use 6)
This compact evergreen shrub bears small glossy leaves. From spring to frost the foliage is flush with salmon-pink flowers. See *Nerium oleander* 'Petite Salmon', p. 137.

Ⓒ Periwinkle (as needed)
A vigorously trailing evergreen ground cover. Bears lavender-purple flowers amid heart-shaped foliage in spring. Space plants 1 ft. apart for solid coverage. See *Vinca major*, p. 150.

Ⓓ Red yucca (use 3)
Spiky foliage gives this shrub a striking presence among billowy neighbors. Coral-pink flowers echo the color of the oleander

Chaste tree **A**

I 'Evergreen Giant' lilyturf

E Victoria regina agave

C Periwinkle

H Trailing rosemary

F Gray santolina

B 'Petite Salmon' oleander

J Mealy cup sage

D Red yucca

SITE: Sunny

SEASON: Summer

CONCEPT: Tough but attractive plants make a colorful, easy-care front yard on a sloping site.

Periwinkle **C**

'Evergreen Giant' lilyturf **I**

'Petite Salmon' **B** oleander

Mealycup sage **J**

G 'Powis Castle' artemisia

blossoms. *Hesperaloe parviflora*, p. 130.

E **Victoria regina agave** (use 3)
A small but bold succulent perennial, it resembles an artichoke bud. See *Agave victoriae-reginae*, p. 119.

F **Gray santolina** (use 10)
Ideal for edges, this evergreen shrub's low mounds of thick leaves bear countless flowers in summer. See *Santolina chamaecyparissus*, p. 145.

G **'Powis Castle' artemisia** (use 11)
A billowy perennial whose foliage will soften the slope's steep face and act

as a foil for the flowers. See *Artemisia* x 'Powis Castle', p. 120.

H **Trailing rosemary** (use 5)
A low, spreading evergreen shrub bearing tiny fragrant quill-like leaves and equally fragrant blue blossoms. See *Rosmarinus officinalis* 'Prostratus', p. 143.

I **'Evergreen Giant' lilyturf** (as needed)
This is the largest version of a popular grassy evergreen ground cover. Plant on 2-ft. centers. See *Liriope muscari* 'Evergreen Giant', p. 135.

See p. 37 for the following:

J **Mealycup sage** (use 30)

1 square = 1 ft.

An Eye-Catching Corner

BEAUTIFY A BOUNDARY WITH EASY-CARE PLANTS

The corner where your property meets your neighbor's and the sidewalk is often a kind of grassy no-man's-land. This design defines that boundary with a planting that can be enjoyed by property owners, as well as passersby. Good gardens make good neighbors, so we've used well-behaved, low-maintenance plants that take the heat and won't make extra work for the person next door—or for you.

Because of its exposed location, remote from the house and close to the street, this is a less personal planting than those in more private and frequently used parts of your property. It is meant to be appreciated from a distance. Dramatic foliage and flowers are the key to its success. At the center is the strikingly bold century plant. Playing off its coarse texture and gray tones are the gray-green foliage of the Mexican bush sage, gaura, and yucca. A patchwork blanket of blooms in yellow, orange, red, and purple offers cheery contrast to the foliage all season long.

Century plant A

'Radiation' lantana E

'Gold Star' esperanza B

Red yucca D

Edging I

'Homestead Purple' verbena H

Plants & Projects

As befits a planting that is some distance from the house, these durable, reliable plants are heat and drought tolerant, requiring little care beyond seasonal pruning and cleanup.

Ⓐ Century plant (use 1 plant)
This regal perennial makes a striking centerpiece with its wide silvery blue leaves ending in single dark-purple spines. See *Agave americana*, p. 119.

Ⓑ 'Gold Star' esperanza (use 1)
Clusters of yellow bell-shaped flowers adorn every branch of this bushy tropical shrub from summer to frost. Attractive bright green leaves. See *Tecoma stans* 'Gold Star', p. 148.

Ⓒ Mexican bush sage (use 2)
This big bushy perennial fills the space behind the century plant with fine green-gray foliage. In fall the plant is topped with long spikes of lavender and white flowers. See *Salvia leucantha*, p. 145.

Ⓓ Red yucca (use 3)
This evergreen perennial bears 3-ft. stalks of coral-red, trumpet-shaped flowers all season. They bloom above clumps of succulent gray-green foliage. See *Hesperaloe parviflora*, p. 130.

Ⓔ 'Radiation' lantana (use 1)
Round clusters of tiny bright-orange and yellow flowers blanket this spreading perennial throughout the growing season. See *Lantana camara* 'Radiation', p. 134.

Ⓕ 'New Gold' lantana (use 3)
This lantana cultivar boasts masses of tiny golden yellow flowers covering dark-green foliage. See *Lantana* x *hybrida* 'New Gold', p. 134.

Ⓖ Gaura (use 3)
An outstanding Texas native, this fine-textured perennial softens the planting with airy masses of small pink and white flowers. See *Gaura lindheimeri*, p. 128.

Ⓗ 'Homestead Purple' verbena (use 3)
Vibrant purple flowers top this perennial's clump of bright-green foliage, forming a colorful mat in front of the century plant. See *Verbena* x *hybrida* 'Homestead Purple', p. 149.

Ⓘ Edging
This decorative border of weathered-gray stones harmonizes with the colors of the foliage and flowers. See p. 162.

See site plan for **Ⓒ**.

Ⓕ 'New Gold' lantana

Ⓖ Gaura

1 square = 1 ft.

Lawn

Sidewalk

SITE: Sunny

SEASON: Fall

CONCEPT: A colorful planting that looks good year-round marks the property line in a neighborly fashion.

A comfortable corner

Why not make the most of a shady corner with a welcoming garden bench under a small tree? Framed by evergreen shrubs and perennials, the design offers a cozy corner for conversing with the neighbors, reading a book, or just sitting and relaxing. A small mound, or "berm," next to the walk helps nestle the bench into the garden setting. (Planted with sedum and daisies, this berm is about 12 in. above grade.) Two or three stepping-stones edge the bench.

Viewed up close or from a distance, the planting offers color in every season: spring blossoms in a palette of pastels; vivid blue, gold, and red flowers in summer; fall foliage and flowers in yellows, pinks, and bronzes; and for winter, evergreens and plenty of cheerful red berries.

Plants & Projects

Ⓐ Texas redbud (use 1 plant)
This lovely small tree provides a pleasant canopy for bench-sitters in every season. Small pink blossoms line bare branches in early spring, giving way to shiny heart-shaped green leaves scattered with light-green bean pods in summer, and bright-yellow leaves in fall. Hints of violet-purple on the gray bark brighten up the branches in dull winter months. See *Cercis texensis*, p. 124.

Ⓑ 'Gulf Stream' heavenly bamboo (use 3)
Prized for its lacy tiers of colorful foliage—emerald green and tipped with orange-bronze new growth in summer, taking on burgundy tones in fall and winter—these compact evergreen shrubs create a decorative fringe behind the bench and along the property line. They bear bright-red berries in winter. See *Nandina domestica* 'Gulf Stream', p. 137.

SITE: Afternoon shade

SEASON: Summer

CONCEPT: A bench and pleasing plants provide a shady spot for catching up on neighborhood news.

1 square = 1 ft.

Bench

Lawn

Sidewalk

See site plan for Ⓖ.

Texas redbud Ⓐ

Texas gold columbine Ⓗ

Ⓑ 'Gulf Stream' heavenly bamboo

Ⓓ Dwarf yaupon holly

Ⓔ 'Goldsturm' black-eyed Susan

Ⓘ Lilyturf

Ⓒ Turk's cap

Ⓙ Stepping-stones

Mealycup sage Ⓕ

C **Turk's cap** (use 1)

A Texas favorite, this perennial forms a low bush of large heart-shaped leaves and red turbanlike flowers in summer. Hummingbirds attracted to the flowers will hover near the bench. Other birds may stop by for the cherrylike berries. See *Malvaviscus arboreus drummondii*, p. 136.

D **Dwarf yaupon holly** (use 2)

This compact evergreen shrub forms a fine-textured globe of olive-green leaves that are free of spines. See *Ilex vomitoria* 'Nana', p. 132.

E **'Goldsturm' black-eyed Susan** (use 5)

Masses of golden "daisies" with dark eyes cover the coarse leaves of this sturdy perennial in early summer. See *Rudbeckia fulgida* 'Goldsturm', p. 143.

F **Mealycup sage** (use 3)

An erect bushy perennial with narrow gray-green leaves. Its many flower spikes are lined with small deep-blue blossoms from spring to fall. See *Salvia farinacea*, p. 144.

G **'Autumn Joy' sedum** (use 3)

A bold-textured perennial that grows in mounds of dull-gray succulent leaves. Tight clusters of tiny buds open pink and fade to tan. See *Sedum* 'Autumn Joy', p. 146.

H **Texas gold columbine** (use 5)

This perennial's lacy leaves form dainty mounds. Yellow-gold flowers nod above the foliage from late spring through summer. See *Aquilegia chrysantha hinckleyana*, p. 119.

I **Lilyturf** (use 46)

This evergreen perennial creates a lush low fringe around the border. See *Liriope muscari*, p. 135.

J **Stepping-stones**

Gray flagstones provide a place to rest your feet. See p. 161.

I Lilyturf

PLANT PORTRAITS

These tough plants provide a splash of color for many months in exchange for just a minimum of care.

● = First design, pp. 40–41

▲ = Second design, pp. 42–43

Century plant
(*Agave americana*, p. 119) ●

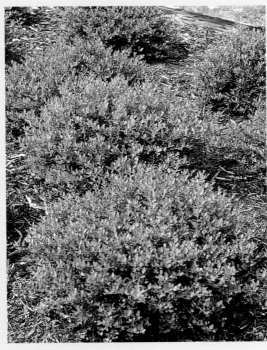

Dwarf yaupon holly
(*Ilex vomitoria* 'Nana', p. 132) ▲

Texas redbud
(*Cercis texensis*, p. 124) ▲

Mexican bush sage (*Salvia leucantha*, p. 145) ●

Lilyturf (*Liriope muscari*, p. 135) ▲

Streetwise and Stylish

GIVE YOUR CURBSIDE STRIP A NEW LOOK

Homeowners seldom give a thought to the part of their property adjacent to the street. Often bounded by a sidewalk, this area is at best a tidy patch of lawn and at worst a weed-choked eyesore. Yet this is one of the most public parts of many properties. Filling this strip with attractive plants and paths from street to sidewalk can give pleasure to passersby and visitors who park next to the curb, as well as enhancing the streetscape you view from the house. (Curbside strips are usually city-owned, so check local ordinances for restrictions before you start a remake.)

This can be a difficult site, subject to summer heat and drought, pedestrian and car traffic, and errant dogs. Plants need to be tough and drought-tolerant to perform well here. (Many towns and cities encourage water-conserving plantings in curbside areas.)

The plants in this design meet both criteria. And they look good, too. There are flowers from late winter to frost in the fall. Foliage in a variety of complementary shades and texture, much of it evergreen, keeps the curbside looking attractive through winter. The 4-ft.-wide path allows ample room for passengers getting in and out of a car.

If your curbside property doesn't include a sidewalk, you can extend the planting farther into the yard and connect the path to the walkway leading to your front door.

SITE: Sunny

SEASON: Fall

CONCEPT: Plants with striking foliage and flowers transform an often neglected area and treat visitors and passersby to a colorful display.

Dwarf **A**
yaupon holly

Fall aster **D**

Gray santolina **G**

'White Beauty' **H**
yarrow

'Cherry Chief' **C**
autumn sage

'Homestead **I**
Purple' verbena

Plants & Projects

Once established, these plants require very little care. You can shear off spent flowers, or better yet, cut and dry the sage, santolina, and rosemary flowers for long-lasting arrangements. An occasional trim will keep the artemisia tidy. Prune the gaura to the ground after a freeze. Cut back the old stems of santolina in early spring.

A Dwarf yaupon holly
(use 5 plants)
This evergreen shrub forms a dense, rounded globe of tiny, spineless, oval leaves that never need shearing. See *Ilex vomitoria* 'Nana', p. 132.

B 'Hill's Hardy' rosemary (use 2)
Fine texture and fragrance distinguish both the foliage and flowers of this upright evergreen shrub. Blue flowers arrive in early spring. See *Rosmarinus officinalis*, p. 143.

C 'Cherry Chief' autumn sage
(use 3)
This bushy perennial's small oval leaves echo the holly's foliage, but are softer and paler. Small red flowers bloom heavily in spring and lightly in summer and fall. See *Salvia greggii* 'Cherry Chief', p. 144.

D Fall aster (use 3)
Lavender-purple daisies literally blanket this carefree perennial's small dull-green leaves in early summer. See *Aster oblongifolius*, p. 120.

E 'Dauphin' gaura (use 3)
With straight stems rising from a base of small pale-green leaves and delicate pink and white flowers, this tall perennial adds an airy presence to the planting. See *Gaura lindheimeri* 'Dauphin', p. 128.

F 'Powis Castle' artemisia
(use 4)
Prized for its foliage, this perennial forms a dense billowing mound of very fine silvery leaves. See *Artemisia* x 'Powis Castle', p. 120.

G Gray santolina (use 8)
This perennial spreads to form a low, dense cushion of fragrant gray leaves along the curb.

Lawn   1 square = 1 ft.

Sidewalk

Driveway

Street

H 'White Beauty' yarrow

J Path

E 'Dauphin' gaura

B 'Hill's Hardy' rosemary

F 'Powis Castle' artemisia

Gray santolina G

'Homestead Purple' verbena I

F 'Powis Castle' artemisia

I 'Homestead Purple' verbena

Bears yellow flowers in summer. See *Santolina chamaecyparissus*, p. 145.

H 'White Beauty' yarrow
(use 13)
The white flowers of this mat-forming perennial edge the walk in spring. Ferny leaves are green all year. See *Achillea millefolium* 'White Beauty', p. 118.

I 'Homestead Purple' verbena
(use 15)
This perennial's deeply cut bright-green leaves and masses of purple flowers will enliven the curbside from spring to frost. See *Verbena x hybrida* 'Homestead Purple', p. 149.

J Path
Interlocking pavers create an attractive, durable, and easily maintained surface. The gray paver shown here ties in with the sidewalk, street, and planting. See p. 161.

Branching out

A small tree and a branching path distinguish this design and give it an informal appeal. The long-lasting deciduous foliage of the evergreen shrubs and perennials is colorful year-round, mixing shades of green, gray, red, and purple. Flowers in white, pink, and yellow complement the foliage and are pretty in their own right.

Like the previous design, this one is a low-maintenance, low-water-use planting. It requires little more than shearing off spent flowers, trimming back the lantana after a freeze, and lightly pruning the spirea and barberry to maintain their size and shape.

Plants & Projects

Ⓐ Wax myrtle (use 1 plant)
A graceful shrub that can be pruned into a shapely multi-trunked tree. In most parts of Texas, foliage stays green through the winter. See *Myrica cerifera*, p. 137.

Ⓑ 'Anthony Waterer' Japanese spirea (use 1)
Clusters of pink flowers top the fine-leaved branches of this attractive deciduous shrub in summer. Needs only light shearing to keep its rounded shape. See *Spirea* x *bumalda* 'Anthony Waterer', p. 147.

Ⓒ Dwarf Japanese barberry (use 6)
This compact shrub has arching branches crowded with small oval maroon-red leaves. See *Berberis thunbergii* 'Crimson Pygmy', p. 121.

Ⓓ Purple wintercreeper (use 4)
This spreading evergreen ground cover fills in the space by the walk with handsome dark-green leaves that turn red in winter. See *Euonymus fortunei* 'Coloratus', p. 127.

Ⓔ 'Weeping White' trailing lantana (use 13)
Clusters of pure white flowers cover this vigorous low-growing perennial from spring to fall. In mild-winter areas plant sometimes blooms all year. See *Lantana montevidensis* 'Weeping White', p. 134.

Ⓕ St.-John's-wort (use 13)
Under the wax myrtle, this evergreen shrub creates a dense, fine-textured carpet, dotted in summer with bright yellow periwinkle-like flowers. Small oval leaves turn reddish purple in winter. See *Hypericum calycinum*, p. 131.

Ⓖ 'Bath's Pink' dianthus (use 7)
Delightfully fragrant pink flowers greet visitors in spring. The rest of the year this perennial's fine blue-green foliage attracts all the attention. See *Dianthus* 'Bath's Pink', p. 127.

See p. 45 for the following:
Ⓗ Path

SITE: Sunny
SEASON: Summer
CONCEPT: Two streetside paths join up with colorful plantings to welcome visitors.

1 square = 1 ft.

PLANT PORTRAITS

These low-maintenance plants will improve any curbside area, while withstanding the rigors of life by the street.

● = First design, pp. 44–45
▲ = Second design, p. 46

'Weeping White' trailing lantana
(*Lantana montevidensis*, p. 134) ▲

'Dauphin' gaura
(*Gaura lindheimeri*, p. 128) ●

Dwarf Japanese barberry
(*Berberis thunbergii*, p. 121) ▲

'Anthony Waterer' Japanese spirea
(*Spirea* x *bumalda*, p. 147) ▲

'Bath's Pink' dianthus
(*Dianthus*, p. 127) ▲

'Powis Castle' artemisia
(*Artemisia*, p. 120) ●

Fall aster
(*Aster oblongifolius*, p. 120) ●

A Garden Path

RECLAIM A NARROW SIDE YARD FOR A STROLL GARDEN

Many residential lots include a slim strip of land between the house and a property line. Usually overlooked by everyone except children and dogs racing between the front yard and the back, this neglected passageway can become a valued addition to the landscape. In this design, a delightful little stroll garden invites adults, and even children, to linger as they move from one part of the property to another.

The wall of the house and a tall fence at the property line create a cozy "room," one that is enhanced by trees, vines, shrubs, and ground covers. Like furnishings in a room, the plantings make the small space seem bigger than it is. A gently curving flagstone path widens the passage visually and lengthens the stroll through it.

In spring, scented blossoms of daffodil, wisteria, and Texas mountain laurel will perfume the entire passage. As these flowers fade, the watermelon pink crapemyrtle will begin its long season of bloom, joined by purple verbena along the fence, bushy mounds of baby blue plumbago where the daffodils had been, and a continuous row of pretty pink salvia. As the trees grow, their boughs will arch over the path, creating a bower heavy with blossoms for much of the year.

Lawn

House

1 square = 1 ft.

Plants & Projects

Install the fence and flagstone path. Then prepare and plant the beds. You'll need to add sturdy trellises or other strong supports for the vines. As the trees grow, prune them so they arch over the path, yet provide headroom for strollers. Once established, the plants require seasonal care as well as pruning to maintain size and shape.

A 'Tonto' crapemyrtle (use 2 plants)
A small deciduous tree deserving of its wide popularity. Attractive dark oval leaves showcase spectacular blossoms from summer to frost. This cultivar bears watermelon-pink flowers. See *Lagerstroemia* x *fauriei* 'Tonto', p. 133.

B Texas mountain laurel (use 1)
Clusters of purple flowers hang from this small glossy evergreen tree in early spring. Passersby on both sides of the fence will appreciate the delightful perfume. Bean pods with bright-red seeds follow the flowers. See *Sophora secundiflora*, p. 146.

C Indian hawthorn (use 4)
A mounding evergreen shrub that produces a dense covering of shiny oval leaves. It offers pink or white flowers in spring and purple-black berries in late summer. Choose a pink-flowering cultivar for this spot. See *Rhaphiolepis indica*, p. 140.

D Tropical plumbago (use 3)
After the daffodils fade, this perennial emerges apple green and bushy. In summer it spills over with big clusters of clear-blue flowers. See *Plumbago auriculata*, p. 139.

E 'Pink' autumn sage (use 6)
These low, bushy mounds of tiny oval leaves bristle with spires of bright-pink flowers all season. Plant this or any pink cultivar. See *Salvia greggii* 'Pink', p. 144.

F Chinese wisteria (use 2)
In spring, this vine will virtually curtain the fence with fragrant violet flowers as large as clusters of grapes. A lacework of green foliage emerges after fragrant blossoms fade, turning yellowish in fall. See *Wisteria sinensis*, p. 151.

G Purple verbena (use 2)
Countless bright clusters of purple flowers rise airily from this perennial's base of dull green leaves. Blooms from midsummer to frost. See *Verbena bonariensis*, p. 149.

H 'Big Blue' lilyturf (use 24)
This perennial makes an attractive edge of grassy dark-green foliage. In summer, small lavender flowers float among the leaves. See *Liriope muscari*, p. 135.

I 'Ice Follies' daffodil (as needed)
Fresh-looking white daffodil flowers with pale yellow centers line the path in early spring. See Bulbs: *Narcissus pseudonarcissus* 'Ice Follies', p. 122.

J Fence
Easy to build, this fence provides privacy and an attractive framework for plants. See pp. 192–193.

K Path
Flagstones in random shapes and sizes trace a graceful curve through the planting. A neutral gray would complement any house. See p. 160.

SITE: Sunny

SEASON: Spring

CONCEPT: Fragrant flowers make an enticing stroll garden in a frequently neglected area.

'Tonto' crapemyrtle **A**

B Texas mountain laurel

J Fence

F Chinese wisteria

Purple verbena **G**

'Big Blue' lilyturf **H**

K Path

I 'Ice Follies' daffodil

See site plan for **D** .

E 'Pink' autumn sage

C Indian hawthorn

PLANT PORTRAITS

Eye-catching plants for an overlooked spot, here are flowers, foliage, and fragrance to make your side-yard stroll garden a favorite.
● = First design, pp. 48–49
▲ = Second design, pp. 50–51

Gold dust aucuba (*Aucuba japonica* 'Variegata', p. 120) ▲

'Ice Follies' daffodil
(Bulbs: *Narcissus pseudonarcissus*, p. 122) ●

'Pink' autumn sage
(*Salvia greggii*, p. 144) ●

Indian hawthorn
(*Rhaphiolepis indica*, p. 140) ●

'Tonto' crapemyrtle (*Lagerstroemia* x *fauriei*, p. 133) ●

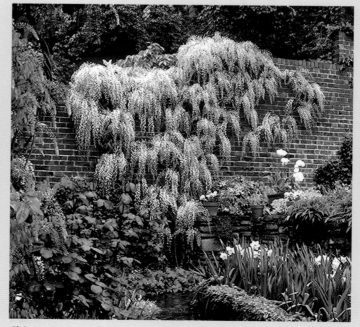

Chinese wisteria (*Wisteria sinensis*, p. 151) ●

A shady corridor

If the side of your house has a shady exposure, try this design. Shade-loving shrubs and ground covers are arrayed in colorful layers along the passage. These "furnishings" are selected primarily for their foliage, ranging from light green to purple-black, fine-textured to coarse, dull to glossy, and low-growing to large and bold. The big leaves of the fatsia and aucuba combine well with ground covers, soft fern fronds, and stiff, swordlike aspidistra. In this evergreen garden, flowers and berries are added enticements. Fragrant jasmine scents the air in spring and purple berries brighten a winter stroll.

SITE: Shady

SEASON: Winter

CONCEPT: Shade-loving plants with lovely foliage highlight this stroll garden.

Plants & Projects

Ⓐ Fatsia (use 1 plant)
A handsome evergreen shrub. Leaves like big hands look wonderful above feathery ferns and other fine-textured plants. See *Fatsia japonica*, p. 127.

Ⓑ American beautyberry (use 1)
This shrub has an open, slightly sprawling habit. Purple berries are showy on bare branches in fall and winter. See *Callicarpa americana*, p. 123.

Ⓒ Gold dust aucuba (use 3)
Speckled and shiny, this evergreen shrub is a striking accent plant, made more so by borders of dark-green lilyturf and purple-black mondo grass. See *Aucuba japonica* 'Variegata', p. 120.

Ⓓ Star jasmine (use 3)
This vine's stiff oval foliage will "wallpaper" the fence with year-round color and texture. Tiny white flowers cover the vine in spring. They'll fill the passage with fragrance. See *Trachelospermum jasminoides*, p. 149.

Ⓔ Cast-iron plant (use 12)
This unusual evergreen plant forms a patch of long leathery leaves that jut from the ground like fence pickets. See *Aspidistra eliator*, p. 120.

Ⓕ Holly fern (use 6)
An evergreen fern distinguished by leathery fronds. It contrasts nicely with the mondo grass and other evergreens. See Ferns: *Cyrtomium falcatum*, p. 128.

Ⓖ Wood fern (use 3)
This is a deciduous fern with a soft shaggy look. Cut back after frost for an attractive brown flat-top. See Ferns: *Thelypteris kunthii*, p. 128.

Ⓗ Black mondo grass (use 12)
Plant this perennial along the path for its unusual color and neat habit. Shear off tops in early spring for new growth. See *Ophiopogon planiscapus* 'Ebony Knight,' p. 138.

See p. 48 for the following:

Ⓘ 'Big Blue' lilyturf (use 24)

Ⓙ Path

Landscape a Low Wall

A TWO-TIERED GARDEN REPLACES A BLAND SLOPE

Some things may not love a wall, but plants and gardeners do. For plants, walls offer warmth for an early start in spring and good drainage for roots. Gardeners appreciate the rich visual potential of composing a garden on two levels, as well as the practical advantage of working on two relatively flat surfaces instead of a single sloping one.

This design places complementary plantings above and below a wall bounded at one end by a set of steps. While each bed is relatively narrow, when viewed from the lower level the two combine to form a border more than 10 ft. deep. Two other design features add depth to the display. A jog in the wall creates a niche for a splashy fountain grass, and the beds are rounded rather than linear. Together with a selection of billowy plants, these features soften the face of the wall and offer pleasing views from many vantage points.

Building the wall that makes this impressive sight possible doesn't require the time or skill it once did. Nor is it necessary to scour the countryside for tons of fieldstone or to hire an expensive contractor. Thanks to precast retaining-wall systems, anyone with a healthy back (or access to energetic teenagers) can install a knee-high do-it-yourself wall in as little as a weekend or two.

Retaining wall and steps ⓙ

Plants & Projects

This planting showcases colorful flowers against curtains of soft silvery green foliage. All the plants tolerate heat and drought and need only a little care to keep them performing at their best. Trim the autumn and mealycup sages lightly through summer to encourage new bloom. The Mexican bush sage and mint marigold will benefit from pruning in late spring and again in midsummer to make them dense and full by showtime in fall.

Ⓐ **'Gracillimus' Japanese maiden grass** (use 1 plant)
This perennial grass graces the steps with narrow arching leaves. Flowers rise another foot above the foliage in late summer. See *Miscanthus sinensis* 'Gracillimus', p. 136.

Ⓑ **Compact Texas sage** (use 3)
A native evergreen shrub with small woolly leaves and a billowy shape. It bears masses of orchid-pink flowers after summer rains. See *Leucophyllum frutescens* 'Compactum', p. 135.

Ⓒ **Mexican bush sage** (use 1)
This big bushy perennial anchors the end of the border and echoes the arching habit of the fountain grass. Slender branches bear gray-green foliage. In autumn, long wands of small purple and white flowers bloom from branch tips. See *Salvia leucantha*, p. 145.

Ⓓ **White autumn sage** (use 3)
This perennial forms a mat of small oval leaves that usually stay green all winter. A profusion of pure-white flowers greets visitors at the steps from spring to fall. See *Salvia greggii* 'Alba', p. 146.

Ⓔ **Mealycup sage** (use 6)
A fringe of blue flower spikes top the narrow grayish leaves of this compact bushy perennial throughout the growing season. Bumblebees will buzz among the blooms. See *Salvia farinacea*, p. 145.

Ⓕ **Soft-tip yucca** (use 1)
This perennial forms an attractive rosette of succulent gray-blue leaves. It puts on a dazzling display of bloom in summer, when clusters of large creamy white bells rise from the center on sturdy stalks. See *Yucca gloriosa*, p. 151.

Ⓖ **Mexican mint marigold** (use 1)
This compact perennial has narrow, emerald green leaves topped with a profusion of small gold flowers. See *Tagetes lucida*, p. 147.

Ⓗ **Fall aster** (use 3)
In autumn, a solid mass of purple daisylike flowers makes this perennial a knockout in front of the gray foliage and white flowers of the sage. See *Aster oblongifolius*, p. 120.

Ⓘ **'Blue Princess' verbena** (use 2)
Lavender-blue flowers blanket this low-growing perennial from spring through fall. It will spread wide enough to surround the yucca in a sea of bloom. See *Verbena* x *hybrida* 'Blue Princess', p. 149.

Ⓙ **Retaining wall and steps**
Prefabricated wall systems make this project easy to install. See p. 172.

Ⓚ **Path**
We've shown gravel here, but use any materials that complement the wall. See p. 160.

White
autumn sage **D**

A 'Gracillimus'
Japanese
maiden grass

H Fall aster

B Compact
Texas sage

G Mexican mint
marigold

C Mexican
bush sage

E Mealycup
sage

F Soft-tip
yucca

I 'Blue
Princess'
verbena

K Path

SITE: Sunny

SEASON: Fall

CONCEPT: A low wall
turns a slope into an
opportunity for a
garden on two levels.

1 square = 1 ft.

Lawn

PLANT PORTRAITS

These plants double the pleasure of a retaining wall with eye-catching flowers and handsome foliage.

● = First design, pp. 52–53
▲ = Second design, pp. 54–55

Black mondo grass (*Ophiopogon planiscapus* 'Ebony Knight', p. 138) ▲

'Gracillimus' Japanese maiden grass (*Miscanthus sinensis*, p. 136) ●

Soft-tip yucca (*Yucca gloriosa*, p. 151) ●

White autumn sage (*Salvia greggii* 'Alba', p. 146) ●

Two tiers in the shade

A retaining-wall planting can be equally alluring in a shady yard. This design uses the same wall-and-step system but keeps the wall straight and nestles the steps into the lawn. Bold shrubs on both levels break up the retaining wall's horizontal plane while bringing the garden together as a whole. These shade-loving plants are chosen for their colorful foliage and flowers in a contrasting palette of rosy purples, cool blues, and cheerful yellows.

Plants & Projects

Ⓐ Chinese fringe flower (use 1 plant)
This evergreen shrub is valued for its luxuriant fringe of dainty pink flowers and its layers of small purple leaves. Where soils are alkaline, substitute American beautyberry. See *Loropetalum chinense rubrum*, p. 136.

Ⓑ Fatsia (use 1)
A bold and beautiful tropical-looking shrub. Glossy evergreen leaves will drape over the wall and nearby plants. See *Fatsia japonica*, p. 127.

Ⓒ American beautyberry (use 1)
This shrub wears a thick coat of pale green foliage most of the year. Clusters of eye-popping purple berries line the branches in late summer. See *Callicarpa americana*, p. 123.

Ⓓ Cast-iron plant (use 3)
An unusual and striking evergreen perennial, it has dark strappy leaves that jut directly from the ground like giant exclamation points. See *Aspidistra elatior*, p. 120.

Ⓔ Holly fern (use 9)
These glossy stands of evergreen fronds will keep the garden lit up through dull winter months. See Ferns: *Cyrtomium falcatum*, p. 128.

Ⓕ Carolina jasmine (use 1)
In no time at all this vine will twine under the redbud and trail over the wall. Tiny lance-like evergreen leaves are almost hidden in spring by sweet-scented yellow flower bells. See *Gelsemium sempervirens*, p. 129.

Ⓖ Louisiana iris (use 3)
This perennial forms an erect clump of narrow arching leaves. Large flowers rise above the foliage in spring. Choose a blue or lavender variety to complement the color scheme. See *Iris x Louisiana* hybrids, p. 132.

Ⓗ Texas gold columbine (use 3)
Plant this evergreen perennial at the front of the border to show off the neat mounds of attractive ferny foliage. Delicate yellow flowers with long spurs rise above the plant in spring. See *Aquilegia chrysantha hinckleyana*, p. 119.

Ⓘ St.-John's-wort (use 3)
This semi-evergreen perennial makes a thick mat of miniature leaves along the wall and cascading over it. Small yellow flowers decorate the plant in summer. Foliage is reddish purple in autumn. See *Hypericum calycinum*, p. 131.

Ⓙ Black mondo grass (use 15)
Slender purple-black leaves give this distinctive plant a bold look that also accents the other purples in the planting. See *Ophiopogon planiscapus* 'Ebony Knight', p. 138.

Ⓚ Dwarf Mexican petunia (use 6)
This low-growing perennial produces tufts of narrow, long, dark-green leaves that are ideal for an informal edging. Slow to emerge in spring, this plant makes up time with a long season of purple bloom. The flowers are funnel-shaped and light purple. See *Ruellia brittoniana* 'Katie', p. 144.

Ⓛ Purple heart (use 1)
Given a chance, the succulent purple foliage of this mat-forming perennial will tumble decorously over the wall. See *Setcreasea pallida*, p. 146.

See p. 52 for the following:
Ⓜ Retaining wall and steps

Chinese fringe flower **A**

C American beautyberry

F Carolina jasmine

I St.-John's-wort

Louisiana iris **G**

Holly fern **E**

D Cast-iron plant

M Retaining wall and steps

Purple heart **L**

Fatsia **B**

H Texas gold columbine

J Black mondo grass

E Holly fern

K Dwarf Mexican petunia

Lawn

Lawn

1 square = 1 ft.

SITE: Shady

SEASON: Spring

CONCEPT: Shade-loving plants surround a garden wall in a shady site.

Angle of Repose

MAKE A BACK-DOOR GARDEN IN A SHELTERED NICHE

Many homes offer the opportunity to tuck a garden into a protected corner. In the front yard, such spots are ideal for an entry garden or a landscaping display that enhances the view of the house from the sidewalk or the street. If the corner is in the backyard, like the site shown here, it can be more intimate, part of a comfortable outdoor "room" you can stroll through at leisure or enjoy from a nearby terrace or window.

This planting introduces shrubs and perennials with a distinctive Southwestern flare. Though not all of them are desert natives, they have the spiky forms and gray-green foliage of desert plants— without the accompanying thorns or spines. Tolerant of heat and drought, they'll do well with good drainage and plenty of sun.

Enjoyable year-round, this garden features the bold, cactuslike foliage of yuccas and prickly pears as well as the softer tones and finer textures of sage and rosemary. The evergreen foliage enhances the garden all year, but particularly before the "desert" begins to bloom in spring. At the first hints of warmth, jonquils and dianthus will entice viewers outdoors with their springtime fragrance. By May the planting will be brimming with flowers in vibrant pinks and yellows, purples and blues. Flowers peak again in fall, after a summer kept colorful by consistent bright clusters of yellow lantana, long-lasting spikes of coral-red yucca, and repeated bursts of pink from the Texas sage bush.

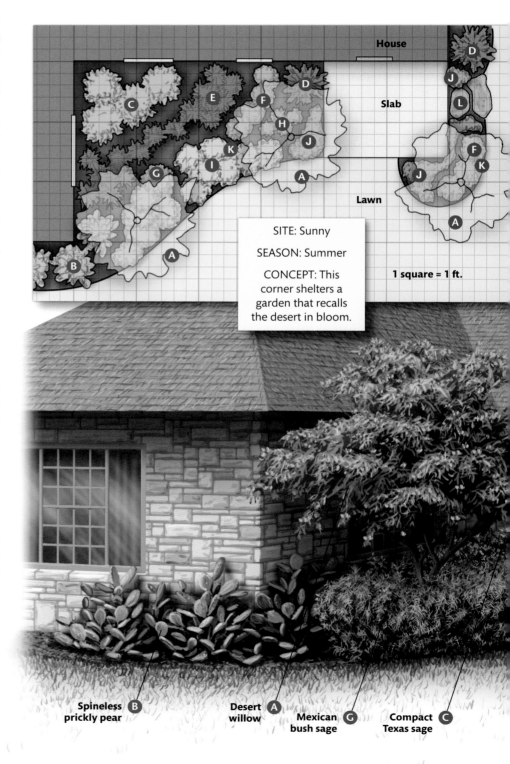

House

Slab

Lawn

SITE: Sunny

SEASON: Summer

CONCEPT: This corner shelters a garden that recalls the desert in bloom.

1 square = 1 ft.

Spineless prickly pear B

Desert willow A

Mexican bush sage G

Compact Texas sage C

Plants & Projects

Once established, these plants will provide years of pleasure. Heat and drought tolerant in summer, they will do best if their roots are kept dry in winter.

Ⓐ Desert willow (use 3 plants)
The fine leaves of this deciduous tree provide an airy canopy over the path without shading out the plants underneath. Showy white, pink, and lavender flowers bloom on and off all season. See *Chilopsis linearis*, p. 125.

Ⓑ Spineless prickly pear (use 3)
A bold cactuslike accent with tiny hidden prickles. This evergreen shrub forms an interesting erect clump of succulent leaf pads, occasionally bearing yellow flowers in summer and showy purple fruit in fall. See *Opuntia lindheimeri*, p. 140.

Ⓒ Compact Texas sage (use 4)
An evergreen shrub that forms a billowy mound of small fuzzy gray leaves on pale stems. This cultivar is a denser, bushier version of the popular Texas sage and has orchid-pink flowers. See *Leucophyllum frutescens* 'Compactum', p. 135.

Ⓓ 'Hill's Hardy' rosemary (use 2)
Both foliage and flowers of this handsome evergreen shrub are fragrant. Most cold tolerant of all the rosemary cultivars. See *Rosmarinus officinalis* 'Hill's Hardy', p. 143.

Ⓔ Red yucca (use 15)
Slow-growing but worth it, these evergreen perennials create a low, striking hedge. Spikes of coral-pink flowers rise from the narrow succulent leaves and bloom from May to frost. See *Hesperaloe parviflora*, p. 132.

Ⓕ 'Pink' autumn sage (use 7)
Massed on both sides of the entry, these fine-textured perennials help tie the planting together. 'Pink' is a large and dependable cultivar with bright pink blooms from spring to fall. Use this or any pink cultivar. Evergreen in warm winters. See *Salvia greggii* 'Pink', p. 144.

Ⓖ Mexican bush sage (use 7)
These bushy perennials will fill the space under the tree with downy gray leaves and stems. The nectar of the white and purple flowers in autumn draws hummingbirds. See *Salvia leucantha*, p. 145.

Ⓗ Mealycup sage (use 4)
For a touch of bright blue, plant this perennial among the pinks and yellows of autumn sage and lantana. See *Salvia farinacea*, p. 144.

Ⓘ 'New Gold' lantana (use 7)
These vigorous perennials will spread to form a continuous border of gold flowers atop small green elliptical leaves. A butterfly favorite. See *Lantana* x *hybrida*, p. 134.

Ⓙ 'Bath's Pink' dianthus (use 18)
This perennial is grown for its thick mat of tiny blue-green leaves and its fragrant pink flowers in early spring. See *Dianthus* 'Bath's Pink', p. 127.

Ⓚ Jonquil (as needed)
Plant these bulbs for fresh grassy foliage and yellow trumpets that announce the arrival of early spring. Sprinkle them throughout, and particularly around plants that are dormant in winter, such as the salvias and lantana. See Bulbs: *Narcissus jonquilla*, p. 124.

Ⓛ Stepping-stones
Flagstones provide access from the slab through the planting to the side yard. See p. 165.

A touch of the tropics

Chosen for a niche in shade, these plants provide the look of a balmy Pacific island. Almost entirely evergreen, the planting will change little from season to season; the interest comes from the many contrasts in plant forms and in foliage texture and color.

Five windmill palms set a dramatic tone across the front of the planting. Their hairy trunks frame views of the plants behind. From front to back, the foliage progresses from fine-textured to coarse and alternates between light and dark colors, finishing with the very bold, very dark foliage of the fatsia. The pattern is repeated on a smaller scale and with some variation on the other side of the entry.

This planting is most effective in late winter, the season shown here.

SITE: Shady

SEASON: Late winter

CONCEPT: Fill a private niche on a shady site with plants that give year-round pleasure.

1 square = 1 ft.

Cast-iron plant **E**   Mondo grass **H**   Fatsia **B**   **A** Windmill palm   **F** Holly fern   **G** 'Big Blue' lilyturf   **E** Cast-iron plant

Plants & Projects

A Windmill palm (use 5 plants)
A dwarf palm tree sporting dark-green fronds and tan trunks matted on the surface with hairy fibers. Trunks provide an interesting contrast to the smooth, glossy foliage of this and the other plants. See *Trachycarpus fortunei*, p. 149.

B Fatsia (use 7)
An evergreen shrub with big leaves that grow in attractive layers. Produces clusters of white flowerballs in fall. See *Fatsia japonica*, p. 127.

C Gold dust aucuba
(use 1 or more)
Year-round, this erect shrub wears a handsome coat of shiny green leaves dusted with yellow spots. Use one, or more if you'd like to extend the planting along the side of house. See *Aucuba japonica* 'Variegata', p. 122.

D Umbrella sedge (use 1)
Often listed as a water plant, this grasslike perennial also thrives in a garden bed and in sun or shade. It makes an eye-catching clump of slender stalks, each one topped with circular spokes of ribbony foliage. See *Cyperus alternifolius*, p. 126.

E Cast-iron plant (use 15)
The stiff leathery leaves of this perennial grow straight up from the ground, forming a dense stand of dark green. See *Aspidistra eliator*, p. 120.

F Holly fern (use 6)
An evergreen fern with thick fronds divided into large glossy leaflets. The stems are fuzzy. See Ferns: *Cyrtomium falcatum*, p. 128.

G 'Big Blue' lilyturf (use 40)
This curving band of grassy perennials links the windmill palms. For a greater color contrast, try one of the variegated cultivars. See *Liriope muscari* 'Big Blue', p. 135.

H Mondo grass (use 60)
Another, darker band of grassy perennials for the front of the palms. See *Ophiopogon japonicus*, p. 138.

See p. 57 for the following:

I Stepping-stones

See site plan for **I**.

C Gold dust aucuba
E Cast-iron plant
Umbrella D sedge
H Mondo grass

PLANT PORTRAITS

Tropical or desertlike, these exotic looking plants provide interest all year.
● = First design, pp. 56–57
▲ = Second design, pp. 58–59

Jonquil (Bulbs: *Narcissus jonquilla*, p. 124) ●

Desert willow (*Chilopsis linearis*, p. 125) ●

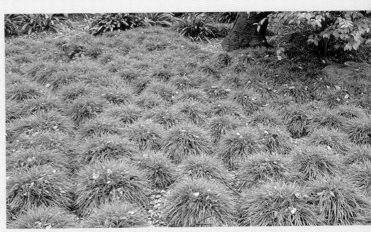

Mondo grass (*Ophiopogon japonicus*, p. 138) ▲

Beautify a Blank Wall

A VERTICAL GARDEN MAKES THE MOST OF A NARROW SITE

Just as a painting enhances a wall in your home, a blank wall outdoors can be decorated with plants. The design shown on these pages transforms a nondescript front entrance by showcasing perennials, vines, and a flowering shrub against an adjacent garage wall. Such entrances are common in suburban homes, but a vertical garden like this is ideal for other spots where yard space is limited.

Selected for a sunny site, these plants offer something in every season. Many are evergreen with foliage that looks fresh year-round. From March to December, flowers enhance the entrance with color and fragrance. In fall, the pomegranate will decorate the wall with large, cream-colored fruits.

The garden has two flowering peaks: spring and autumn. Fragrant white flowers of jasmine greet visitors to the front door early in spring. Chiming in later are the bold blossoms of the pomegranate, iris, and daylily and the more delicate blooms of dianthus and sage. Daylilies and sages continue to flower through the heat of summer, joined by santolina's bright-yellow buttonlike blooms. Expect another round of bloom that covers much of the color wheel when the weather turns cool in fall.

SITE: Sunny

SEASON: Spring

CONCEPT: Handsome plants arrayed against a blank wall make a picture that pleases year-round.

Plants & Projects

Training the pomegranate and the jasmine are the most demanding aspects of this planting. As the pomegranate grows, select horizontal branches that grow parallel with the wall and fasten them to wires attached to the wall. Prune to restrict growth to the wires. Train the jasmine vines by securing the runners to the trellises. The perennials are generally carefree.

A 'Wonderful' pomegranate (use 1 plant)
This upright deciduous shrub is easily trained against a wall. It bears bright-green glossy foliage and dazzling orange-red flowers in spring. A bounty of sweet, juicy pomegranates follows. Leaves are colorful in fall. See *Punica granatum* 'Wonderful', p. 140.

B Star jasmine (use 2)
This twining climber will cover the trellis year-round in small, shiny, dark-green leaves. It bears abundant and fragrant pinwheel-shaped white flowers in spring. See *Trachelospermum jasminoides*, p. 149.

C Mealycup sage (use 5)
From spring to fall, this upright perennial produces showy blue flower spikes that rise in clusters from clumps of slender gray-green leaves. See *Salvia farinacea*, p. 144.

D Autumn sage (use 3)
This bushy perennial has tiny oval leaves that contrast with the strappy foliage of the daylilies nearby. Colorful flower spikes surround the plant all season. We've shown a purple variety, but pink, white, or red are also available. See *Salvia greggii*, p. 144.

E Gray santolina (use 4)
This evergreen perennial forms a tight mound of narrow silver-gray foliage, just right for borders and tucked into corners.

Small yellow flowers top the foliage in summer. See *Santolina chamaecyparissus*, p. 145.

F Bearded iris (use 3)
Prized for handsome swordlike foliage as well as large lavender blossoms, this perennial is a standout against the daintier dianthus. It often blooms again in autumn. See *Iris* x *germanica*, p. 132.

G 'Black-Eyed Stella' daylily (use 5)
A popular perennial for hot sunny spots. Forms a clump of long, slender evergreen leaves crowned all summer with golden trumpet-shaped flowers tinged dark red in the centers. See *Hemerocallis* 'Black-Eyed Stella', p. 130.

H 'Bath's Pink' dianthus (use 15)
Sprinkled with small pink flowers in spring, this perennial trims the walk the rest of the year with a fringe of fine silvery foliage. See *Dianthus* 'Bath's Pink', p. 127.

Bearded iris **F**

Gray santolina **E**

'Bath's Pink' dianthus **H**

B Star jasmine

E Gray santolina

D Autumn sage

G 'Black-Eyed Stella' daylilly

A 'Wonderful' pomegranate

C Mealycup sage

G 'Black-Eyed Stella' daylilly

D Autumn sage

H 'Bath's Pink' dianthus

Driveway

Garage

E

B

D

G

A

B

G

D

F

C

E

H

H

Walkway

1 square = 1 ft.

House

Door

PLANT PORTRAITS

These perennials and shrubs fill a blank wall with handsome foliage and pretty flowers for many months of the year.

● = First design, pp. 60–61
▲ = Second design, pp. 62–63

Golden bamboo
(*Phyllostachys aurea*, p. 139) ▲

'Black-Eyed Stella' daylily
(*Hemerocallis*, p. 130) ●

'Picturata' aucuba
(*Aucuba japonica*, p. 120) ▲

English ivy
(*Hedera helix*, p. 129) ▲

'Kyoto Dwarf' mondo grass
(*Ophiopogon japonicus*, p. 140) ▲

Dressing up a shady wall

A shadier site calls for a different palette of plants. The basic idea of this design remains the same as the previous one—incorporate wall space to make the best use of a narrow plot.

Here the focus is on foliage. All the plants are evergreen or nearly so, and they offer a continuous array of colors, textures, and architectural qualities that brighten a dark space and deepen a narrow one. The result is a planting as bright and attractive in winter as it is the rest of the year.

Impressive canes of golden bamboo fill the corner with color, while dark-leaved ivy along a trellis provides a ruffled backdrop for two bold-leaved shrubs, the variegated aucuba and the tropical-looking fatsia. The border is trimmed in grassy ground covers of differing textures and colors. Summer flowers of the fatsia and lilyturf are seasonal treats.

Plants & Projects

Ⓐ Golden bamboo (use 1 plant)
This giant grass forms a striking clump of golden-yellow canes topped with straplike leaves. See *Phyllostachys aurea*, p. 139.

Ⓑ Fatsia (use 1)
Valued for its dressy foliage, this evergreen shrub also produces fuzzy white flower clusters in late summer and small black berries in fall. See *Fatsia japonica*, p. 127.

Ⓒ 'Picturata' aucuba (use 2)
A perfect complement for the bamboo, this durable evergreen shrub bears gold-splashed foliage edged in green. Red berries in winter. See *Aucuba japonica* 'Picturata', p. 120.

SITE: Shady

SEASON: Winter

CONCEPT: Evergreen foliage in a variety of textures and colors offers a warm welcome even in winter.

1 square = 1 ft.

Trellis H

English ivy D

'Big Blue' lilyturf E

'Kyoto Dwarf' mondo grass G

'Picturata' aucuba C

Fatsia B

'Big Blue' lilyturf E

Black mondo grass F

Golden bamboo A

D English ivy (use 6)
This vigorous evergreen vine will cling tightly to the trellis and wall. Of the many cultivars available, we've chosen one with large dark-green leaves that showcase the bright foliage of other evergreens, especially the aucuba and fatsia. See *Hedera helix*, p. 129.

E 'Big Blue' lilyturf (use 15)
Neat low mounds of fine-textured dark-green foliage make this evergreen perennial an attractive year-round ground cover. Lavender flowers are a summer bonus. This cultivar has larger flowers than the species. See *Liriope muscari* 'Big Blue', p. 135.

F Black mondo grass (use 14)
The dark-purple to black foliage of this ornamental evergreen plant makes a dramatic ground cover around the golden bamboo. See *Ophiopogon japonicus* 'Ebony Knight', p. 140.

G 'Kyoto Dwarf' mondo grass (use 50)
Dark green and very low growing, this evergreen plant adds a fine finish to the planting along the walk. See *Ophiopogon japonicus* 'Kyoto Dwarf', p. 140.

H Trellis
You can support the English ivy with the sturdy homemade trellis shown here, or buy one ready-made at a garden center. See p. 182.

Backyard Makeover

GET A LOT OUT OF A SMALL, FROST-FREE LOT

Space is at a premium on many suburban lots, but this needn't cramp your outdoor living style. The design shown here makes use of the entire area in a small backyard to provide opportunities for open-air gatherings as well as family relaxation and play. (The rendering is shown as if viewed from the house, which is indicated on the plan.)

At the center is a large flagstone patio bordered by grassy verges where children can play or adults can kick off their shoes and recline. A continuous garden bed meanders along a privacy fence enclosing the lot. As the shade tree matures, its generous canopy will accommodate a table or recliners. To cater outdoor feasts, there's a barbecue. A small pool and fountain provide a cooling presence and the music of bubbling water.

Curving gently around the perimeter, the plantings comprise a pleasing array of trees, shrubs, and trellised vines. Several "boulders" add to the natural composition and provide a few extra places to sit.

Many of the plants originate in exotic parts of the world and are chosen for their proven performance in frost-free areas. South America's native tipu tree is a striking focal point, with long clusters of spring flowers and fine-textured foliage. Equally eyecatching are the diverse and sculptural palms, the extraordinary flowers of the tropical bird of paradise, and the flamboyant blossoms of dwarf ixora.

Plants & Projects

Ambitious do-it-yourselfers can install the entire design. If you're less energetic, have a landscaping service put in the hardscape and do the planting yourself. A layer of small river-washed rocks mulches the beds, complementing the look of the plants and helping to conserve water.

A Tipu tree (use 1 plant)
Long clusters of yellow- to apricot-colored blossoms dangle among this small evergreen tree's fine-textured leaves in spring and early summer. Long seedpods add interest in autumn and winter. See *Tipuana tipu*, p. 148.

B Mediterranean fan palm (use 1)
This compact palm fits nicely under the tree and thrives in its shade. It forms a clump of trunks crowned with coarse blue-gray fronds, each looking

SITE: Sunny

SEASON: Spring

CONCEPT: A large patio and gorgeous plants make the most of a small backyard.

C Bottle palm

Bird of H Paradise

I 'Flower Carpet Pink' rose

F Arabian jasmine

Tipu tree A

I 'Flower Carpet Pink' rose

M Barbecue

J Annuals

Annuals J

'Thai Dwarf' E ixora

'Flower Carpet I Pink' rose

like a giant handheld fan. See *Chamaerops humilis*, p. 124.

C **Bottle palm** (use 1)
Another palm with great structural appeal. The trunk starts swollen and then narrows before branching into a shaggy bright green crown. See *Nolina recurvata*, p. 137.

D **'New Gold' Bougainvillea** (use 1)
This vigorous climber is clothed in golden flowers spring and summer. Leaves add texture and color in winter. See *Bougainvillea*, p. 121.

E **'Thai Dwarf' ixora** (use 2)
In a sheltered spot, this beautiful shrub promises a bounty of large colorful flowers. Evergreen foliage. See *Ixora* 'Thai Dwarf', p. 132.

F **Arabian jasmine** (use 2)
Two of these white-flowering vines are enough to perfume the entire backyard on summer nights. Evergreen. See *Jasminum sambac*, p. 132.

G **Madagascar palm** (use 1)
This shrub produces a single thorned trunk topped with straplike dull green leaves. See *Pachypodium lamerei*, p. 138.

H **Bird of Paradise** (use 2)
This evergreen perennial forms a wide clump of long-stemmed bluish green leaves and an abundance of large and unusual orange flowers. See *Strelitzia reginea*, p. 147.

I **'Flower Carpet Pink' rose** (use 13)
Shear this ground cover rose once in winter to keep it compact and blooming vigorously. Forms a nearly continuous mass of pink. See *Rosa*, p. 148.

J **Annuals**
Grow your favorites in large pots and narrow beds next to the house to enliven the patio. Ivy geranium is shown here.

K **Paving**
Choose a flagstone that complements the color of your home. See p. 160.

L **Water feature**
A small fiberglass pool and a simple fountain add interest at a modest cost. See p. 168.

M **Barbecue**
You can install a custom grill of stone or adobe as shown here or use a movable gas unit.

Gateway Garden

ARBOR, FENCE, AND PLANTINGS MAKE AN INVITING ENTRY

Entrances are an important part of any landscape. They can welcome visitors onto your property; highlight a special feature, such as a rose garden; or mark the passage between two areas with different character or function. The design shown here can serve in any of these situations.

A picket fence set amid shrubs and perennials creates a friendly and attractive barrier, just enough to signal the boundary of the front yard. The simple vine-covered arbor provides welcoming access.

Uncomplicated elements are combined imaginatively in this design, creating interesting details to catch the eye and an informal, happy-to-see-you overall effect. The arbor will be covered with cheerful yellow flowers in spring, and the fence with fragrant honeysuckle blossoms in summer. For winter color, both offer evergreen foliage. A multilayered planting in front of the fence offers contrasts in foliage texture as well as pretty flowers, and enough structure to be inviting after the blossoms fade.

Coral honeysuckle **E**

'Gracillimus' Japanese maiden grass **C**

'Goldsturm' black-eyed Susan **G**

Russian sage **F**

Mealycup sage **J**

'Stella d'Oro' daylily **I**

Plants & Projects

For many people, a picket fence and vine-covered arbor represent old-fashioned neighborly virtues. The structures and plantings are easy to install. You can extend the fence and plantings as needed.

Ⓐ Carolina jasmine (use 2 plants)
A lovely evergreen vine for the arbor. Sweetly fragrant clear-yellow flowers bloom among the masses of shiny leaves in early spring. See *Gelsemium sempervirens*, p. 129.

Ⓑ Firebush (use 1)
Summers set this perennial ablaze with orange-red flowers. New clusters keep coming until

frost. It is planted near the arbor so you can catch a glimpse of hummingbirds as you come and go. See *Hamelia patens*, p. 129.

Ⓒ 'Gracillimus' Japanese maiden grass (use 1)
This fine-textured grass makes an attractive anchor at one end of the planting. Stalks of creamy white flower plumes rise above the foliage in fall. See *Miscanthus sinensis* 'Gracillimus', p. 136.

Ⓓ 'Radiation' lantana (use 1)
This perennial spreads to form a 3-ft. mound of coarse green leaves topped with many small,

round clusters of orange and yellow flowers. Blooms prolifically all season. See *Lantana camara* 'Radiation', p. 134.

Ⓔ Coral honeysuckle (use 4)
Unlike the more invasive honeysuckles, this native vine is mannerly, climbing up the fence in neat tiers of rounded blue-green leaves. Clusters of coral-colored flowers radiate from the foliage in summer and sometimes fall. See *Lonicera sempervirens*, p. 137.

Ⓕ Russian sage (use 4)
These perennials make a big splash when planted together. They offer silvery foliage and

blue flowers to cool down the border's many hot colors. See *Perovskia atriplicifolia*, p. 139.

Ⓖ 'Goldsturm' black-eyed Susan (use 1)
A popular perennial companion of ornamental grasses. It forms a robust stand of dark leaves that are blanketed in summertime with bright-gold flowers. See *Rudbeckia fulgida* 'Goldsturm', p. 145.

Ⓗ Cigar plant (use 2)
An upright perennial with the look of a dwarf oleander. It forms a dense bush bearing multiple branches of narrow foliage that terminate in small

Carolina jasmine **A**

Cigar plant **H**

K Arbor and fence

B Firebush

E Coral honeysuckle

D 'Radiation' lantana

Mealycup sage **J**

Mealycup sage **J**

Lawn

Driveway

Walkway

Sidewalk

1 square = 1 ft.

tubelike orange and yellow flowers in autumn. See *Cuphea micropetala*, p. 126.

I **'Stella d'Oro' daylily** (use 9) Trumpet flowers the color of ripe pineapples crown these grassy perennials in summer. One of the best ever-blooming daylilies. See *Hemerocallis* 'Stella d'Oro', p. 130.

J **Mealycup sage** (use 18) Beautiful in front of a border, this upright perennial bears spikes of small blue flowers above gray-green leaves. See *Salvia farinacea*, p. 144.

K **Arbor and fence** Thick posts give this simple arbor a sturdy visual presence, and the low picket fence adds character. Both can be stained or painted. Cedar or redwood can be left to age with the weather, shown here. See p. 186.

SITE: Sunny

SEASON: Summer

CONCEPT: Shrubs, perennials, and flowering vines accent a traditional picket fence and simple entry arbor.

Say hello with roses

Not every entry calls for a fence. This design offers a traditional welcome with a rose garden. A border of tea roses and other flowering shrubs and perennials serves as a fragrant and colorful barrier on each side of a rose-covered entry arbor. The formal symmetry (an element often associated with rose gardens) is enhanced by boxwoods trimmed into pyramids at the foot of the arbor. The roses will bloom for many months. In spring they're joined by pink dianthus and blue iris and in late summer and fall by purple asters and sage. The boxwood's evergreen foliage provides green in winter.

Tea roses are less difficult than many people fear, but they require regular attention.

SITE: Sunny

SEASON: Fall

CONCEPT: Fragrant roses and other flowers provide a sweet welcome.

Plants & Projects

A **'Climbing Old Blush' China rose** (use 2 plants)
This delicate-looking rose is nonetheless a vigorous climber. It bears apple-green foliage and a steady bloom of baby-pink semidouble flowers, especially in spring. See *Rosa chinensis* 'Climbing Old Blush', p. 142.

B **'Gilbert Nabonnand' tea rose** (use 2)
The silky flowers of this bushy rose are pale pink and very fragrant all season. Petals are semidouble. See *Rosa x odorata* 'Gilbert Nabonnand', p. 142.

1 square = 1 ft.

'Climbing Old Blush' China rose **A**

Arbor **J**

'Gilbert Nabonnand' tea rose **B**

'Martha Gonzales' rose **C**

Bearded iris **H**

Mexican bush sage **D**

D Mexican bush sage

C 'Martha Gonzales' rose

E Littleleaf boxwood

F 'Powis Castle' artemisia

E Littleleaf boxwood

F 'Powis Castle' artemisia

G Fall aster

I 'Bath's Pink' dianthus

C **'Martha Gonzales' rose** (use 6)
  Wine red flowers cover this reliable dwarf
  rose in spring and fall. New shoots and
  leaves are also red. See *Rosa chinensis*
  'Martha Gonzales', p. 142.

D **Mexican bush sage** (use 2)
  This tall perennial adds height at the trellis.
  Bears spikes of purple-and-white flowers in
  fall. See *Salvia leucantha*, p. 145.

E **Littleleaf boxwood** (use 2)
  Plant these dense, glossy evergreen shrubs
  in front of the arbor and trim them into
  pyramids to enhance the formal look of this
  arbor entry. See *Buxus microphylla*, p. 123.

F **'Powis Castle' artemisia** (use 2)
  Prized for its foliage texture and color, this
  perennial forms silvery pillows beside the
  boxwoods. See *Artemisia* x 'Powis Castle',
  p. 120.

G **Fall aster** (use 2)
  Another fine-textured gray-green perennial
  to complement the boxwoods. For many
  weeks in fall it bursts into eye-catching
  lavender-purple bloom. See *Aster oblongifolius*, p. 120.

H **Bearded iris** (use 2)
  This perennial's foliage adds a spiky presence to the planting as well as showy blue
  flowers in spring. See *Iris* x *germanica*,
  p. 132.

I **'Bath's Pink' dianthus** (use 10)
  This perennial spreads to form low, wide
  tufts of very fine-textured foliage. Delicate
  pink flowers blanket the gray-green leaves
  in spring. See *Dianthus* 'Bath's Pink', p. 127.

See p. 67 for the following:

J **Arbor**

B 'Gilbert
Nabonnand'
tea rose

G Fall aster

H Bearded iris

I 'Bath's Pink'
dianthus

PLANT PORTRAITS

Combining compelling fragrance, lovely
flowers, and handsome foliage, these plants
create a distinctive entry.
● = First design, pp. 66–67
▲ = Second design, pp. 68–69

'Martha Gonzales' rose
(*Rosa chinensis*, p. 142) ▲

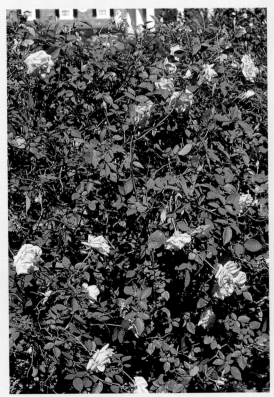

'Gilbert Nabonnand' tea rose
(*Rosa* x *odorata*, p. 142) ▲

'Climbing Old Blush' China rose
(*Rosa chinensis*, p. 142) ▲

Littleleaf boxwood
(*Buxus microphylla*, p. 123) ▲

Elegant Symmetry

MAKE A FORMAL GARDEN FOR YOUR BACKYARD

Formal landscaping often lends dignity to the public areas around a home. (See pp. 28–29.) Formality can also be rewarding in a more private setting. There, the groomed plants, geometric lines, and symmetrical layout of a formal garden can help to organize the surrounding landscaping, provide an elegant area for entertaining, or simply be enjoyed for their own sake.

Formal need not mean elaborate. This elegant design is no more than a circle inside a square. Concentric low hedges of clipped boxwood define the circle; a gravel path around the perimeter defines the square. The path continues through the center, opening into a small square decorated with a terra-cotta planter set on a grassy carpet.

The tallest elements in the design are four white-flowering trees interplanted with pyramidal evergreens. Enclosed in semicircular hedges and surrounded by grassy ground covers, white roses, and stately purple and gold perennials, these trees and shrubs create the effect of an enchanted *bosque*, a French word for a small, formal wood.

Even more than other types of landscaping, formal gardens work well only when carefully correlated with other elements in the landscape, including structures and plants. A round garden can be difficult to integrate. Relate it to rectilinear elements, such as a fence or hedges. And repeat plants used in the design elsewhere in your landscape to tie things together.

Plants & Projects

Of all gardens, a formal garden most obviously reflects the efforts of its makers. After the hedge has filled in, this garden requires attention mostly to keep it looking neat—shearing the hedges, pruning, deadheading the perennials, and seasonal cleanup.

Ⓐ 'Diana' althea (use 4 plants)
Pruned here as small trees, they wear a healthy coat of green leaves. In summer and fall they bear beautiful white hibiscus blossoms. See *Hibiscus syriacus* 'Diana', p. 131.

Ⓑ Compact Carolina cherry laurel (use 4)
A native evergreen shrub, it offers shiny green leaves and spikes of scented white flowers in spring. Shear to maintain a formal shape. See *Prunus caroliniana* 'Compacta', p. 140.

Ⓒ 'Marie Pavie' polyantha rose (use 4)
Clusters of small white roses cover this shrub rose from spring to frost. Buds have a pink cast. If this cultivar

'Diana' althea Ⓐ

Dwarf Mexican petunia Ⓙ

'Green Beauty' littleleaf boxwood Ⓓ

'Marie Pavie' polyantha rose Ⓒ

SITE: Sunny

SEASON: Early summer

CONCEPT: This self-contained planting could fill a small backyard or join other features on a larger property.

Lawn

1 square = 1 ft.

See site plan for Ⓚ.   Ⓜ Mondo grass

isn't available, consider 'White Pet' or 'Marie Daly'. See *Rosa* x *polyantha* 'Marie Pavie', p. 142.

D **'Green Beauty' littleleaf boxwood** (use 68)
A dense habit and fine texture make this evergreen shrub ideal for shearing into clipped hedges. See *Buxus microphylla* 'Green Beauty', p. 123.

E **Yellow variegated agave** (use 1)
Similar to yucca but shorter, this shrub creates a bold centerpiece above a planting of fine-leafed grass. See *Agave americana* 'Marginata', p. 119.

F **'Trailing Lavender' lantana** (use 6)
Lantanas are prized for their continuous and lavish bloom. This cultivar frames the central walkway with lacy clusters of lavender-purple flowers from spring to frost. See *Lantana montevidensis* 'Trailing Lavender', p. 134.

G **Texas gold columbine** (use 6)
This perennial's bright yellow flowers float above soft mounds of fernlike foliage in spring. Blooms are abundant and long lasting. See *Aquilegia chrysantha hinckleyana*, p. 119.

H **Purple verbena** (use 6)
Masses of wispy purple flowers wave above low clumps of foliage. This perennial comple-

ments the gold columbine. See *Verbena bonariensis*, p. 149.

I **St.-John's-wort** (use 16)
This mounding semievergreen shrub forms a dense mass of medium-green foliage that turns colorful in fall. Yellow flowers appear in summer. See *Hypericum calycinum*, p. 133.

J **Dwarf Mexican petunia** (use 20)
A beautiful and durable perennial ground cover. Clusters of purple petunialike blooms appear at the center of neat leafy mounds. See *Ruellia brittoniana* 'Katie', p. 144.

K **White rainlily** (use 48)
Planted among the lilyturf, this bulb makes white flowers after late summer rains. See Bulbs: *Zephyranthes candida*, p. 122.

L **'Big Blue' lilyturf** (use 30)
This grasslike perennial makes a neat edging along the path. Bears spikes of small lavender flowers. See *Liriope muscari* 'Big Blue', p. 135.

M **Mondo grass** (use 100)
This perennial will gradually grow into a continuous mat of very fine leaves. See *Ophiopogon japonicus*, p. 138.

N **Walkway**
Crushed stone is easy to install and suits the simple lines of this design. The pink granite we've shown here weathers to a terra-cotta pink. See p. 160.

H Purple verbena

I St.-John's-wort

E Yellow variegated agave

A 'Diana' althea

B Compact Carolina cherry laurel

Walkway **N**   **F** 'Trailing Lavender' lantana   **L** 'Big Blue' lilyturf   **G** Texas gold columbine   'Marie Pavie' polyantha rose **C**   **M** Mondo grass

Garden oasis

Palms and a pool give this garden a tropical look. The layout takes its inspiration from a compass or sundial. Four columnar palm trees planted outside the perimeter path mark the four directions of the compass. Interior paths lead from the living "columns" to a small lily pond at the center.

The planting beds are designed with the sun's path in mind. Two beds on the side of the afternoon sun are planted with bold shrubs and perennials that look cool even in the heat. The beds receiving morning light feature delicate roses and fine-textured grasses. Added water will produce more foliage and flowers.

1 square = 1 ft.

Lawn

Plants & Projects

Ⓐ Windmill palm (use 4 plants) A handsome little palm tree bearing a crown of dark-green fronds and a shaggy trunk. Easy to grow. See *Trachycarpus fortunei*, p. 149.

Ⓑ 'Mutabilis' China rose (use 2) This rose forms a 4-ft. bush of dark-green leaves and red shoots. The flowers are single, five-petaled, and change from pale yellow to orange to pink. See *Rosa chinensis* 'Mutabilis', p. 142.

Ⓒ 'Gold Star' esperanza (use 2) A very showy tropical-looking shrub. The foliage is bright green and has a crisp look. Golden bell-like flowers bloom in clusters from May to Novem-

SITE: Sunny

SEASON: Late summer

CONCEPT: A small pond becomes the focal point for a formal setting.

Ⓐ Windmill palm

See site plan for Ⓚ.

Gray Ⓗ santolina

'Mutabilis' Ⓑ China rose

'Gold Star' Ⓒ esperanza

Path Ⓝ

Tropical Ⓕ plumbago

'Morning Light' Ⓔ Japanese maiden grass

Ⓜ 'Big Blue' lilyturf

Pond Ⓛ

Ⓖ Purple heart

'Bath's Pink' Ⓘ dianthus

Ⓙ Dauben water lily

Ⓓ Soft-tip yucca

ber. Deciduous in most parts of Texas. See *Tecoma stans* 'Gold Star', p. 148.

D Soft-tip yucca (use 4)
A bold accent plant, this perennial bears long pointed sword-like leaves with bent tips. It sends up branched stalks of large white flowers in summer. See *Yucca gloriosa*, p. 151.

E 'Morning Light' Japanese maiden grass (use 4)
A must for a cool oasis, this grass forms a fountain of arching light-green foliage. See *Miscanthus sinensis* 'Morning Light,' p. 136.

F Tropical plumbago (use 8)
This perennial will fill the space with small, oval, bright-green leaves. Bears tight clusters of cool blue flowers in the heat of summer. See *Plumbago auriculata*, p. 139.

G Purple heart (use 8)
This perennial ground cover creates a thick mat of colorful, interesting foliage. Pale-pink flowers bloom throughout the season. See *Setcreasea pallida* 'Purple Heart', p. 146.

H Gray santolina (use 20)
A handsome low-growing shrub. Thick gray foliage looks like lavender. Yellow flowers in the summer. See *Santolina chamaecyparissus*, p. 145.

I 'Bath's Pink' dianthus (use 32)
Another excellent edging, this perennial forms a year-round mat of short, very narrow silver foliage. Spring flowers are pink and fragrant. See *Dianthus* 'Bath's Pink', p. 127.

J Dauben water lily (use 1)
A small plant for a small-scale pond. Lavender flowers bloom among floating leaves nonstop in summer heat. See p. 151.

K Stepping-stones
Gray limestone makes a decorative edging around the santolina. See p. 160.

L Pond
Use a round fiberglass shell for this small pool. See p. 168.

See p. 71 for the following:

M 'Big Blue' lilyturf (use 30)

N Path

PLANT PORTRAITS

These well-behaved, low-care shrubs, bulbs, and perennials bring form, texture, flowers, and scent to a formal garden.
● = First design, pp. 70–71
▲ = Second design, pp. 72–73

Dauben water lily
(Water plants: *Nymphaea*, p. 151) ▲

'Green Beauty' littleleaf boxwood (*Buxus microphylla*, p. 123) ●

'Diana' althea
(*Hibiscus syriacus*, p. 131) ●

'Marie Pavie' polyantha rose
(*Rosa x polyantha*, p. 142) ●

Yellow variegated agave
(*Agave americana* 'Marginata', p. 119) ●

White rainlily
(Bulbs: *Zephyranthes candida*, p. 122) ●

A Beginning Border

FLOWERS AND A FENCE MAKE A CAREFREE DESIGN

A mixed border can be one of the most delightful of all gardens. Indeed, that's usually its sole purpose. Unlike many other types of landscape plantings, a traditional border is seldom yoked to any function beyond that of providing as much visual pleasure as possible.

This border is designed for a beginning or busy gardener. In parts of Texas, watering is one of the most formidable garden tasks. To reduce the time and cost associated with this chore, we've selected low-water-use plants for this border. Durable and carefree, they'll maximize the time you spend enjoying the garden.

Behind the planting, a simple fence screens out distractions and provides a unifying frame for the display. The border is meant to be viewed from the front, so taller plants go in back. A small flowering tree in the center serves as a colorful focal point.

The planting offers a selection of flowers in blues, reds, pinks, yellows, and creamy whites. Blooming over many months, there are flowers borne in spiky clusters as well as large feathery plumes, pendent bells, and bright cheerful "daisies."

The garden's foliage is at least as compelling as its flowers. A range of textures and colors contrast with and complement one another. At the back of the planting, the striking spiky yucca contrasts with the bushy green mounds of autumn sage and fall aster. These plants in turn are framed by airy masses of silvery green and blue foliage. Similar juxtapositions of color and texture are repeated on a smaller scale at the front of the planting.

If you want a larger border, just plant more of each plant to fit the space, or repeat parts of the design.

SITE: Sunny

SEASON: Summer

CONCEPT: Use the fence as a backdrop for this gorgeous border.

1 square = 1 ft.

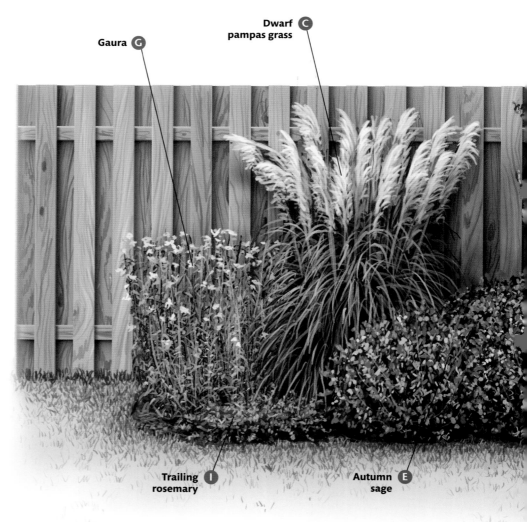

Gaura **G**

Dwarf pampas grass **C**

Trailing rosemary **I**

Autumn sage **E**

Plants & Projects

Once established, this planting will require almost no supplemental water and little other care. The only maintenance will be removing spent flowers during the summer and annual pruning of the chaste tree, fall aster, and santolina.

A Chaste tree (use 1 plant)
When in full summer bloom, this vigorous shrub bristles with fragrant lavender-blue flowers. The narrow deciduous leaves are dark green above and gray-green below. Prune into a tree if you like, or cut it back to a few feet in early spring to keep it compact and shrublike. See *Vitex agnus-castus*, p. 150.

B Soft-tip yucca (use 2)
This evergreen shrub forms a mound of attractive blue-gray swordlike foliage terminating in soft, rather than stiff, tips. In summer and fall, it sends up very tall stalks of nodding, lily-like white flowers. See *Yucca gloriosa*, p. 151.

C Dwarf pampas grass (use 1)
A small version of a stunning ornamental grass. Forms a dense clump of slender arching evergreen blades topped with creamy flowers the size of feather dusters. See *Cortaderia selloana* 'Pumila', p. 126.

D Russian sage (use 3)
This bushy perennial's small silvery leaves and slender blue flower stalks are a nice contrast to the surrounding greens. See *Perovskia atriplicifolia*, p. 139.

E Autumn sage (use 4)
These perennials form rounded mounds of bright foliage and flowers. Choose red or coral blooms for best effect. Evergreen in most of the state. See *Salvia greggii*, p. 144.

F Fall aster (use 1)
Another round shape for an otherwise spiky garden, this native perennial sports a dense growth of pale-gray foliage on wiry stems. Lavender-purple flowers in fall echo the color of the chaste tree and Russian sage blooms. Looks best when trimmed a couple of times during the growing season. See *Aster oblongifolius*, p. 120.

G Gaura (use 1)
A tough heat-tolerant Texas native, it produces surprisingly delicate masses of pink and white flowers above slender swaying stems. See *Gaura lindheimeri*, p. 128.

H Red yucca (use 3)
This mini yucca has slender gray-green leaves adorned with many stalks of small, coral-pink trumpet-shaped flowers. See *Hesperaloe parviflora*, p. 130.

I Trailing rosemary (use 2)
An evergreen shrub forming a low clump of sinuous branches lined with tiny pinelike leaves. Blooms mostly in early spring but the small blue flowers may appear sporadically throughout the year. See *Rosmarinus officinalis* 'Prostratus', p. 143.

J Gray santolina (use 3)
This compact shrub reinforces the silver-gray theme. Small, fragrant, toothed leaves grow in low mounds. In summer they sport bright-yellow button flowers. Cut back to about 6 in. in early spring to maintain a nice round shape. See *Santolina chamaecyparissus*, p. 145.

K Fence
A tall fence provides a backdrop for the border and privacy for you. See p. 190.

Autumn blooms

This border focuses on flowers. It requires more frequent watering than the previous one but otherwise needs little care. Flowers in purples, pinks, blues, and yellows open in spring and peak again in fall. The blossoms are enhanced by their juxtaposition—for example, lantana combined with garden phlox and daisy mums—and by handsome foliage in shades of green and gray. Silvery Texas sage makes a luminous backdrop for the pink and purple flowers of phlox and verbena. And the holly's dark lustrous foliage helps highlight the blues and yellows of salvia and daylily. If you'd like to keep the border in bloom year-round, plant winter annuals among dormant perennials. Evergreen shrubs and perennials provide plenty of colorful contrasts to please less energetic gardeners.

Plants & Projects

A **Burford holly** (use 1 plant) A bold accent, this evergreen shrub has sparkling deep-green leaves brightened by showy red berries in fall and winter. See *Ilex cornuta* 'Burfordii', p. 132.

B **Compact Texas sage** (use 1) Evergreen shrub with a tidy, rounded habit. Lavender flowers bloom among silvery white leaves in summer. See *Leucophyllum frutescens* 'Compactum', p. 135.

C **'Indigo Spires' salvia** (use 2) This vigorous perennial's long spires of dark purple-blue flowers bloom for months above silvery green triangular leaves. A great specimen plant. See *Salvia* x 'Indigo Spires', p. 145.

D **'Confetti' lantana** (use 1) Bursting with pink and yellow flowers from spring to frost, this perennial is the perfect companion for garden phlox and daisy mums. See *Lantana camara* 'Confetti', p. 134.

E **'Powis Castle' artemisia** (use 1) This perennial forms a mound of silver-lace foliage that looks good year-round. Shear it occa-

SITE: Sunny

SEASON: Fall

CONCEPT: Flowers are the main show in this mixed border.

Lawn

1 square = 1 ft.

'Indigo Spires' salvia **C**
Burford holly **A**
E 'Powis Castle' artemisia
F 'John Fanick' garden phlox
Compact **B** Texas sage
'Confetti' **D** lantana
'Indigo Spires' salvia **C**
Fence **M**
'Homestead **J** Purple' verbena
I 'Country Girl' daisy mum
Daylily **H**
F 'John Fanick' garden phlox
L Stepping-stones
G Bearded iris
K 'Bath's Pink' dianthus
J 'Homestead Purple' verbena
'Bath's Pink' **K** dianthus

PLANT PORTRAITS

These well-behaved, low-care shrubs, bulbs, and perennials bring form, texture, flowers, and scent to a formal garden.

● = First design, pp. 74–75

▲ = Second design, pp. 76–77

sionally to maintain a pleasing round shape. See *Artemisia* x 'Powis Castle', p. 120.

F **'John Fanick' garden phlox** (use 5)
A floriferous perennial, it produces long-lasting clusters of small pink flowers with dark-pink eyes from spring through fall. See *Phlox paniculata* 'John Fanick,' p. 139.

G **Bearded iris** (use 9)
Spectacular flowers and striking foliage make this perennial a must for the flower border. It blooms in spring and may repeat in fall. Shop for a reblooming cultivar in yellow or white for this garden. See *Iris* x *germanica*, p. 132.

H **Daylily** (use 6)
Carefree perennials that form mounds of grassy foliage topped by vase-shaped flowers. Shop for newer varieties that rebloom in fall. Soft-yellow flowers would look good here. See *Hemerocallis* hybrids, p. 130.

I **'Country Girl' daisy mum** (use 5)
This perennial's pretty pink flowers add color to the border in the fall. Prune halfway in spring and again in early summer to keep the clump compact. See *Chrysanthemum* x 'Country Girl', p. 125.

J **'Homestead Purple' verbena** (use 5)
Plant this perennial among the stepping-stones for a thick carpet of vibrant purple flowers. A trim twice a year keeps it tidy. See *Verbena* x *hybrida* 'Homestead Purple', p. 149.

K **'Bath's Pink' dianthus** (use 11)
This fine-textured evergreen perennial for the front of the border forms a low dense mat of silvery needlelike foliage topped with fragrant pink flowers in spring. See *Dianthus* 'Bath's Pink', p. 127.

L **Stepping-stones**
Flagstones placed around the birdbath provide access for cleaning and filling. See p. 160.

See p. 75 for the following:

M **Fence**

'Country Girl' daisy mum (*Chrysanthemum*, p. 125) ▲

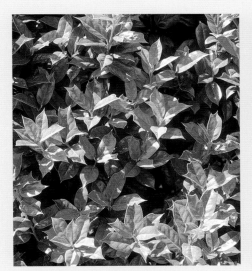
Burford holly (*Ilex cornuta* 'Burfordii', p. 132) ▲

'John Fannick' garden phlox (*Phlox paniculata*, p. 139) ▲

Gray santolina (*Santolina chamaecyparissus*, p. 145) ●

Year-In-Year-Out Border

PERENNIALS AND A WALL MAKE A TRADITIONAL DESIGN

Using durable plants that are easy to establish and maintain, this border is intended for a beginning or busy gardener. Behind the planting, providing a solid backdrop, is a simple wall. The border is meant to be viewed from the front, so taller plants go at the back. Draped over the wall, a trumpet vine adds a swath of dark-green leaves to the backdrop, dappled for weeks in late summer with lovely deep-pink flowers.

The planting offers a selection of flowers in blues, reds, pinks, and purples. Blooming over many months, there are small flowers borne in spiky clusters as well as bright cheerful daisies.

The garden's foliage is at least as compelling as its flowers. A range of textures and colors contrast with and complement one another. At the back of the planting, the striking spiky purple leaves of New Zealand flax contrast with the bushy green mound of the autumn sage. These plants are in turn framed by lacy masses of silver-gray foliage. Similar juxtapositions of color and texture are repeated on a smaller scale at the front of the planting.

If you want a larger border, just plant more of each plant to fit the space, or repeat parts of the design.

'Atropurpureum' **A**
New Zealand flax

Mexican **B**
bush sage

Sunrose **L**

'Powis Castle' **G**
artemisia

K 'Burgundy'
gazania

Plants & Projects

Removing spent flowers and seasonal pruning are the main chores in this garden. (To allow for maintenance, leave a space between the plants at the front of the border and those at the back, as shown on the site plan.) In winter, cut the gaura and Russian sage almost to the ground, cut the germander sage back by one-third, and prune the trumpet vine to control its size. Once established, the plants require little supplemental water.

A **'Atropurpureum' New Zealand flax**
(use 1 plant)
A bold, colorful accent, this perennial offers long, reddish purple, straplike leaves. From late spring to midsummer, branched stalks of reddish flowers rise above the foliage. See *Phormium tenax*, p. 139.

B **Mexican bush sage** (use 1)
This perennial has silver-gray foliage. It bears purple-and-white flowers from midsummer into fall. See *Salvia leucantha*, p. 145.

C **Gaura** (use 1)
Another wispy perennial, its graceful arching stems bear small leaves and spikes of small pink-and-white flowers from spring through fall. See *Gaura lindheimeri*, p. 128.

D **Autumn sage** (use 5)
This bushy perennial's green foliage bristles with striking spikes of red flowers from spring into fall. See *Salvia greggii*, p. 144.

E **Russian sage** (use 1)
From early summer into fall, small lavender-blue flowers seem to float amidst this perennial's stiff gray-green stems and silvery foliage. See *Perovskia atriplicifolia*, p. 139.

F **'Mme. Galen' trumpet vine** (use 1)
This deciduous vine bears large compound leaves on thick stems. Clusters of salmon flowers bloom in late summer. Stake it the first year; after that its aerial rootlets will cling to the wall. See *Campsis x tagliabuana*, p. 124.

G **'Powis Castle' artemisia** (use 3)
This perennial makes a mound of lacy silver foliage that looks good year-round. It is an excellent companion for the colorful gazania and New Zealand flax. See *Artemisia*, p. 120.

H **Germander sage** (use 1)
Forming a low, spreading mass of small silvery leaves, this perennial bears wispy spikes of bright-blue flowers from summer into fall. See *Salvia chamaedryoides*, p. 144.

F 'Mme. Galen' trumpet vine

SITE: Sunny

SEASON: Early summer

CONCEPT: Easy-care perennials with colorful flowers and foliage make this border ideal for beginning and busy gardeners alike.

E Russian sage

C Gaura **J** Blue marguerite Autumn sage **D** **I** 'Majestic' lilyturf **H** Germander sage

I **'Majestic' lilyturf** (use 3)
This evergreen perennial makes a clump of dark-green leaves topped by tall purple flowers in summer. See *Liriope muscari*, p. 135.

J **Blue marguerite** (use 3)
Blue daisies nod above the spreading foliage throughout the year (if you deadhead them). See *Felicia amelloides*, p. 127.

K **'Burgundy' gazania** (use 4)
This perennial flower produces large reddish purple daisies during late spring and in early summer. Dark-green foliage remains attractive for months. See *Gazania*, p. 128.

L **Sunrose** (use 3)
Small, bright-colored flowers sparkle in spring and early summer on the evergreen foliage of this small shrub. See *Helianthemum nummularium*, p. 129.

Wall

Lawn

1 square = 1 ft.

Garden in the Round

CREATE A PLANTING WITH SEVERAL ATTRACTIVE FACES

SITE: Sunny

SEASON: Summer

CONCEPT: A free-floating garden offers beauty all around, and a bonus of butterflies.

In domestic landscapes, plantings are often meant to be viewed from the front, similar to a wall-mounted sculpture in raised relief. However, the planting shown here forms an island bed that you can stroll around. Plants displayed in the round present different scenes from several vantage points. This is an excellent option for those who want to squeeze more gardening space from a small lot, add interest to a rectangular plot, or divide a large area into smaller outdoor "rooms."

A bed that floats free of any anchors requires a sensitivity to scale. To be successful, the bed must neither dominate its surroundings nor be lost in them. The plants here, with their bold textures and bright colors, have presence when viewed from a distance, while also offering a visual feast on close inspection. A festive parade of flowers begins in spring and continues through November. First up are pink-and-yellow daylilies, followed closely by the showy purples of the chaste tree, salvia, and verbena. Joining them are vivid yellows of lantana, esperanza and rudbeckia, and the calmer pinks of roses, yarrows, and gaura.

Among the garden's delights will be countless butterflies, attracted to the flowers of almost all plants here, in particular those of the chaste tree, verbena, and lantana. Position a small decorative birdbath among the blooms, and let it double as a butterfly basin.

See site plan for **I** and **K** .

A Chaste tree

Mexican bush sage D

Gaura E

'Goldsturm' H
black-eyed Susan

Plants & Projects

This planting offers flowers and foliage that look good with a minimum of care. Prune the chaste tree into a tree form to allow space and light for nearby plants. To keep the gaura looking fresh, remove stems that have played out their blooms. Cut back the Mexican bush sage by a third in late spring to keep it from getting floppy in fall due to the weight of the flower spikes.

A Chaste tree (use 1 plant)
A fast-growing deciduous shrub or small tree with arching branches and dark-green leaves. It defies its common name by flowering prolifically from May to November. In full bloom the showy lavender-blue blossoms hide most of the tree. See *Vitex agnus-castus*, p. 150.

B 'Gold Star' esperanza (use 1)
Big, bright-yellow, bell-like flowers dangle from the tips of this bushy perennial's many branches from summer to frost. Flowers have a pleasant, light fragrance. See *Tecoma stans* 'Gold Star', p. 148.

C 'Belinda's Dream' rose (use 3)
These bushy roses will fill the space behind the daylilies with luxuriant dark-green foliage and abundant fragrant pink blossoms from early spring to hard frost. See *Rosa* x 'Belinda's Dream', p. 142.

D Mexican bush sage (use 5)
These bushy perennials skirt the chaste tree with slender gray-green leaves. Spikes of lavender flowers will echo the blossoms just above them in fall. See *Salvia leucantha*, p. 145.

E Gaura (use 3)
A favorite of butterflies, this fine-textured perennial forms a base of small pale-green leaves from which numerous slender stems rise, bearing pink-and-white flowers that appear to float above the plant. See *Gaura lindheimeri*, p. 128.

F 'Confetti' lantana (use 1)
Festive clusters of bicolored flowers in pink and yellow cover this bushy perennial from spring to frost. See *Lantana camara* 'Confetti', p. 134.

Lawn

1 square = 1 ft.

G Daylily (use 11)
This popular perennial forms a grassy mound of narrow foliage. Numerous, large, trumpet-shaped flowers rise on sturdy stalks and open just above the foliage from pickle-like buds. A gaily colored pink, yellow, or lavender cultivar would look best here. See *Hemerocallis*, p. 130.

H 'Goldsturm' black-eyed Susan (use 5)
A golden blanket of dark-eyed "daisies" covers this perennial in early summer. See *Rudbeckia fulgida* 'Goldsturm', p. 145.

I 'Fire King' yarrow (use 7)
This perennial forms a mat of fine fernlike foliage topped with flat, lacy flowerheads in shades of hot pink. See *Achillea millefolium* 'Fire King', p. 118.

J Homestead Purple' verbena (use 4)
Masses of purple flowers and the butterflies they attract hover among the bright-green leaves of this perennial all season. See *Verbena* x *hybrida* 'Homestead Purple', p. 149.

K Narcissus (use as needed)
Small trumpet-shaped flowers open in clusters on stalks that rise above dark-green leaves. Each stalk may produce as many as 20 flowers. Common cultivars have white petals and a yellow cup. Plant throughout the bed for a carpet of bloom in spring. See Bulbs: *Narcissus tazetta*, p. 120.

L Butterfly basin
A small birdbath can also serve up food and drink for butterflies. Fill it with water, or leave bits of fruit to ferment for a sugary treat.

'Gold Star' **B** esperanza

F 'Confetti' lantana

L Butterfly basin

J 'Homestead Purple' verbena

C 'Belinda's Dream' rose

G Daylily

An island garden for the birds

This design uses an existing shade tree as an anchor for a free-floating island bed and adds a smaller tree at its opposite end for balance. The trees are underplanted with shrubs and mid-height perennials. Lower-growing perennials fill the rest of the gently curved bed in repeating waves of contrasting foliage and flower. Like the previous design, this one affords attractive views from all sides.

Plants are chosen not only for their lush woodsy look but also for the birdlife they'll attract. The redbud offers flowers in early spring, attractive seasonal foliage, and a welcome perch for songbirds year-round. The unusual flowers of the Turk's cap open just in time for migrating hummingbirds. And the decorative seeds of beautyberry and inland sea oats keep ground-feeding birds feasting in autumn and winter.

This garden requires little maintenance beyond annual pruning. The columbines and ferns naturally shed their stems and can be thinned out as needed. To maintain its bushy shape and encourage more flowers, the Turk's cap can be cut back by about a third after each flowering spurt.

Turk's cap **C**

D Wood fern

I Birdbath

Inland **F** sea oats

Holly fern **E**

Texas gold **G** columbine

1 square = 1 ft.

Existing shade tree

Lawn

SITE: Shady

SEASON: Fall

CONCEPT: Stroll around this planting to enjoy the plants and the birds they attract.

Plants & Projects

A **Redbud** (use 1 plant)
A deciduous understory tree with a rounded crown, colorful fall leaves, and a burst of vivid-pink bloom in early spring. See *Cercis canadensis*, p. 124.

B **American beautyberry** (use 1)
This deciduous shrub has an open habit and draping branches lined with tapered leaves. Bright-purple berries appear in tight, round clusters on every leaf node in late summer. The berries are especially showy on bare branches. See *Callicarpa americana*, p. 123.

C **Turk's cap** (use 5)
This hibiscus relative will form a dark leafy mass under the shade tree. Small red-orange flowers resembling a Turkish fez decorate the shrub all season. See *Malvaviscus arboreus drummondii*, p. 138.

A Redbud

B American beautyberry

H Dwarf Mexican petunia

PLANT PORTRAITS

These distinctive plants will bring color and texture to any garden in the round.

● = First design, pp. 80–81

▲ = Second design, pp. 82–83

'Belinda's Dream' rose (*Rosa*, p. 142) ●

'Fire King' yarrow (*Achillea millefolium*, p. 118) ●

D Wood fern (use 10)
Light-green fronds add a cool fresh look to the garden from spring through fall. See Ferns: *Thelypteris kunthii*, p. 128.

E Holly fern (use 22)
In contrast to most ferns, this one has leathery dark evergreen foliage that looks more like holly leaves. Adds greenery to the garden when the other plants are dormant. See Ferns: *Cyrtomium falcatum*, p. 128.

F Inland sea oats (use 5)
Forming a small patch of prairie between the trees, this grass is most interesting in late summer, when long oatlike seedheads dangle on arching stalks among the foliage. See *Chasmanthium latifolium*, p. 125.

G Texas gold columbine (use 10)
Yellow flowers nod in spring above this perennial's dainty mounds of fernlike foliage. See *Aquilegia chrysantha hinckleyana*, p. 119.

H Dwarf Mexican petunia (use 18)
A tough perennial gound cover, its dark-green leaves create an informal fringe around the redbud, with clusters of small, petunialike purple flowers opening in the center of each plant. See *Ruellia brittoniana* 'Katie', p. 144.

I Birdbath
This island bed will attract lots of birdlife, so place a favorite birdbath under the tree for their refreshment.

'Lavender Bonanza' daylily (*Hemerocallis*, p. 130) ●

A Shady Hideaway

BUILD A COZY RETREAT IN A CORNER OF YOUR YARD

One of life's pleasures is sitting in a shady spot reading or just looking out onto your garden. If your property is long on lawn and short on shade, a chair under an arbor can provide a cool respite from the heat or the cares of the day. Tucked into a corner of the yard and set among attractive shrubs, vines, and perennials, the arbor shown here is a desirable destination even when the day isn't sizzling.

A small tree and an overhead vine create a cozy enclosure, affording privacy as well as shade. Plantings in front of the arbor and extending along the property lines integrate the hideaway with the lawn and make a handsome scene when viewed from the house. The design is also effective in an open corner or backed by a property-line fence. The arbor is small; it's easy to make it wider and longer by extending the plantings.

Flowers contribute warm colors. Festive yellows, pinks, and reds start the year off and continue until the first frost. Along with a canopy of honeysuckle blossoms, there will be showy hibiscus flowers and lantanas by the bench. Masses of black-eyed Susans and red pomegranate flowers join up in summer. And in fall, deciduous foliage adds to the colorful mix. This is primarily a warm-season planting, but pomegranate fruits and holly berries will make the hideaway well worth a winter visit.

Property line

Lawn

1 square = 1 ft.

Plants & Projects

The arbor and plants can be installed in a few weekends. Once the plants are established, seasonal pruning and cleanup should keep this durable planting looking good year-round.

A **Possumhaw holly** (use 1 plant)
This fast-growing deciduous tree makes a handsome screen for the hideaway. Smooth oval leaves turn yellow in fall. When they drop, they expose silvery branches with bright red, orange, or yellow berries, the color depending on the cultivar. See *Ilex decidua*, p. 132.

B **Compact pomegranate** (use 3)
A low-growing form of a popular deciduous shrub. Lustrous foliage showcases red carnationlike flowers in summer and small ornamental fruits in fall. See *Punica granatum* 'Nana', p. 140.

C **Dwarf Japanese maiden grass** (use 2)
One of the most compact fountain grasses. Abundant cream-colored flowers rise above long leaves in summer. Foliage turns tawny in winter. See *Miscanthus sinensis* 'Adagio', p. 136.

D **Texas star hibiscus** (use 2)
This perennial forms a large airy clump of slender, deeply divided, glossy leaves borne on red-tinged stems. Brilliant red five-petaled flowers open daily during the summer and fall. See *Hibiscus coccineus*, p. 131.

E **Firebush** (use 2)
Small slender flowers dangle at the ends of this perennial's many branches from summer to frost. Dull green leaves turn red in fall. See *Hamelia patens*, p. 129.

F **Turk's cap** (use 4)
This shrubby perennial will tolerate the eventual shade under the tree canopy, providing a lush screen of dark-green leaves studded with small red turban-like flowers. See *Malvaviscus arboreus drummondii*, p. 136.

G **Cigar plant** (use 2)
Adding a vertical element to the planting, this perennial spreads to form a patch of upright stems topped with long narrow leaves. Thin orange and yellow flowers complement the firebush blossoms in summer. See *Cuphea micropetala*, p. 126.

H **'Goldstrum' black-eyed Susan** (use 3)
This popular perennial's abundant, golden, dark-eyed daisies bloom abundantly in summer, with plenty to spare for flower arrangements. See *Rudbeckia fulgida* 'Goldsturm', p. 143.

I **'New Gold' lantana** (use 2)
Tiny golden flowers in tight round clusters cover the foliage of this spreading perennial from late spring to frost. See *Lantana x hybrida* 'New Gold', p. 134.

J **Mexican mint marigold** (use 3)
Plant this perennial next to the bench for fragrant foliage and a fall display of rich yellow flowers. On your way into the house snip a few anise-flavored leaves for cooking and a handful of flowers for fall bouquets. See *Tagetes lucida*, p. 147.

K **Coral honeysuckle** (use 2)
Whorls of scarlet flowers decorate this popular vine from late spring to fall. Attractive blue-green foliage is evergreen. See *Lonicera sempervirens*, p. 135.

L **Arbor**
This simple structure can be built in a weekend or two. See p. 189.

M **Paving**
Flat fieldstones in tones of gray complement the arbor and the planting. See p. 160.

SITE: Sunny

SEASON: Summer

CONCEPT: Enjoy a colorful array of plants while you relax under a shady arbor.

Possumhaw holly **A**

Coral honeysuckle **K**

Arbor **L**

Texas star hibiscus **D**

See site plan for **F** .

Mexican mint marigold **J**

Dwarf Japanese maiden grass **C**

I 'New Gold' lantana

B Compact pomegranate

Paving **M**

Firebush **E**

Cigar plant **G**

'Goldsturm' black-eyed Susan **H**

PLANT PORTRAITS

Privacy, shade, flowers, foliage, and fragrance—these plants provide all the necessities for a relaxing backyard retreat.

● = First design, pp. 84-85
▲ = Second design, pp. 86-87

Compact pomegranate
(*Punica granatum* 'Nana', p. 140) ●

Narcissus (Bulbs: *Narcissus tazetta* 'Grand Primo', p. 122) ▲

Mexican mint marigold
(*Tagetes lucida*, p. 147) ●

Polyantha rose (*Rosa* x *polyantha* 'Marie Daly', p. 142) ▲

Homegrown hideaway

Instead of building your garden retreat, you can grow it. A small tree and midsize shrubs replace the arbor in the previous design. Their lush greenery provides a sense of enclosure and privacy year-round, and the cool flower colors (blues, pinks, and whites) will soothe the senses even as the temperature rises.

Reliably evergreen, the wax myrtle's deliciously scented leaves will cast dappled shade over the bench all year. The camellias, viburnums, and abelias are evergreen too, their dark glossy foliage a perfect foil for pink and white blossoms. There will be flowers in every season: sweet-scented viburnum in early spring, roses from May to October, camellias in November, and narcissus for snow-white blooms in winter.

Plants & Projects

Ⓐ Wax myrtle (use 1 plant)
This small evergreen tree offers a fragrant and shady canopy for bench sitters. Leaves are smooth and slender. See *Myrica cerifera*, p. 137.

Ⓑ 'Shi Shi Gashira' camellia (use 3)
This low, compact, and lustrous evergreen shrub bears double rose-colored flowers in late fall. See *Camellia sasanqua* 'Shi Shi Gashira', p. 123.

Ⓒ 'Spring Bouquet' viburnum (use 1)
Pink buds open into scented white flowers when this evergreen shrub blooms in early spring. See *Viburnum tinus* 'Spring Bouquet', p. 150.

Ⓓ 'Edward Goucher' glossy abelia (use 3)
This evergreen shrub forms a low mound of small, pointed, glossy leaves tinged purple-bronze in winter. Pink flowers in summer lead to creamy pink seedheads later on. See *Abelia grandiflora* 'Edward Goucher', p. 118.

E **Polyantha rose** (use 3)
Apple-green foliage topped with pale-pink semidouble flowers make this dwarf rose a standout next to the path. See *Rosa* x *polyantha* 'Marie Daly', p. 142.

F **Tropical plumbago** (use 4)
The clear blue flowers of this shrubby perennial add cool color to the planting in hot summer months. See *Plumbago auriculata*, p. 139.

G **'Indigo Spires' salvia** (use 1)
This lush, vigorous perennial makes a bushy mound of triangular leaves topped all season with long spikes of blue-purple flowers. See *Salvia* x 'Indigo Spires,', p. 145.

H **'Blue Princess' verbena** (use 2)
Plant this low-growing perennial up front for a season-long border of lavender-blue flowers. See *Verbena* x *hybrida* 'Blue Princess', p. 149.

I **'Bath's Pink' dianthus** (use 5)
This evergreen perennial's pincushion-like blue-gray foliage adds texture and color to the border. Masses of small pink flowers blanket the plant in spring. See *Dianthus* 'Bath's Pink', p. 127.

J **'Grand Primo' narcissus** (use 40)
Scatter bulbs of this small daffodil around the planting, especially the plumbago and salvia, for grassy foliage and white flowers after the perennials freeze back. See Bulbs: *Narcissus tazetta* 'Grand Primo', p. 122.

See p. 84 for the following:

K **Paving**

Property line

Lawn

SITE: Sunny

SEASON: Fall

CONCEPT: Planting your own retreat can be as therapeutic as sitting and enjoying the results.

1 square = 1 ft.

Wax myrtle **A**

See site plan for **J**.

'Spring Bouquet' viburnum **C**

Tropical plumbago **F**

Polyantha rose **E**

'Blue Princess' verbena **H**

'Indigo Spires' salvia **G**

Paving **K**

'Shi Shi Gashira' camellia **B**

'Edward Goucher' glossy abelia **D**

I 'Bath's Pink' dianthus

An Outdoor "Living" Room

PATIO AND SHADY ARBOR PROVIDE OPEN-AIR OPPORTUNITIES

In Texas, opportunities for outdoor living abound. This design demonstrates how a patio next to the house can become a true extension of your living space with the addition of an arbor, a fence, and plants that create an attractive setting—and attract hummingbirds as well.

At one end of an informal patio, a vine-covered arbor, anchored by a small tree, provides a cool shady spot for dining or relaxing. At the opposite end, a wooden fence bordered by flowers offers privacy as well as a colorful display to be enjoyed from the patio or the house. Together the fence, arbor, patio, and plants nicely mingle the indoors with the outdoors.

From early spring to late fall, the plantings will provide colorful accompaniments to your patio activities. Blossoms of fragrant jasmine open first. By May, the patio will boast long-lasting flowers and nectar-seeking hummingbirds.

Scale is particularly important when you're landscaping near the house. This design can be adapted to suit houses and properties in a range of sizes. The flagstone patio can be altered by adding or removing irregular pavers. And the plantings can be extended or reduced along the edges.

> SITE: Sunny
>
> SEASON: Summer
>
> CONCEPT: Arbor, paving, and plants provide a pleasant ambiance for outdoor relaxation and entertaining.

'Lemon Drop' **K** lantana

Texas star **D** hibiscus

Star jasmine **C**

Fence **O**

'David Verity' **J** cigar plant

Autumn sage **I**   Firebush **E**   **I** Autumn sage

Plants & Projects

This design will keep your yard busy with winged creatures. Hummingbirds are drawn to the trumpet creeper, Texas star hibiscus, firebush, red yucca, Turk's cap, autumn sage, and the cigar plant. Butterflies are fond of Turk's cap and the two lantanas. The planting is also carefree.

A **'Bubba' desert willow** (use 1 plant)
The willowy foliage of this small deciduous tree showcases orchidlike purple flowers on and off throughout the summer. See *Chilopsis linearis* 'Bubba', p. 125.

B **'Mme. Galen' trumpet creeper** (use 1)
A vigorous, leafy, deciduous vine laden from summer to fall with clusters of showy salmon red flowers. A dense canopy of foliage provides shade for the patio in warm months. See *Campsis x tagliabuana* 'Mme. Galen', p. 124.

C **Star jasmine** (use 6)
An evergreen vine bearing dark green glossy leaves and clusters of sweetly fragrant blossoms in springtime. The white flowers resemble small stars or pinwheels. See *Trachelospermum jasminoides*, p. 149.

D **Texas star hibiscus** (use 1)
Dazzling star-shaped red flowers bloom at the tips of this bushy perennial's leafy green branches all season long. See *Hibiscus coccineus*, p. 131.

E **Firebush** (use 3)
This perennial forms a neat mound of dark-green foliage. Numerous small firecracker red flowers bloom from summer to frost. Stems and new growth are tinged red. See *Hamelia patens*, p. 129.

F **'Dallas Red' lantana** (use 3)
Swirls of tight-knit tiny red-and-orange blossoms create a fine-textured backdrop for the holly fern. New flower clusters are yellowish orange inside and red outside. See *Lantana camara* 'Dallas Red', p. 134.

G **Red yucca** (use 1)
A bold year-round accent, this yucca relative forms a large

N Arbor

B 'Mme. Galen' trumpet creeper

See site plan for F.

H Turk's cap

O Fence

Door   House

M Containers

H

K

D

C

P

E

B

L

F

N

E

J

G

I   E   I

A

I

K

1 square = 1 ft.   Lawn

A 'Bubba' desert willow

E Firebush

M Containers

Holly fern L

I Autumn sage

Red yucca G

K 'Lemon Drop' lantana

P Patio

clump of narrow succulent leaves. It is especially striking when in summer and fall bloom under the desert willow. Flowers are coral pink. See *Hesperaloe parviflora*, p. 130.

H Turk's cap (use 4)
Plant this perennial near the patio to enjoy its summer-to-frost display of unusual red flowers. Dense and upright, it will fill the corner with handsome dark green palmate leaves. See *Malvaviscus arboreus drummondii*, p. 136.

I Autumn sage (use 7)
Plant this perennial by the flagstones. Branch tips bear red blooms the size and shape of lipsticks. Flowers are especially abundant in spring and fall. See *Salvia greggii*, p. 144.

J 'David Verity' cigar plant (use 3)
A perfect companion for sage and firebush. Upright stems are topped with narrow leaves and a profusion of orange flowery "cigars" all summer long. See *Cuphea* x 'David Verity', p. 126.

K 'Lemon Drop' lantana (use 6)
This vigorous spreading perennial lays out a thick carpet of cheery yellow flowers next to the patio from late spring to late fall. See *Lantana* x *hybrida* 'Lemon Drop', p. 134.

L Holly fern (use 4)
An unusual fern with coarse-textured evergreen fronds resembling holly leaves. Provides a dense, durable, knee-high border on the shady side of the patio. See Ferns: *Cyrtomium falcatum*, p. 128.

M Containers (as needed)
Bring butterflies right on to your patio with colorful plants in handsome pots. We suggest using Texas-made Grub's white-clay pots. The three smaller pots are planted with 'New Gold' lantana (1 plant in each) and the larger pot with 'Ruby Glow' red penta (3 plants for full effect). Both flowers are magnets for butterflies.

N Arbor
This large arbor will serve as a sunscreen for the patio even before the trumpet vine fills in. See p. 188.

O Fence
A simple structure creates an attractive screen for flowers as well as for privacy. See p. 192.

P Patio
Flagstones set on a sand-and-gravel base make a durable informal patio. See p. 166.

PLANT PORTRAITS

While lending privacy, shade, color, and fragrance to your outdoor room, this selection of plants attracts butterflies and other wildlife on the wing.

● = First design, pp. 88–89
▲ = Second design, pp. 90–91

'David Verity' cigar plant
(*Cuphea*, p. 126) ●

'Mme. Galen' trumpet creeper
(*Campsis* x *tagliabuana*, p. 124) ●

'Dallas Red' lantana
(*Lantana camara*, p. 134) ●

'Bubba' desert willow
(*Chilopsis linearis*, p. 125) ●

'Whirling Butterflies' gaura
(*Gaura lindheimeri*, p. 130) ▲

Butterfly viewing

This design creates an outdoor room that beckons butterflies along with friends and family. The live oak will provide pleasant shade for a portion of the patio, while playing host to duskywings, hairstreaks, and many other butterfly species. Long-blooming flowers are a feast for the eye and for skippers, swallowtails, and roving monarchs. Other plants play their part too. Texas sage and holly fern shelter butterflies from storms; maiden grasses serve as nurseries for eggs and larvae; and pots of leafy edibles, such as dill, parsley, and fennel, give the pupa (caterpillars) something to munch.

Here are a few tips to increase your butterfly population once they discover your patio. Place decorative rocks or logs in the flower beds for them to rest on and spread their wings. Butterflies need to soak up warmth from the sun to become active. Protect their life stages, eggs, larva, and pupa by avoiding the use of pesticides on plants. And remember, some leaf eating is desirable and beneficial in a butterfly garden.

Plants & Projects

Ⓐ Live oak (use 1 plant)
This large native tree forms a thick canopy of small hollylike evergreen leaves that will eventually shade the whole patio. If you'd like less shade, plant a smaller oak such as Texas red oak or lacey oak. See *Quercus virginiana*, p. 140

Ⓑ Butterfly rose (use 1)
This delicate bush rose flowers all season. The profusion of single silky blossoms change color as yellow to orange to pink. New

shoots and leaves are flushed purple; mature leaves are dark green. See *Rosa chinensis* 'Mutabilis', p. 142.

C Compact Texas sage (use 3)
This native evergreen shrub is grown for striking purple bell-shaped flowers that open after summer rains. Woolly silver-gray leaves make a handsome informal year-round screen. See *Leucophyllum frutescens* 'Compactum', p. 135.

D Dwarf Japanese maiden grass (use 3)
The foliage of this small, fine-textured grass spills over like a fountain. These distinct yet overlapping clumps create a smooth transition to the lawn. See *Miscanthus sinensis* 'Adagio', p. 136.

E 'Whirling Butterflies' gaura (use 4)
From spring through fall, this graceful perennial sends up many slender stems of delicate "floating" flowers. They both resemble and attract butterflies. See *Gaura lindheimeri* 'Whirling Butterflies', p. 130.

F Fall aster (use 2)
This carefree native perennial puts on a dazzling show of lavender-purple "daisies" from early fall to frost. Their nectar draws roving monarchs. See *Aster oblongifolius*, p. 122.

G 'Homestead Purple' verbena (use 1)
This sprawling perennial forms a lacy mat of evergreen leaves and bright-purple flowers. It blooms nonstop from spring to fall if deadheaded regularly. See *Verbena* x *hybrida* 'Homestead Purple', p. 149.

H Purple verbena (use 3)
This perennial's lavender-purple flowers are borne aloft tall, stiff stems. A magnet for butterflies from spring to frost. See *Verbena bonariensis*, p. 149.

I Coreopsis (use 5)
Plant these perennials to weave a gold "daisy" chain through the border in spring. See *Coreopsis lanceolata*, p. 126.

J 'Trailing Lavender' lantana (use 5)
This evergreen shrub's weeping branches are laden with clusters of small lavender-purple flowers in summer. See *Lantana montevidensis* 'Trailing Lavender', p. 134.

K Containers (as needed)
Plant dill, parsley, carrots, fennel, and anise to attract swallowtail butterflies; abutilons, hibiscus, and mallows for skipper butterflies.

L Water basin
A shallow dish makes an ideal birdbath for butterflies. Place some sand in the bottom; add a few pebbles for butterflies to land on; fill it with water; and watch what happens.

M Paving
Shown here is a brick patio laid in a simple basketweave pattern. See p. 160.

See p. 89 for the following:

N Holly fern (use 20)

O Autumn sage (use 4)

SITE: Sunny

SEASON: Spring

CONCEPT: A butterfly garden brings this outdoor room to life.

A Live oak
N Holly fern
Compact C Texas sage
Holly N fern
'Homestead G Purple' verbena
Fall F aster
'Trailing Lavender' J lantana
Water L basin
E 'Whirling Butterflies' gaura
G 'Homestead Purple' verbena
M Paving
Containers K
Coreopsis I
Autumn O sage
B Butterfly rose
H Purple verbena
D Dwarf Japanese maiden grass

1 square = 1 ft.

Formal Outdoor Living

CREATE SHADY ENTERTAINING SPACE ON THIS FORMAL PATIO

D Chinese wisteria

J Arbor

F 'Tuscan Blue' rosemary

C 'Green Beauty' boxwood

G Serbian bellflower

B Bear's breeches

A 'Meyer' lemon

C 'Green Beauty' boxwood

I Annuals

K Paving

H Ground covers for informal paving

In Texas, opportunities for year-round outdoor living abound. This design demonstrates how a patio next to the house can become a true extension of your living space with the addition of an arbor and plants that create an attractive outdoor setting.

At one end of a formal patio, a vine-covered arbor provides a shady, cool spot for dining or relaxing. At the opposite end, random paving and a seat-height curved stone wall invite informal gatherings when the heat of the day has passed.

A neatly trimmed boxwood hedge, clipped trees, and shrubs in terra-cotta pots reinforce the formality of the grid-work paving, while annuals and ground covers spilling onto the pavement soften the effect. Backing the curved seating wall, a loose hedge of rosemary is an informal echo of its boxwood counterpart.

Easily accessed and viewed from the house, the arbor, patio, and plants nicely mingle the indoors with the outdoors.

Scale is particularly important when you're landscaping near the house. This design can be adapted to suit houses and properties in a range of sizes. The grid-work patio can be altered by adding or removing rows of pavers. And the plantings can be extended or reduced along the edges.

SITE: Sunny

SEASON: Summer

CONCEPT: Arbor, paving, and plants provide shade and a pleasant ambiance for outdoor relaxation and entertaining.

1 square = 1 ft.

L Seating wall

E 'Goodwin Creek Gray' lavender

Plants & Projects

The patio and arbor are sizable projects, but their rewards are large, too. Grow the lemon trees in 3-ft.-diameter terra-cotta pots, the rosemary in deep pots, 12 in. in diameter. Prune these plants to emphasize their natural shapes: a loose ball for the lemons, a narrow column for the rosemary. Keep the boxwood hedge neatly clipped. Train a single stem of each wisteria to twist up its arbor post.

A **'Meyer' lemon** (use 5 plants)
The evergreen foliage of these small trees showcases fragrant white flowers and tangy yellow fruits borne on and off all year. Bellflowers planted in the pots provide additional interest. See *Citrus*, p. 125.

B **Bear's breeches** (use 6)
As if this perennial's big, bold, deeply divided green leaves aren't striking enough, in late spring spikes of white or deep pink flowers rise several feet above the foliage. See *Acanthus mollis*, p. 118.

C **'Green Beauty' boxwood** (use 20)
The small leaves and compact habit of this evergreen shrub make it ideal for the formal, neatly clipped hedge edging the arbor. See *Buxus microphylla* var. *japonica*, p. 123.

D **Chinese wisteria** (use 4)
A vigorous deciduous vine with lacy leaves and clusters of fragrant purple, lavender, or white flowers in spring. See *Wisteria sinensis*, p. 151.

E **'Goodwin Creek Gray' lavender** (use 9)
This evergreen shrub's mounding gray foliage makes an attractive informal hedge. Bears spikes of blue flowers in early summer. See *Lavandula*, p. 133.

F **'Tuscan Blue' rosemary** (use 4)
Trim this evergreen shrub to a tall, narrow column. Foliage is aromatic; light-blue flowers bloom in winter and spring, sometimes in fall. See *Rosmarinus officinalis*, p. 143.

G **Serbian bellflower** (use 31)
This spreading perennial is used as a ground cover and as an underplanting in the lemon tree pots (3 per pot). In spring and early summer, blue flowers float about a foot above the foliage on slender stalks. See *Campanula poscharskyana*, p. 124.

H **Ground covers for informal paving** (as needed)
Planted in the gaps between the flagstones, these perennials accent the informality of this end of the design. Snow-in-summer (*Cerastium tomentosum*, p. 124)

has silver leaves and bears white flowers in early spring. Coralbells (*Heuchera*, p. 131) features neat tufts of round leaves topped from spring to late summer by red flowers. Creeping thyme (*Thymus praecox* ssp. *arcticus*, p. 148) withstands light traffic and smells good when you step on it.

I **Annuals** (as needed)
Change the plantings of annuals in the beds around the potted trees and shrubs for seasonal interest. In summer (the season shown here), try phlox, snapdragons, and purple basil.

J **Arbor**
This large arbor is designed to serve as a sunscreen for the area beneath even without a foliage canopy. See p. 176.

K **Paving**
Use flagstone pavers, 24 in. square, in the formal area. Press rounded pebbles into the gaps between pavers for added interest. Irregular flagstones pave the informal area. See p. 160.

L **Seating wall**
This low wall provides seating and should be constructed with mortared fieldstone. If your budget doesn't allow hiring a mason, buy commercially made curved wooden or precast concrete benches.

Splash Out

MAKE A HANDSOME WATER GARDEN IN A FEW WEEKENDS

A water garden adds a new dimension to a home landscape. It can be the eye-catching focal point of the entire property or a quiet out-of-the-way retreat. A pond can be a hub of activity—a place to garden, watch birds and wildlife, raise ornamental fish, or stage an impromptu paper-boat race. It just as easily affords an opportunity for some therapeutic inactivity; a few minutes contemplating the ripples on the water's surface provides a welcome break in a busy day.

A pond can't be moved easily, so choose your site carefully. Practical considerations are outlined on pp. 168–171 (along with instructions on installation and on planting water plants). In addition to those considerations, think about how the pond and its plantings relate to the surroundings. Before plopping a pond down in the middle of the backyard, imagine how you might integrate it, visually if not physically, with nearby plantings and structures.

The plantings in this design are intended to settle the pond comfortably into an expanse of lawn. Flagstone paving invites visitors to stroll up to the pond's edge. Framing the pond and path are a small broadleaf evergreen tree and perennial ground covers planted in contrasting waves of color and texture. A full season of flowers in complementary blues, purples, and golds will draw hummingbirds and butterflies as surely as they delight the eye.

SITE: Sunny

SEASON: Summer

CONCEPT: Water is a welcome presence in the landscape, especially when surrounded by lovely plants.

Lawn   1 square = 1 ft.

Plants & Projects

Installing a pond is arduous but simple work, requiring several weekends of energetic digging. Lay out and install the paving at the same time as the pond. Once established, the plants require only seasonal care. The pond will need regular attention to keep a healthy balance of water plants and fish (if you have them) in order to maintain oxygen levels and to keep algae in check. Consult local or mail-order suppliers to help you determine the right mix.

Ⓐ Wax myrtle (use 1 plant)
This small tree adds graceful height to the pond planting. Fragrant leaves are fairly small, smooth, leathery, and evergreen; they won't litter the pond in fall. See *Myrica cerifera*, p. 137.

Ⓑ 'Gracillimus' Japanese maiden grass (use 3)
An ornamental grass with a weeping habit. Flower plumes rise high above the foliage in late summer and last through winter. See *Miscanthus sinensis* 'Gracillimus', p. 136.

Ⓒ Mealycup sage (use 12)
This perennial's grayish green foliage is topped with many blue flower spikes visited by hummingbirds and butterflies. To keep it blooming all season, remove flowers as they fade. But don't discard them—they make wonderful dried flowers. See *Salvia farinacea*, p. 144.

Ⓓ St.-John's-wort (use 5)
Bright-yellow flowers with showy stamens top this dense, mounding shrub in summer. Some will eventually cascade

'Big Blue' Ⓖ lilyturf

'Stella d'Oro' Ⓔ daylily

over the edge of the pond. The overlapping leaves are small and oval, turning reddish purple in fall and last through winter. See *Hypericum calycinum*, p. 131.

E **'Stella d'Oro' daylily** (use 20) For small fountains of grassy foliage near water's edge, plant these perennials en masse. Clusters of golden trumpets open daily in spring and often repeat in fall. See *Hemerocallis 'Stella d'Oro'*, p. 130.

F **'Blue Pacific' shore juniper** (use 3) An evergreen shrub bearing bright blue-green trailing foliage that will fall softly over the flagstone edging and into the pond. See *Juniperus conferta* 'Blue Pacific', p. 133.

G **'Big Blue' lilyturf** (use 30) Evergreen and lush-looking, this perennial's foliage makes an attractive grassy outer edge to the planting. Bears lavender flowers in summer, followed by black berries in fall. See *Liriope muscari* 'Big Blue', p. 135.

H **'Homestead Purple' verbena** (use 6) This perennial spreads out to form an edging of felty leaves interlaced with bright purple flowers. Cut back occasionally to encourage a new flush of bloom. See *Verbena* x *hybrida* 'Homestead Purple', p. 149.

I **Louisiana iris** (use 3) This plant forms a tall clump of pale green swordlike leaves that can survive half-submerged in water. Bright yellow flowers rise a foot above the leaves in spring. Foliage is attractive year-round. See *Iris* x *Louisiana hybrids*, p. 151.

J **Umbrella sedge** (use 2) Plant this bold grasslike water plant for its many unusual green stalks topped with ribbons of foliage, arranged like the spokes of an umbrella. See *Cyperus alternifolius*, p. 126.

K **Water lily** (use 1) No pond is complete without these lovely floating flowers. Pointed petals open in layers above saucer-shaped leaf pads. We've shown a pink-flowering cultivar here. See Water plants: *Nymphaea*, p. 150.

L **Pond** You can make this pond with a commercially available flexible liner. See p. 166.

M **Paving** A flagstone edge widens into a natural path around the front of the pond. See p. 160.

Patio pool

A little pond can make a big splash in a well-chosen setting. And it provides all the pleasures of water gardening without the energy or space required to install and maintain a larger pond. Within its confines you can enjoy water plants, fish, or even a small fountain.

The scale of this pond is just right for a small patio or as part of a larger patio planting. We've included a low fence along the perimeter of the patio, but the design would work just as well without it. The pond design is simple and inexpensive. We recommend using a 4-ft. diameter fiberglass tub sunk into the ground and planted all the way to the edge.

The planting displays an exuberant collection of foliage and flowers. We've selected plants that mound and arch, dangle and droop to create billowy, colorful contours around the small pool.

Plants & Projects

A **'Pink Dawn' chitalpa**
(use 1 plant)
This small fast-growing deciduous tree provides an open airy backdrop for the patio planting as well as decorative gray bark, attractive pale green leaves, and pink ruffled flowers. See x *Chitalpa tashkentensis* 'Pink Dawn', p. 127.

B **Compact Texas sage** (use 4)
Silver-gray foliage suffused with orchid pink blooms distinguish this evergreen shrub. It provides a soft background for the flower display in summer and a privacy screen during winter. See *Leucophyllum frutescens* 'Compactum', p. 135.

1 square = 1 ft.

Lawn

Patio

SITE: Sunny

SEASON: Summer

CONCEPT: Copious plants around a small pond create a focal point on a patio.

A **'Pink Dawn' chitalpa**

B **Compact Texas sage**

C **Autumn sage**

Coral **H** **vine**

G **Tropical plumbago**

K **'Gracillimus' Japanese maiden grass**

J **Low fence**

H **Coral vine**

D **Trailing rosemary**

Dwarf Japanese garden juniper **E**

I **Pond**

M **Water lily**

L **Umbrella sedge**

F **'Blue Princess' verbena**

D **Trailing rosemary**

C **Autumn sage** (use 2)
Loose clusters of pretty flowers bloom at the tips of this bushy perennial's branches all season. Choose a cultivar with pink flowers for this planting. See *Salvia greggii*, p. 146.

D **Trailing rosemary** (use 2)
An attractive evergreen shrub, it forms a sprawling mound of needle-thin leaves that are both fragrant and tasty. Small blue flowers appear in spring and off and on through the year. See *Rosmarinus officinalis* 'Prostratus', p. 143.

E **Dwarf Japanese garden juniper** (use 3)
This beautiful compact shrub forms a blue-green mat of dense evergreen needles, layered sprays of which will eventually spill over the edge of the pond. See *Juniperus procubens* 'Nana', p. 133.

F **'Blue Princess' verbena** (use 5)
This perennial produces clusters of small flowers from spring through fall (year-round in areas with mild winters). Its lavender-blue flowers complement the color scheme well. See *Verbena* x *hybrida* 'Blue Princess', p. 149.

G **Tropical plumbago** (use 5)
This perennial contributes baby blue flowers and fresh green foliage to the planting. See *Plumbago auriculata*, p. 139.

H **Coral vine** (use 2)
Grown for its showy panicles of tiny heart-shaped pink blossoms. Plant two of these vines and train them along the fence. They will cover it quickly. See *Antigonon leptopus*, p. 119.

I **Pond**
Bury a 4-ft.-diameter watertight tub and add water plants or a fountain, as you wish. See p. 168.

J **Low fence**
This variation on a picket fence frames the pond and patio nicely. See p. 190.

See pp. 94–95 for the following:

K **'Gracillimus' Japanese maiden grass** (use 1)

L **Umbrella sedge** (use 1)

M **Water lily** (use 1)

PLANT PORTRAITS

Whether growing in the water or nearby, these plants combine fresh foliage and lovely flowers for your poolside pleasure.
● = First design, pp. 94–95
▲ = Second design, pp. 96–97

'Blue Pacific' shore juniper
(*Juniperus conferta*, p. 133) ●

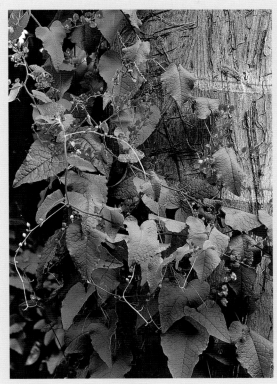
Coral vine
(*Antigonon leptopus*, p. 119) ▲

Dwarf Japanese garden juniper
(*Juniperus procubens* 'Nana', p. 133) ▲

Water lily
(Water plants: *Nymphaea*, p. 150) ● ▲

'Pink Dawn' chitalpa
(x *Chitalpa tashkentensis*, p. 127) ▲

Poolside Pleasures

PLANTINGS ENHANCE YOUR SWIMMING POOL

Swimming pools are an increasingly common backyard amenity in many Texas communities. On a suburban lot, a pool is often the dominant backyard presence. Too often, however, the backyard pool is little more than an aquatic gym surrounded by a slab of concrete and lawn.

This design shows that a planting of trees, shrubs, and perennials and a little hardscaping can work magic to enhance all your outdoor activities, whether you're escaping with a good book, entertaining friends, working in the garden, or playing in the pool. (The rendering shows the design as seen from the house, which is indicated on the plan.)

Tall shrubs on the perimeter heighten the sense of enclosure and privacy provided by the fence, which building codes usually require around a pool. The paving surrounding the pool extends at each end to accommodate a table and chairs for entertaining and recliners for relaxing. An arbor creates a little niche along one side. Low-growing plants lining the surround add color and texture to the setting. And there's still ample lawn for playing games and lounging.

Plants & Projects

The plants in this design are chosen not only for their year-round good looks, but also because they are well-behaved around a pool. All are low-maintenance evergreens that hold on to their foliage throughout the year, producing as little litter as possible. You won't be fishing leaves out of the water as you would with deciduous trees and shrubs.

Ⓐ 'Majestic Beauty' Indian hawthorne (use 5)
Trimmed into small trees with overlapping crowns, these evergreen shrubs are decorated with huge clusters of fragrant pearl-pink flowers in spring. Choose single-trunked shrubs for this planting. See *Rhaphiolepis indica* 'Majestic Beauty', p. 140.

Ⓑ Fraser photinia (use 15)
Growing 8 ft. tall and 6 ft. wide, these naturally rounded shrubs overlap to form a coarse dark-leafed hedge. In spring they form a solid bank of white flowers. Note that one is trained flat to the wall as a decorative backdrop for the arbor. See *Photinia x fraseri*, p. 139.

SITE: Sunny

SEASON: Spring

CONCEPT: A poolside filled with flowers and foliage lets you go for a swim in the garden.

Fraser photinia Ⓑ

'Majestic Beauty' Indian hawthorne Ⓐ

Ⓒ **'Royal Princess' heavenly bamboo**

Ⓘ **Asian jasmine**

Ⓖ **'Russian Rhapsody' daylily**

Bigleaf hydrangea Ⓓ

C **'Royal Princess' heavenly bamboo** (use 19)
Airy reddish green foliage covers this narrow, upright evergreen shrub. It bears small pink flowers in spring and summer. See *Nandina domestica*, p. 137.

D **Bigleaf hydrangea** (use 2)
A rounded deciduous shrub clothed in large, deep-green, leaves and huge, ball-shaped flowers through summer. Varieties abound in blue, pink, or white flowers. See *Hydrangea macrophylla*, p. 131.

E **Sasanqua camellia** (use 3)
This evergreen shrub produces lovely flowers from late fall into winter. Choose from a range of colors. See *Camellia sasanqua*, p. 123.

F **Pink azaleas** (use 7)
Masses of pink flowers cover this compact slightly spreading shrub in spring. Small dark-green leaves are attractive all year. See *Rhododendron*, p. 141.

G **'Russian Rhapsody' daylily** (as needed)
This grassy perennial is bright green and topped with showy purple flowers in summer. Plant about 12 in. apart for a seamless poolside fringe. See *Hemerocallis*, p. 130.

H **Winter-blooming bergenia** (as needed)
Large round leaves with wavy margins distinguish this evergreen perennial. Pink flowers form on short thick spikes in winter. Plant the clumps 18 in. apart for a continuous border. See *Bergenia crassifolia*, p. 121.

I **Asian jasmine** (as needed)
A dense, sprawling ground cover with small, dull green leaves and star-shaped white flowers. For complete coverage in a season, plant on 12 in. centers. See *Trachelospermum asiaticum*, p. 148.

J **Arbor**
Easily built, this attractive structure provides a central focal point and a welcome sun screen by the pool. See p. 176.

See site plan for **E** .

J Arbor

B Fraser photinia

C 'Royal Princess' heavenly bamboo

F Pink azaleas

H Winter-blooming bergenia

D Bigleaf hydrangea

G 'Russian Rhapsody' daylily

Down to Earth

HARMONIZE YOUR DECK WITH ITS SURROUNDINGS

'Morning Light' **E**
Japanese maiden grass

Texas **A**
mountain
laurel

Russian **F**
sage

Mexican mint **H**
marigold

Carolina **D**
jasmine

'Pink' **K**
autumn sage

Yarrow **L**

'Powis Castle' **J**
artemisia

Gaura **G**

'John Fanick' **I**
garden phlox

'Hill's Hardy' **C**
rosemary

A backyard deck is a perfect spot for enjoying the garden. Too often, however, the deck offers little connection to its surroundings. Perched on bare posts above a patch of lawn, it is a lonely outpost rather than an inviting gateway to the world of plants and wildlife.

This design nestles the deck into its immediate surroundings while preserving the vista from the deck and the windows. The one exception to the low landscape of shrubs, vines, and ground covers is a

small tree, whose fragrant spring flowers and attractive foliage will improve rather than screen the view.

Decreasing in height from the deck to the ground, the planting makes it easier for the eye to move between levels. Japanese maiden grasses and rosemary rise railing-high on one side of the deck, and glossy abelias fill in the other. Around the grasses is an airy border of Russian sage. A lower edging of fine-leaved yarrow frames the front of the deck.

Striking to look at, this deckside planting appeals to other senses as well. In March and April the large flower clusters of Texas mountain laurel will give off their distinctive fragrance. (Some liken it to grape soda.) The spring air will also carry the heady perfume of Carolina jasmine. Many of the plants also have fragrant leaves, releasing their pungence to the touch or on their own when days are hot. A few are flavorful too, adding zest to culinary dishes.

House

Deck

E

Lawn

1 square = 1 ft.

SITE: Sunny

SEASON: Fall

CONCEPT:
A garden of earthly delights surrounds a low deck.

L Yarrow

I 'John Fanick' garden phlox

B Glossy abelia

Plants & Projects

You'll need to water young plants to get them established. But after a year or two, these durable perennials and shrubs will require infrequent supplemental watering and little care beyond routine seasonal pruning and clean up.

A Texas mountain laurel (use 1 plant)
Fragrant purple flowers will entice you outdoors in early spring. This native shrub or tree has interesting gnarled branches and shiny evergreen foliage. See *Sophora secundiflora*, p. 146.

B Glossy abelia (use 3)
Another shrub with scented blossoms and luxuriant semi-evergreen foliage. Honeysuckle-like flowers are pinkish white and bloom from spring to fall. See *Abelia x grandiflora*, p. 118.

C 'Hill's Hardy' rosemary (use 4)
This attractive evergreen shrub deserves a spot by the steps. Crush a few leaves in your hand as you go by to release their pungent aroma. The piney branches are dotted with fragrant lavender-blue flowers in late winter and spring. See *Rosmarinus officinalis* 'Hills Hardy', p. 143.

D Carolina jasmine (use 2)
A popular evergreen vine bearing small, medium-green,

lance-shaped leaves. The perfume of its small yellow flowers will intoxicate on early spring days. See *Gelsemium sempervirens*, p. 129.

E 'Morning Light' Japanese maiden grass (use 6)
A variegated (gray to medium green) ornamental grass that grows into a fountain-shaped mound. In fall large buff-colored tassels may rise above a porch railing. The dried flowers are showy into late winter. See *Miscanthus sinensis*, p. 136.

F Russian sage (use 8)
This erect perennial forms a vase of silvery see-through stems and small aromatic gray leaves. Tiny pale-blue flowers bloom along stem tips from spring through summer. See *Perovskia atriplicifolia*, p. 139.

G Gaura (use 7)
Masses of delicate white to pink flowers float above low clumps of pale-green foliage from spring through summer. A favorite of butterflies. See *Gaura lindheimeri*, p. 128.

H Mexican mint marigold (use 13)
Golden daisylike blossoms smother these upright peren-

nials in autumn. Leaves and flowers are aromatic, and tasty too. See *Tagetes lucida*, p. 149.

I 'John Fanick' garden phlox (use 11)
Big, fragrant clusters of long-blooming flowers make this perennial a great one to plant near patios and decks. This mildew-resistant cultivar bears pink flowers from spring to July. See *Phlox paniculata* 'John Fanick', p. 139.

J 'Powis Castle' artemisia (use 3)
This perennial's silvery foliage makes a beautiful foil for the pale-pink gaura flowers and the deeper pink of the autumn sage. See *Artemisia x* 'Powis Castle', p. 120.

K 'Pink' autumn sage (use 7)
Fine-textured bushy perennial with small oval medium-green leaves and spikes of bright-pink flowers. Blooms nonstop from March to October. See *Salvia greggii* 'Pink', p. 144.

L Yarrow (use 36)
The dense ferny foliage of this mounding perennial makes a fine edging. You can choose among many flower colors. Blooms in spring. See *Achillea millefolium*, p. 118.

Decked-out Deck

MAKE YOUR DECK AN INVITING GATEWAY TO THE OUTDOORS.

SITE: Sunny

SEASON: Early summer

CONCEPT: A pleasing mix of durable plants integrates a low deck with its hillside surroundings.

In the design shown here, a low deck nestles in a planting of trees, shrubs, and perennials. The plants provide shade and privacy as well as lovely flowers and foliage and the birds and other wildlife attracted to them. Conceived for a dry, hilly site with a backyard that slopes down from the deck, the planting makes effective use of terrain where play areas are impractical and a manicured lawn or traditional garden beds are difficult to maintain. (The planting can easily be adapted for sites that are steeper or more level than the gradual slope shown here.)

The plants are chosen for their ability to thrive in the hot, dry conditions found in many parts of Texas. Western redbud, manzanita, and ceanothus are joined by tough plants that are ideal for semiarid regions. There are flowers for much of the year, and a mixture of evergreen and deciduous foliage provides delightful colors and textures year-round. The planting makes a seamless transition to the surrounding cover of native grasses and wildflowers that naturally colonize such hillsides. Mow a path through this "volunteer" ground cover and extend the planting as far as you wish down the hill.

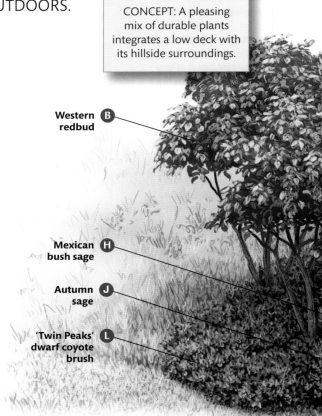

Western redbud **B**

Mexican bush sage **H**

Autumn sage **J**

'Twin Peaks' dwarf coyote brush **L**

Plants & Projects

You'll need to water young plants to get them established. But after a year or two, these durable perennials, trees, and shrubs will require infrequent supplemental watering and a minimum of care. Prune the shrubs (particularly the hop bushes and the butterfly bush) to keep them from overgrowing their neighbors. Shear the dwarf coyote brush each spring. Divide any perennials that become crowded.

A Chitalpa (use 1 plant)
This attractive deciduous tree has a wide crown of airy foliage and bears eye-catching clusters of ruffled pink or white flowers in early summer. See x *Chitalpa tashkentensis*, p. 125.

B Western redbud (use 3)
Tiny magenta flowers line the bare branches of this small multitrunked deciduous tree in spring. Bright-green summer foliage turns yellow in fall. See *Cercis occidentalis*, p. 124.

C Purple hop bush (use 3)
Native to the Southwest, this tough evergreen shrub has bronze-green foliage that turns purple in winter. See *Dodonaea viscosa* 'Purpurea', p. 127.

D 'Julia Phelps' ceanothus (use 4)
This popular evergreen shrub displays clusters of blue flowers against a backdrop of deep-green foliage in spring. See *Ceanothus*, p. 124.

E 'Howard McMinn' manzanita (use 7)
Lining the path, this evergreen shrub forms mounds of shiny dark-green foliage. Small white-to-pink spring flowers produce red berries. See *Arctostaphyllos densiflora*, p. 119.

F 'Black Knight' butterfly bush (use 1)
This deciduous shrub makes a fountain-shaped clump of long arching stems. Clusters of dark-purple flowers form at the ends of the stems from midsummer

through fall. See *Buddleia davidii*, p. 121.

G 'Happy Wanderer' hardenbergia (use 1)
The stems and distinctive bright-green foliage of this evergreen vine twine around the deck railing. Bears pinkish-purple flowers in late winter and early spring. See *Hardenbergia violacea*, p. 129.

H Mexican bush sage (use 8)
A shrubby perennial, its gray-green foliage contrasts nicely with the dark-evergreen leaves of nearby plants. Long spikes of purple-and-white flowers bloom from late spring to fall. See *Salvia leucantha*, p. 145.

I 'Tuscan Blue' rosemary (use 4)
The needlelike dark-green leaves of this evergreen shrub add interesting texture to the planting. Small deep-blue flowers appear in late winter and early spring. See *Rosmarinus officinalis*, p. 143.

J Autumn sage (use 11)
This bushy perennial's medium-green leaves are topped from spring to fall with airy spikes of red flowers. Place two plants in each of the planters on the wide steps leading up to the deck. See *Salvia greggii*, p. 144.

K 'Yellow Wave' New Zealand flax (use 4)
This evergreen perennial's colorful spray of swordlike leaves is topped in summer by tubular red flowers on tall stalks. See *Phormium tenax*, p. 139.

L 'Twin Peaks' dwarf coyote brush (use 10)
The dense foliage of this low, spreading evergreen shrub makes a fine ground cover. See *Baccharis pilularis*, p. 121.

M Path
A path mowed through the native grasses and wildflowers on the hillside will be easier to maintain than a path of wood chips or other loose material.

'Black Knight' F
butterfly bush

'Happy G
Wanderer'
hardenbergia

Chitalpa A

'Yellow Wave' K
New Zealand flax

Purple C
hop bush

H Mexican
bush sage

E 'Howard McMinn'
manzanita

J Autumn sage

M Path

D 'Julia Phelps'
ceanothus

'Tuscan Blue' I
rosemary

'Howard McMinn' E
manzanita

House

Deck

J
Planters
J

C

C

G

H

K

B

I

K

L

D

A

B

F

I

K

J

H

B

D

E

L

H

M

J

E

1 square = 1 ft.

Native grasses
and wildflowers

Planting in the Pines

SURROUND YOUR WOODLAND DECK WITH FLOWERING SHRUBS

This simple patio planting is intended for a home (or home away from home) located on a wooded slope. Permanent residences and weekend retreats alike often feature backyard terraces or decks nestled in the pines, where fresh mountain air, cool evenings, and wildlife can be enjoyed year-round.

Numerous desirable ornamental plants thrive in dry mid-elevations. This design features drought-tolerant and fire-resistant trees and shrubs that look beautiful and natural in a setting of mature conifers.

Western redbuds that are planted around the deck create a leafy canopy among the bare trunks of taller pines. Beneath and around them are a selection of lower-growing shrubs displaying contrasting bold and fine-textured foliage and springtime flowers. The entire planting is edged in a foot-high swath of bright green foliage.

Like the surroundings, the planting will be in full bloom in spring, with masses of white, yellow, and pink flowers. The evergreen foliage looks fresh throughout the rest of the year.

Wildfires are always a concern in dry areas. To protect your home, keep areas near the house well irrigated and keep vegetation 15 to 20 feet from the house. For other tips on how to keep your home safe from wildfires, contact your local fire department or state Department of Forestry.

Western redbud **A**

SITE: Partial shade

SEASON: Late spring

CONCEPT: A deck set in a forest of pines nestles in a planting of spring-flowering shrubs.

'Ken Taylor' **C**
flannel bush

'Emerald Carpet' **E**
bearberry

Patio

Deck

1 square = 1 ft.

'Emerald Carpet' **E**
bearberry

B Bush
anemone

'Majorca Pink' **D**
rosemary

Plants & Projects

Preparing the planting beds and
installing the shrubs can be done
in a few weekends. Then sit back
and enjoy the display. Once established, these plants require little
care beyond seasonal pruning.

A **Western redbud** (use 4 plants)
Native to the foothills, this small
tree is so vivid in bloom it stops
drivers along the roads in spring.
The purplish-pink flowers give
way to bright green deciduous

leaves that turn yellow in fall.
Purplish seedpods decorate the
bare branches in winter. See
Cercis occidentalis, p. 124.

B **Bush anemone** (use 4)
One of the loveliest chaparral
shrubs, its dark glossy leaves
with whitish undersides create
a beautiful backdrop in spring
for masses of showy white
flowers sporting bright-yellow
centers. See *Carpenteria
californica*, p. 124.

C **'Ken Taylor' flannel bush**
(use 4)
Cup-shaped golden yellow-
to-orange flowers stand out
brightly against this evergreen
shrub's felty, dark-green leaves.
See *Fremontodendron* 'Ken
Taylor', p. 128.

D **'Majorca Pink' rosemary**
(use 4)
Lavender-pink flowers continuously adorn this tough, upright
evergreen shrub during late

winter into early spring. See
Rosemarinus 'Majorca Pink',
p. 143.

E **'Emerald Carpet' bearberry**
(use 12)
This low-spreading shrub forms
a dense, slightly mounding
carpet of small oval leaves that
remain bright green throughout
the year. It makes an exceptional
choice for a ground cover. See
Arctostaphylos 'Emerald Carpet',
p. 119.

Link for a shadier edge

If an adjacent woodland shades your property, try this design, which features plants tolerant of shady conditions. The concept is the same as in the previous design—layers of plants increasing in height toward the woods—but the layout is somewhat different. A wider path ambles to the right; a flowering trellis marks the entry into the woods; and foliage textures and colors take the place of flowers, providing interest in all seasons.

The planting is at its most colorful in fall and winter, when masses of burnished heavenly bamboo stand out against the light greens of ferns and the deeper greens of holly and euonymous. Fall is also emblazoned with the reds and purples of countless berries, fruits we fondly associate with woodland outings.

SITE: Shady

SEASON: Fall

CONCEPT: Attractive evergreen shrubs guarantee year-round color at this shady woodland edge.

Plants & Projects

A **Possumhaw holly** (use 2 plants) This native deciduous shrub has year-round appeal. In season, it wears a thick coat of glossy foliage. When shed, it exposes silver-gray twigs laden with long-lasting red berries. Birds love to eat them. See *Ilex decidua*, p. 132.

B **Manhattan' euonymus** (use 12) These evergreen shrubs make a handsome framework for the other plantings, eventually growing into a dense, irregular mound 8 to 10 ft. tall. The foliage stays dark green and shiny all year. See *Euonymus kiautschovicus* 'Manhattan', p. 127.

C **American beautyberry** (use 3) A shrub with a somewhat open and arching habit. The inconspicuous flowers produce eye-popping purple berries that last long after the leaves drop. See *Callicarpa americana*, p. 123.

D Dwarf yaupon holly (use 14)
This shrub's olive-green foliage complements the other leaf colors. See *Ilex vomitoria* 'Nana', p. 132.

E Coral honeysuckle (use 1)
A native vine that blooms in shade. It bears showy whorls of red-orange flowers, followed by pretty red berries in fall and winter. Gray-blue leaves are attractive and usually evergreen. See *Lonicera semper-virens*, p. 135.

F Gulf Stream' heavenly bamboo (use 3)
This compact evergreen shrub makes a colorful ground cover. Fine-textured leaves are tinged bronze, orange, and purple, turning bright red in winter. See *Nandina domestica* 'Gulf Stream', p. 137.

G 'Harbour Dwarf' heavenly bamboo (use 26)
A lower-growing version of heavenly bamboo (wider than tall) with larger, less-colorful foliage than 'Gulf Stream'. It produces small red berries in the center of the plant. See *Nandina domestica* 'Harbour Dwarf', p. 137.

H Wood fern (as needed)
A vigorous spreading perennial fern. The fronds are bright green and deeply cut. Plant as many of them as needed on 2-ft. centers. See Ferns: *Thelypteris kunthii*, p. 128.

I Inland sea oats (use 32)
This native grass makes a natural transition to the woods. Grows in ever-larger clumps and also spreads from seed. Long seed heads resemble oats and dangle and dance from arching stems in fall. See *Chasmanthium latifolium*, p. 125.

J Snowflake (as needed)
White flowers planted among the ferns are lovely in early spring. Plant several hundred bulbs if possible. See Bulbs: *Leucojum aestivum*, p. 122.

K Arbor
Placed at the entry to the woods, this simple cedar arbor invites visitors for a woodland stroll. See p. 185.

See p. 113 for the following:

L Path

PLANT PORTRAITS

With handsome foliage and flowers, these plants are effective against a woodland backdrop.

● = First design, pp. 112–113
▲ = Second design, pp. 114–115

'Hana Jiman' sasanqua camellia
(*Camellia sasanqua*, p. 123) ●

Louisiana iris
(*Iris* x *Louisiana* hybrids, p. 132) ●

'Harbour Dwarf' heavenly bamboo
(*Nandina domestica*, p. 137) ▲

'Manhattan' euonymus
(*Euonymus kiautschovicus*, p. 127) ▲

'Goldflame' Japanese spirea
(*Spiraea* x *bumalda*, p. 147) ●

Plant Profiles

When you are ready to install your new landscape design, you will find this section a great reference for selecting the plants for your project. Plants are key, and here you'll find descriptions of all the ones used in all of the designs, along with helpful advice for planting and maintaining them. What's more, the trees, shrubs, perennials, grasses, bulbs, and vines that are included have all proven themselves as dependable performers in Texas. They offer a wide spectrum of lovely flowers and fruits and most add something special to your home's landscape for at least two seasons.

Using the plant profiles

All of these plants are proven performers in many of the soils, climates, microclimates, and other conditions commonly found in Texas. But they will perform best if planted and cared for as explained in the Guide to Installation, beginning on p. 152. In the following descriptions and recommendations, "full sun" means a site that gets at least eight hours a day of direct sun throughout the growing season. "Partial sun" and "partial shade" both refer to sites that get direct sun for part of the day but are shaded the rest of the time by a building, fence, or tree. Plants preferring partial sun or shade often do best with morning sun and afternoon shade. "Full shade" means sites that don't receive direct sunlight.

The plants are organized here alphabetically by their scientific name. If you are browsing, page references direct you to the designs in which the plants appear. Numbers in **bold italic** type indicate the page where you can find a photo of the plant.

In the writeups, we've noted plants that have been designated Texas Superstar® **plants by the Texas Cooperative Extension and the Texas nursery industry because of their proven performance throughout the state.**

Abelia x *grandiflora*

GLOSSY ABELIA. This easy-to-grow semievergreen shrub bears countless small white flowers from early summer until frost and attracts many butterflies. The lustrous, small, pointed leaves are dark green in summer and purple-bronze in winter. It grows a sprawling 5 ft. wide and tall. The cultivar 'Edward Goucher' (pp. 32, 86) has showy pink flowers and grows a smaller 3 to 4 ft. tall and wide. Both need full sun to partial shade and grow with an arching habit. Pages: 22, 101, **103**.

Acanthus mollis

BEAR'S BREECHES. A perennial with dark-green leaves that grow up to 2 ft. long. Tall spikes of white to pinkish purple flowers bloom in late spring, reaching 2 to 3 ft. above the foliage. Grows best in moist shade but can take some sun. Page: 93.

Achillea millefolium

YARROW. This is a long-blooming, cool-season perennial with flat clusters of small flowers on 1 ft. stalks. The foliage is gray-green, growing in a dense mat about 6 in. tall. The species (p. 101) has white flowers and is very vigorous. 'Fire King' (pp. 81, **83**) has hot-pink flowers. 'Apple Blossom' (pp. 32, **32**) has light-pink flowers; if it isn't available, a good substitute is 'Rosea'. 'White Beauty' (p. 45) has pure-white flowers. Yarrow needs full sun and tolerates most soils. Cut off blooms when they fade, or before; they make good cut flowers.

Abelia x *grandiflora* 'Edward Goucher'
GLOSSY ABELIA

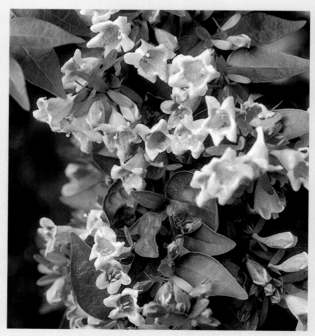

Abelia x *grandiflora*
GLOSSY ABELIA

Agave

CENTURY PLANT. These are bold evergreen succulents with thick spiny leaves in fantastic architectural rosettes. (Be careful to avoid the sharp spines on the tips of the leaves.) Rare flowering stalks occur after many years, giving rise to the popular name, century plant. Mother plants die upon flowering, followed by new suckers at their base. *A. americana* (pp. 41, 43) has striking blue-green foliage and grows 5 ft. tall and wide. Yellow variegated agave (*A. americana* 'Marginata', pp. 41, **43**, 71, **73**) has green and yellow leaves and is slightly smaller than the species. *A. victoriae-reginae* (pp. **38**, 39) has green-and-white leaves and grows only 1 ft. tall and wide. Agaves require full sun and good drainage. Twin-flower agave (*A. geminiflora*, p. 35) forms a tight rosette 2 to 3 ft. round of stiff, narrow green leaves with yellow bell-shaped flowers.

Agapanthus

AGAPANTHUS, LILY-OF-THE-NILE. Flowering perennials with arching, straplike leaves and ball-shaped clusters of blue-and-white flowers in late spring and summer. *A. 'Peter Pan'* (p. 28) is a dwarf variety with leaves reaching only 12 in. tall and blue flowers on stalks up to 18 in. tall. Plant in full sun or light shade and well-drained soil. Evergreen in mild-winter climates; goes dormant in cold winters.

Alyogyne huegelii

BLUE HIBISCUS. Evergreen shrub with blue-to-purple flowers borne on and off throughout the year. Grows 5 to 8 ft. tall and has dark-green leaves. Best adapted to coastal areas. Plant in full sun. Page: 28.

Anisodontea x hypomandarum

CAPE MALLOW. Fast-growing evergreen shrub with a long season of bloom. Small pink flowers with dark veins appear almost year-round in mild-winter areas. (Bloom time is shorter in inland and foothill areas.) Grows 6 ft. tall. Full sun. Page: 28.

Annuals

Gardeners in Texas use annuals generously to provide bright patches of colorful flowers throughout the year. They're fast-growing plants that bloom abundantly for months, and when they're finished, they are easy to uproot and replace with something else. One of the fun things about growing annuals is that you can try different kinds from year to year.

Annuals in Texas can be divided into three groups. Winter, or cool-season, annuals are planted when the weather starts to cool in the fall. They live through the winter, perhaps blooming off and on, and put on a good show in spring. This group includes pansies, snapdragons, violas, sweet alyssum, dusty miller, and dianthus.

Spring, or warm-season, annuals are planted in early spring and again in early fall. They grow best during the milder temperatures of spring and fall and only occasionally endure hot temperatures. This group includes petunias, begonias, verbena, ageratum, nicotiana, marigolds, and salvia.

Summer, or hot-season, annuals are the most useful during the scorching Texas summers. They are usually native to tropical climates and are planted during late spring and early summer. This group includes lantana, Mexican heather, purslane, vinca, ornamental sweet potato, Persian shield, blue daze, and purple fountain grass.

Antigonon leptopus

CORAL VINE. A vigorous vine that climbs by tendrils, it bears airy panicles of coral-pink heart-shaped flowers among apple-green foliage in summer and autumn. Grows best in full hot sun. Grow it as an annual in northern areas or substitute coral honeysuckle. Also known as queen's crown and Mexican love vine. Page: 97, **97**.

Aquilegia chrysantha hinckleyana

TEXAS GOLD COLUMBINE. This native perennial bears fragrant golden flowers with long spurs. Blooms in early spring on 2-ft. stalks above neat clumps of blue-green leaves. The plant is relatively short-lived but self-seeds easily. Grows best in light shade and well-drained soil. Tends to go dormant in summer; cut it back when it does. Designated a **Texas Superstar**®. Pages: 31, 43, 54, 71, 83, 103, 109.

Arctostaphylos

MANZANITA. Evergreen shrubs with shiny red bark, lustrous deep-green foliage, and small white-to-pink flowers in spring followed by red berries. *A. densiflora* 'Howard McMinn' (p. 104) grows 5 to 6 ft. tall and spreads a little wider. *A. 'Emerald Carpet'* (Bearberry, p. 111) grows 8 to 14 in. high by 5 ft. wide and has brilliant-green leaves. Best used in dry areas and on slopes where there is infrequent watering. Plant in fall in full sun to partial shade.

Aquilegia chrysantha hinckleyana
TEXAS GOLD COLUMBINE

Artemisia x 'Powis Castle'
ARTEMISIA

Aspidistra elatior
CAST-IRON PLANT

Aster oblongifolius
FALL ASTER

Artemisia x 'Powis Castle'

'POWIS CASTLE' ARTEMISIA. A beautiful accent plant, this shrubby perennial is grown for fragrant, silvery, finely divided foliage. Flowers rarely, if ever. It forms a dome-shaped mound 2 ft. tall and 3 ft. wide. Plant in full sun with good drainage. Tolerates dry soil but grows faster when watered during dry summers. Cut back lightly in early spring and fall to encourage new growth and to keep plant compact. Pest free. Pages: 23, 33, 39, 44, **47**, 69, 76, 78, 101.

Aspidistra elatior

CAST-IRON PLANT. An unusual evergreen perennial valued for its tolerance of deep shade. It forms a dense patch of stiff, dark, pointed leaves that grow directly from the ground and reach 3 ft. tall. Spreads slowly into a weed-proof colony about 2 ft. wide. Purple to gray-white flowers are solitary and mostly hidden in the foliage. Cast-iron plant grows well in full or partial shade with occasional summer watering. Pest and disease free. Cut back the old growth in early spring before the new leaves emerge. The bold foliage is often used in floral arrangements. Pages: 51, 54, 59, 113.

Aster oblongifolius

FALL ASTER. This carefree native perennial bears showy lavender-purple daisylike flowers from early fall until the first hard freeze. The plant spreads to form a dense clump 2 ft. tall and 3 ft. wide. Fall aster thrives in full sun or partial shade with well-drained soil. It is drought tolerant and has no known pest problems. Prune to the ground after the first hard freeze. In late spring, cut new stems back by one-third to keep plants from getting floppy and to encourage more flowers in fall. Divide plants every few years in early spring. Pages: 21, 32, 44, **47**, 52, 69, 75, 91.

Aucuba japonica

AUCUBA. These are showy evergreen shrubs with thick erect stems sporting large, lustrous, leathery leaves. They generally grow around 4 ft. tall and 3 ft. wide. The cultivar 'Variegata', also known as gold dust aucuba (pp. **50**, 51, 59), has green leaves sprinkled with yellow dots. The leaves of 'Picturata' (p. **62**, 62) are splashed with yellow blotches. Aucubas are some of the best shrubs for dark shady areas. They will not tolerate hot, exposed, sunny sites. Provide monthly watering during dry summers. Plants are generally pest free. Prune lightly in late winter to control size.

Baccharis pilularis 'Twin Peaks'

'TWIN PEAKS' DWARF COYOTE BRUSH. Evergreen shrub valuable as a ground cover for sunny, dry, low-maintenance areas. Grows 10 to 24 in. high and spreads 6 ft. wide, with a dense cover of small green leaves. It is a male selection that doesn't produce messy seeds. Needs little water near the coast, once a month in warmer areas. Page: 104.

Bergenia crassifolia

WINTER-BLOOMING BERGENIA. A low-growing perennial with large, dark-green, wavy-edged leaves that are evergreen except in cold-winter areas. In January and February, tall stems bear clusters of pink flowers. Plant in partial shade (or full sun where summers are cool). Will withstand poor conditions but looks best grown in good soil and with regular watering. Page: 99.

Berberis thunbergii 'Crimson Pygmy'

DWARF JAPANESE BARBERRY. A deciduous shrub grown for its colorful foliage and compact, spreading habit. Stiff, spiny stems are lined with small leaves that are burgundy in summer and bright crimson in fall. Grows into a dense mound 2 ft. tall and 3 ft. wide or can be trimmed into a small hedge. Needs full sun, well-drained soil, and occasionally water during dry periods. Expect no insect or disease problems. Shear as needed to maintain a desired shape. Pages: 46, **47**.

Bignonia capreolata 'Tangerine Beauty'

'TANGERINE BEAUTY' CROSS VINE. This vigorous evergreen vine grows to a generous 15 ft. tall and wide. In spring, the entire plant turns into a mass of beautiful trumpetlike orange flowers with yellow throats. Scattered bloom continues through the growing season. Excellent for covering walls, trellises, and fences. Cross vine is a Texas native and requires little care or water. It is rarely plagued by insects or disease. Pages: 22, **102**, 103.

Bougainvillea

BOUGAINVILLEA. One of the most spectacular flowering plants, it blooms in striking shades of white, pink, red, orange, yellow, or purple in late spring and summer. Foliage is evergreen. Habit varies by variety, of which there are many. Most are sprawling vinelike plants that can spread over 20 ft. wide and need lots of room. Others are smaller and more shrublike. 'New Gold' (pp. 35, 65) has bronzy yellow flowers and grows 5 to 6 ft. tall with the support of a trellis. The shrublike 'Rosenka' (p. 35) forms an arching mound 4 ft. tall and 5 ft. wide and bears gold flowers aging to pink. Bougainvilleas are reliably hardy only in mild climates. Widely grown elsewhere, they may lose leaves or die back partially in colder areas. Can also be grown in pots or treated as summer annuals in cold climates. Plant in spring in full sun, or light shade in hot areas.

Buddleia davidii

BUTTERFLY BUSH. A fast-growing shrub that blooms from midsummer through fall and is sometimes evergreen where winters are mild. Arching shoots make a vase-shaped clump. Spikes of small white, pink, lilac, blue, or purple flowers form at the end of each stem. The flowers have a sweet fragrance and really do attract butterflies. 'Black Knight' (p. 104) has purple flowers. 'Nanho Blue' (p. 28) reaches 4 to 5 ft. tall and is a better choice for small spaces. Both need full sun and well-drained soil. Cut down old stems to 1-ft. stubs in late winter to early spring to promote vigorous growth and maximum flowering. Plants will grow 5 to 8 ft. tall and wide by the end of the summer.

Bulbs

The bulbs recommended in this book are perennials that come up year after year and bloom in late winter or early spring. Buy bulbs from a garden center or catalog in late summer or fall. Plant them promptly in a sunny or partly shaded bed in moderately well-drained soil. As a rule, plant at a depth two times the bulb's height. After bulbs flower in spring, their leaves continue growing until some time in May, when they gradually turn yellow and die down to the ground. In subsequent years, remove (or ignore, if you choose) the old leaves after they turn yellow. Most bulbs can be divided every four to five years if you want to grow them elsewhere. Dig them as the foliage is turning yellow; shake or pull them apart; and replant them right away. Perennial bulbs are great for naturalizing in meadows and borders, for edging flower beds and fences, and as pockets of color among shrubs and ground covers. See the box on p. 122 for information on specific bulbs.

Aucuba japonica
AUCUBA

Bignonia capreolata
'Tangerine Beauty'
CROSS VINE

Recommended bulbs

Narcissus tazetta, **Narcissus**

This enduring perennial bulb blooms between late fall and early spring. Extremely fragrant white flowers open in dense clusters on 1 to 1½ ft. stalks and make great cut flowers. The dark-green foliage occurs in clumps 1 ft. wide and tall, emerging in the fall and going dormant during the summer. 'Avalanche' (p. 103, **103**) has creamy-white flowers with lemon yellow cups. 'Grand Primo' (pp. **86**, 87) is a southern heirloom with creamy white flowers and pale-yellow cups; if unavailable, use 'Avalanche' as a substitute. Paperwhite (*N. tazetta papyraceous*) has pure-white flowers and can be used as a substitute in the milder areas below Interstate 10. Tazetta narcissus are pest free and require no irrigation. Pages: 81, 113.

Narcissus pseudonarcissus 'Ice Follies'
DAFFODIL

N. pseudonarcissus **'Ice Follies', 'Ice Follies' daffodil**

Along with the golden yellow cultivars 'Carlton' and 'Fortune', this is one of the few daffodils that does well in Texas. A spring-blooming perennial bulb, it has wide, ruffled, yellow trumpets fading to creamy white. The extremely showy blooms rise 1 ft. among blue-green foliage and make great cut flowers for display in the home. Daffodils require full sun and good drainage. Divide them every 5 to 10 years to keep them blooming. Pages: 31, 48, **50**.

N. jonquilla, **Jonquil**

This early spring bulb has heavenly scented small golden-yellow flowers above dark-green rushlike foliage. Goes dormant during the summer, re-emerging with fresh foliage in the winter. It has no pest problems and prefers dry summers. 'Trevithian' and 'Sweetness' are commonly available. Pages: 57, **59**.

Narcissus tazetta
NARCISSUS

Leucojum aestivum, **Snowflake**

This dependable perennial bulb delights with clusters of tiny white bells on 1 ft. stalks in early spring. The healthy green foliage emerges in early winter and goes dormant in summer. Snowflakes are great for introducing bright patches of early bloom among ground covers and landscaped beds. They grow in sun or shade and in moist or dry conditions. This foolproof bulb is pest free and requires no supplemental watering. Pages: 27, 115.

Zephyranthes candida, **White rainlily**

This hardy little bulb produces dark-green grasslike foliage during the cool months of the year. In late summer the leaves often die back in exchange for showy white crocuslike flowers in the fall. White rainlily grows less than a foot tall and wide. It will grow in full sun or partial shade and tolerates dry or boggy soil. It has no serious insect or disease problems and can be used to naturalize in beds or as a border substitute for lilyturf or monkeygrass. Pages: 71, **73**.

Leucojum aestivum
SNOWFLAKE

Buxus microphylla

LITTLELEAF BOXWOOD. This evergreen shrub forms a dense mass of small glossy leaves that makes it ideal for shearing into formal globes, cones, hedges, or topiary. If left alone, it grows into a neat soft mound 4 to 5 ft. tall. Leaves turn brownish in cold winters. The cultivar 'Green Beauty' (pp. 71, **73**) forms a globe 3 to 4 ft. tall and keeps its bright-green foliage in winter. Japanese boxwood (*B. microphylla* var. *japonica*) 'Green Beauty' (p. 93) has small leaves that stay bright green all winter. It forms a compact globe up to 4 ft. tall. Boxwoods grow relatively slowly, so buy the largest plants you can afford. They need well-drained soil and grow best in full or partial sun. Use mulch to protect their shallow roots and water regularly during periods of drought. Shear in late spring to desired shape. Pages: 69, **69**, 93.

Callicarpa americana

AMERICAN BEAUTYBERRY. This native deciduous shrub has a lax habit, spreading 4 ft. wide and tall. Tapered dull green leaves line the slightly arching branches. In fall, they give way to profuse clusters of vivid violet-purple berries. Beautyberry is pest free and drought tolerant. Irrigation may be needed during periods of drought to maintain attractive foliage. Thin one-third of the older branches to the ground each spring to promote a denser appearance. Pages: 21, 51, 54, 82, 114.

Camellia sasanqua

SASANQUA CAMELLIA. This is a much-sought-after evergreen shrub with glossy foliage and beautiful white, pink, or rose flowers in the fall. There are many cultivars from which to choose (pp. 26, **26**, 99). They differ in flower color, size, and form (single or double), as well as in overall plant habit, hardiness, and mature size. They range from 3 ft. tall and wide to 8 ft. tall and 6 ft. wide. The lower-growing forms are useful for mass plantings; the taller forms are ideal for hedges. 'Hana Jiman' (pp. 113, **115**) grows 6 ft. tall and 4 ft. wide and bears semidouble white flowers edged in pink. 'Shi Shi Gashira' (pp. 86, 109, **109**) has rose-colored semidouble flowers and stays a more compact 3 ft. tall and wide. 'Yuletide' (pp. 31, **32**) has red flowers and grows 6 ft. tall by 3 ft. wide. Sasanquas need moist, well-drained, acid soil; a layer of mulch; and a site that is shaded from midday sun. They are relatively pest free and more forgiving than the winter-flowering *C. japonica*. If needed, prune and fertilize immediately after flowering.

Buxus microphylla
LITTLELEAF BOXWOOD

Camellia sasanqua
SASANQUA CAMELLIA

Callicarpa americana
AMERICAN BEAUTYBERRY

Cercis canadensis
REDBUD

Campanula

BELLFLOWER. A large group of useful flowering perennials (a few are annuals) that vary in plant habit and flower form. Plant them in flower beds, rock gardens, or containers. Spreading types are useful as small-scale ground covers. Serbian bell-flower (*C. poscharskyanna*, p. 93) is spreading and has flower stalks about 1 ft. tall. Blooms in spring to early summer in shades of blue to lavender. All grow best in partial shade but can take full sun near the coast.

Campsis x tagliabuana 'Mme. Galen'

'MME. GALEN' TRUMPET CREEPER, or VINE. This hummingbird favorite is a vigorous deciduous vine with a stout woody trunk, large compound leaves, and clusters of salmon-red flowers from summer until frost. Trumpet vine needs full sun, room to grow, and only occasional watering during summer droughts. Once established, it can climb and cover a trellis, fence, or wall with no further assistance or care. It grows at least 10 ft. tall and can reach 20 to 30 ft. Pages: 78, 88, **90**.

Carpenteria californica

BUSH ANEMONE. This evergreen shrub is grown for its lovely, lightly fragrant white flowers with yellow centers, which are displayed in late spring and early summer against handsome, glossy, dark-green leaves. Grows upright 4 to 6 ft. high and equally as wide. Plant in full sun except in the hottest areas, where partial shade is best. Page: 111.

Ceanothus

CEANOTHUS, WILD LILAC. Evergreen shrubs useful in dry landscapes, especially on slopes. Blue or (rarely) white flowers appear in early spring. Leaves are deep green. 'Julia Phelps' (p. 104) reaches 4 to 7 ft. tall and up to 9 ft. wide and has deep-blue flowers. Plant ceanothus in full sun in fall. Do not water once established.

Cerastium tomentosum

SNOW-IN-SUMMER. A perennial often used as a ground cover, with slivery evergreen foliage and masses of white flowers in early summer. Forms a low mat 6 to 8 in. high, with stems that trail 2 to 3 ft. wide. Requires full sun or partial shade and well-drained soil. Water regularly. Shear off the top of the plant, cutting it back by about one-half, right after it blooms. Page: 93.

Cercis

REDBUD. This small, early-spring flowering, deciduous tree is native to East Texas and performs best in the piney woods region. It produces clusters of bright purple-pink flowers along bare twigs in early spring before the heart-shaped leaves unfold. Medium-green foliage turns gold in the fall. 'Forest Pansy' (*C. canadensis*, pp. 102, 109, **109**, 113) has purple foliage that turns dark green in the summer. Texas redbud (*C. texensis*, pp. 42, **43**) has thick shiny leaves. Native to central and north Texas, this redbud is adapted to the drier areas of Texas with alkaline soils but performs well throughout the state. Redbuds are generally available with single or multiple trunks and may reach 20 to 25 ft. tall and wide. They require well-drained soil and regular watering in the summer but have few pests. Western redbud (*C. occidentalis*, pp. 104, 111) is a good choice for dry or natural landscapes. It is often grown as a large multitrunked shrub. Magenta flowers are followed by seedpods some people find unsightly. Leaves turn yellow in fall. Grows 10 to 20 ft. tall. Thrives in poor, dry soils. Page: 31.

Chamaerops humilis

MEDITERRANEAN FAN PALM. A bushy palm with coarse, blue-green, palm-shaped leaves arising from the tops of multiple stalks. Yellow flowers are borne in long panicles in spring but are mostly hidden in the dense foliage. Grows 6 to 10 ft. tall and half as wide. The Mediterranean fan palm is an adaptable plant that does as well in full sun as it does in partial shade and in moderately fertile to poor soils. Page 64.

Chasmanthium latifolium

INLAND SEA OATS. This is a native perennial grass that forms erect leafy clumps about 2 ft. tall, topped with loose clusters of flat seed heads that dance in the breeze from midsummer through winter. All parts are green in summer and russet or tan in the winter. Grows in sun or shade and adapts to almost any soil. Cut to the ground in spring before the new growth emerges. This vigorous, pest-free plant can reseed and naturalize quite prolifically. To reduce the number of seedlings, pull or hoe them as they appear, apply a heavy layer of mulch in the area, use a selective post or preemergent herbicide, or remove the seed heads before they shatter. The dainty seed heads are great for flower arrangments. Pages: 21, 83, 193, 109, 115.

Chilopsis linearis

DESERT WILLOW. This small native deciduous tree sports narrow willowlike leaves and showy tubular flowers from spring throughout the summer. Flower colors range from pure white to lavender to deeper purple. Desert willow can reach 15 ft. tall and wide and makes a good substitute for crapemyrtle in extremely dry areas. It performs well throughout the state in sunny, well-drained locations. The more compact 'Bubba' (pp. 88, **90**) has greener leaves and dark wine-purple flowers. Desert willow has few pests and is very drought tolerant. Pages: 34, 57, **59**.

x Chitalpa tashkentensis 'Pink Dawn'

'PINK DAWN' CHITALPA. A hybrid of catalpa and chilopsis, this narrow-leaved deciduous tree quickly grows 20 to 30 ft. tall. Large clusters of ruffled, trumpet-shaped pink flowers bloom in early summer. Plant in full sun. Grows best with occasional water in hot-summer climates. Chitalpa may be defoliated by catalpa worms or fungal leaf spot but survives with little care. Pages: 28, 96, **97**, 104.

Chyrsactinia mexicana

DAMIANITA. This tough little evergreen shrub stands up well to desert heat and is useful for lining walkways and borders. It forms a densely branched 2 ft. mound of highly aromatic, dark-green, needle-like leaves. Small, fragrant, golden yellow "daisies" are borne in spring and fall, and sometimes through the summer where temperatures are mild. Grows in full sun. Needs little water but will bloom more with occasional irrigation. Page: 35.

Chrysanthemum leucanthemum

OX-EYE DAISY. This vigorous cool-season perennial produces loads of white daisies on 2-ft. stems in spring; the flowers are a great addition to bouquets. Prefers full sun and adequate moisture and has few pest problems. Remove flowers after they finish blooming to encourage more of them. To produce more plants, divide the leafy clumps in fall. Ox-eye daisy is the best substitute for Shasta daisies in Texas. Pages: 33, 37.

Chrysanthemum x 'Country Girl'

'COUNTRY GIRL' DAISY MUM. This daisy mum is a cool-season perennial that produces a profusion of pink daisies on 2 ft. stems in the fall. It is one of the few chrysanthemums that performs as a reliable perennial in Texas. Requires full sun, good drainage, and regular watering in the summer. Plants may need staking when in bloom. After bloom, cut the spent stalks to their base. To promote heavier bloom in fall, shear the plant by half several times during the summer. Daisy mum has no pest problems. Page: 77, **77**.

Citrus

CITRUS. These evergreen trees offer handsome dark-green leaves, fragrant spring flowers, and colorful, edible fruits in winter. The many varieties vary in adaptation, tree height, and form. Check with local nurseries for the best varieties for your area. Good landcape varieties include 'Meyer' lemon (p. 93), which forms a compact tree seldom over 8 ft. tall. Plant in full sun and well-drained soil. Water and fertilize frequently for quality fruit. Prune to keep the center of the tree open or to maintain size. Protect trees if temperature drops below 30°F for prolonged periods.

Clematis terniflora

SWEET AUTUMN CLEMATIS. One of very few clematis species that perform well throughout Texas. This vigorous perennial vine climbs 25 ft. or higher. It bears medium-green compound leaves and billows of small, very fragrant white flowers in late summer and fall. Grows best in full sun to partial shade in moist soil conditions. It has very few pest problems and only requires supplemental watering during droughts. Prune in early spring, cutting back partway or close to the ground. It can become invasive in East Texas. Often sold under the name *C. paniculata*. Pages: 103, 107, **109**.

Chasmanthium latifolium
INLAND SEA OATS

Chrysanthemum leucanthemum
OX-EYE DAISY

Clematis terniflora
SWEET AUTUMN CLEMATIS

Coreopsis lanceolata
COREOPSIS

Cortaderia selloana 'Pumila'
DWARF PAMPAS GRASS

Cuphea
CUPHEA

Coreopsis lanceolata

COREOPSIS. A native Texas wildflower, coreopsis explodes each spring with masses of golden yellow daisylike flowers. Forms a clump 1 ft. tall and 1½ ft. wide of bright-green linear leaves and slender flower stalks. A warm-season perennial, coreopsis grows best in full sun with modest irrigation. Tolerates most soil types and has very few pest problems. Looks best if the spent blossoms are sheared off after bloom. Pages: 37, 91.

Cortaderia selloana 'Pumila'

DWARF PAMPAS GRASS. An evergreen clumping grass growing 5 ft. tall and 4 ft. wide with long linear leaves that have very sharp margins. In the summer, plumes of white flowers rise above the foliage. They make excellent dried flowers. Dwarf pampas grass thrives in hot sun and in almost all soil types. Irrigation is only neccessary during prolonged summer droughts. In early spring, you can cut the grass low to the ground to eliminate the old, unsightly foliage. Pages: 37, 75.

Cuphea

CUPHEA. These are showy plants from the tropics that are often grown as perennials or annuals in Texas gardens. Cigar plant (*C. micropetala*, pp. 66, 84) is a warm-season perennial that covers itself with yellow and orange tubular flowers each fall as the days grow short. It makes a bold clump 4 ft. tall and 3 ft. wide. The hybrid 'David Verity' (pp. 89, **90**) grows a more compact 2½ ft. tall and wide and blooms all summer with smaller orange flowers. Both attract hummingbirds in profusion. Mexican heather (*C. hyssopifolia*, p. 23) is a tender perennial that is usually treated as an annual in the northern two-thirds of the state. It grows 1 ft. tall and wide and bears lavender-pink flowers all summer long. Cupheas are very tough plants that prefer full sun and tolerate most soil conditions. They are drought tolerant as well, requiring water only during periods of prolonged drought.

Cyperus alternifolius

UMBRELLA SEDGE. This evergreen perennial forms bold clumps 4 ft. tall and 3 ft. wide, topped with lacy green, leafy umbrellas. It grows extremely well in sun or shade in any soil type, including poorly drained. It is often grown as an aquatic. Umbrella plant has no known pests and can become invasive in South Texas. In northern areas or during severe winters, it may die back to the ground or not return. Consider using it as an annual or replacing it with a hardy fern. Pages: 59, 95.

Dasylirion longissima
MEXICAN GRASS TREE. An evergreen shrub forming a grassy fountain of narrow, olive-green, succulent leaves. With age it bears spikes of tiny white flowers in early summer and develops a treelike trunk. Usually reaches 4 to 5 ft., but may get as tall as 10 ft. Grows best in full sun or light shade and needs good drainage. Its smooth tropical appearance is especially attractive in desert areas. Page: 35.

Dianthus 'Bath's Pink'
'BATH'S PINK' DIANTHUS. This low-growing perennial forms a dense, grassy mat of gray-green foliage 6 in. tall and 1 to 2 ft. wide. Fragrant flowers like tiny pink carnations carpet the plant during the spring. Needs full sun and well-drained soil. Water only when the soil is dry. After blooming, shear off the flower stalks and cut the plants back halfway. Fresh new foliage will soon develop. Divide every few years during the fall to keep the plants vigorous. Pages: 23, 31, 46, 57, 60, 69, 73, 77, 87.

Dodonaea viscosa 'Purpurea'
PURPLE HOP BUSH. A tough evergreen shrub that can withstand difficult conditions, including poor soil, heat, wind, and drought. Narrow leaves are bronzy green, picking up a stronger purplish tone in winter. Flowers are inconspicuous, but seedpods are interesting late in summer. Grows 10 to 15 ft. tall, about 8 ft. wide. Ideal hedge or screen. Best foliage color when planted in full sun. Page: 104.

Euonymus fortunei 'Coloratus'
PURPLE WINTERCREEPER. This shrub is a durable spreading ground cover. Its glossy evergreen leaves turn purplish red during winter. Wintercreeper grows 1 to 2 ft. tall and spreads 5 to 6 ft. wide. It adapts to sun or shade and needs a well-drained soil with regular irrigation during the summer. Shear or prune at any time to provide a uniform surface. Wintercreeper is relatively pest free and less prone to scale than golden euonymus. Page: 46.

Euonymus kiautschovicus 'Manhattan'
'MANHATTAN' EUONYMUS. An evergreen shrub with thick, glossy, rounded, medium-green leaves and small but showy pink and orange fruits that ripen

Cyperus alternifolius
UMBRELLA SEDGE

in the fall. It grows naturally as an upright shrub, reaching about 5 ft. tall and wide, but it can be sheared, pruned, or trained as you choose. Tolerates sun or shade and any well-drained soil. It is relatively pest free and requires irrigation only during dry periods. Pages: 114, **115**.

Euphorbia hybrids
Euphorbias are evergreen shrubs that come in a variety of sizes, shapes, and colors; some have the appearance of thorny palm trees; others are busy and thornless. Crown of thorns (*E. milii*) is a compact shrub growing 18 in. tall and wide. Evergreen leaves cluster at ends of thorny stems and are topped with red flower bracts all year. Page: 35.

Fatsia japonica
FATSIA. This bold evergreen shrub grows around 4 ft. tall and wide and prefers shade to prevent leaf burn. It sports large, shiny, tropical-looking leaves all year and small rounded clusters of white flowers in early spring; the flowers become black berries. Fatsia requires well-drained soil and regular watering. It has no common pest problems. It may get leaf burn during severe winters. Pages: 26, 51, 54, 59, 62, 109.

Felicia amelloides
BLUE MARGUERITE. Dependable perennial covered with small, blue, daisylike flowers for a long season, usually starting in late winter and spring. Some bloom year-round in warm-winter areas. Grows about 18 in. tall and 3 to 4 ft. wide. Plant in full sun and water regularly. Often grown as an annual. Great in pots. Remove spent flowers to promote more bloom. Cut back by half in late summer. Page: 79.

Dianthus 'Bath's Pink'
DIANTHUS

Fatsia japonica
FATSIA

Cyrtomium falcatum
HOLLY FERN

Thelypteris kunthii
WOOD FERN

Ferns

These are carefree long-lived perennials. Despite their delicate appearance, several are among the most durable plants you can grow. Most ferns prefer shade, but some do well in partial shade or even full sun. They grow best in well-drained soil that's been amended with extra organic matter. You can divide them every few years in early spring if you want more plants, or leave them alone for decades. If you want to keep the foliage fresh and green, you can cut all the fronds off at the crown each spring before the new fiddleheads start to unfurl.

Holly fern (*Cyrtomium falcatum*, pp. 27, 31, 51, 54, 59, 83, 89, 109) is a showy evergreen fern with fronds divided into large, glossy, hollylike leaflets. It forms dense clumps about 2 ft. tall and wide. Holly fern prefers good drainage, regular watering, and is resistant to most pests. In more northern areas, mulch well during cold winters. Wood fern (*Thelypteris kunthii*, pp. 51, 83, 103, 115) is without a doubt the toughest, most versatile fern for Texas; it prefers some shade but will also perform fairly well in full sun. The lacy apple-green fronds grow in clumps 2 ft. tall and wide. Like most ferns, this one requires regular watering during the summer to look its best.

Fouquieria splendens

OCOTILLO. This distinctive desert shrub forms a wiry clump of upright, gray-green, thorned, and furrowed branches. Tubular orange-red flowers form quickly at branch tips after spring rains and attract humingbirds. The deciduous gray-green leaves are small and fleshy, and drop during dry spells. Ocotillo can reach 20 to 25 ft. tall. It makes an attractive silhouette in desert gardens or an impenetrable barrier. Grows in full sun and well-drained soil. Page: 35.

Fremontodendron 'Ken Taylor'

'KEN TAYLOR' FLANNEL BUSH. A smaller cultivar of a large showy evergreen shrub found in dry woodlands and mountain slopes. Golden yellow cup-shaped flowers bloom continuously from spring to fall among dark-green, lobed leaves, leathery above and downy below. Flowers are followed by bristly seedpods. Grows 4 to 6 ft. tall and about twice as wide. Requires full sun and excellent drainage, making it ideal for a hillside location. Page 111.

Gardenia jasminoides 'Daisy'

'DAISY' GARDENIA. An intensely fragrant evergreen flowering shrub, it produces single white blossoms in summer above shiny dark-green foliage. Like all gardenias, 'Daisy' prefers partial sun, acidic soil, and regular watering. Feed with acid-type "azalea" fertilizer and apply iron to improve foliage that yellows. In areas that have alkaline soils, amend the soil with sphagnum peat moss, composted pine bark, and sand, or ask at your local nursery about choosing a more suitable alternative. Pages: 31, **32**.

Gaura lindheimeri

GAURA. This native Texas perennial forms a loose clump of graceful arched stems bearing pale pink-and-white flowers from spring through fall. Gaura normally reaches about 3 ft. tall and wide. 'Whirling Butterflies' (pp. **90**, 91) is slightly more compact. 'Dauphin' (pp. 44, **47**) is slightly more upright. Gaura needs full sun, well-drained soil, and regular watering during droughts. Looks best if sheared occasionally after bloom cycles. Cut it to the ground after the first frost. Pages: 41, 75, 78, 81, 101.

Gazania 'Burgundy'

'BURGUNDY' GAZANIA. Clumping evergreen perennials with daisylike flowers. 'Burgundy', with wine-colored flowers, is just one of many varieties that bloom in festive shades of yellow, orange, red, and purple. They make excellent small-scale ground covers. Upright blooms reaching 6 to 10 in. high appear mostly in spring and early summer. Can

Gaura lindheimeri
GAURA

Gelsemium sempervirens
CAROLINA JASMINE

Hamelia patens
FIREBUSH

bloom year-round in mild-winter areas. Dark-green leaves have hairy, gray-green undersides. Tough plants that adapt to most soils but look best with occasional water in summer. Plant in full sun. Page: 79.

Gelsemium sempervirens
CAROLINA JASMINE. This is a Texas native evergreen vine beloved for its fragrant display of small bell-shaped yellow flowers in late winter and early spring. The small lancelike leaves are neat and green all year. This vine can climb trees but is usually trained to grow against a fence or trellis. Carolina jasmine can also be used as a ground cover but will need pruning yearly to keep it within bounds. This plant needs full or partial sun. Pages: 25, 54, 66, 101.

Hamelia patens
FIREBUSH. This colorful tropical shrub is normally grown in Texas as a tender perennial, usually reaching around 3 to 4 ft. tall and wide. In milder areas, it can grow even larger. Firebush bears red-orange trumpet-shaped flowers from summer to frost against red-tinged leaves that turn maroon as cool temperatures set in. Hummingbirds adore this plant. Extremely heat and drought tolerant. Cut to the ground after the first frost. In northern areas, mulch the crown heavily or grow it as a wonderful summer annual. Firebush has been designated a **Texas Superstar®**. Pages: 25, 66, 84, 88.

Hardenbergia violacea 'Happy Wanderer'
'HAPPY WANDERER' HARDENBERGIA. A useful evergreen that can be grown as a vine or a shrub. It produces clusters of pinkish purple flowers in late winter and early spring. Grown as a vine, it will twine around a trellis or up a fence, reaching about 10 ft. high. As a shrubby ground cover, it forms a mound 1 to 2 ft. high and spreads about 10 ft. wide. Plant in full sun or, in hot climates, partial shade. Needs well-drained soil. Page: 104.

Hedera helix
ENGLISH IVY. This is a vigorous vine with large, lobed evergreen leaves and woody stems that send out roots and cling to any surface they touch. It spreads fast as a ground cover or climbs to cover a fence, wall, or tree trunk. There are slower-growing fancy kinds with fine-cut or variegated leaves, as well as the regular plain green ones. Grows in partial sun or full shade. English ivy takes a year or two to become established, then lasts forever. Mow or prune it back whenever it grows out of bounds. Pages: **62**, 63.

Helianthemum nummularium
SUNROSE. Flowering evergreen shrublets with small, bright-colored spring flowers in various shades of white, yellow, orange, pink, and red. Grows 6 to 8 in. high, 2 to 3 ft. wide. This small shrub needs full sun and well-drained soil. Good on dry banks. Page: 79.

Hemerocallis hybrids
DAYLILY

Hemerocallis 'Stella d'Oro'
DAYLILY

Hesperaloe parviflora
RED YUCCA

Hemerocallis hybrids

DAYLILY. Among the most popular of perennials, daylilies display large lilylike flowers above dense clumps of narrow, arching leaves. Almost all daylilies today are hybrids (pp. 32, 77, 81) sold as named cultivars. There are many thousands to choose from. Some are evergreen; others die back in winter. Some are low-growing, while others have flower stalks reaching 3 ft. tall. Flowers last only a day but are replaced daily. They come in many shades of white, yellow, orange, red, and purple, and bloom from several weeks to several months. Mix early-blooming, midseason, and late-blooming varieties to ensure months of color. 'Stella d'Oro' has golden-yellow flowers (pp. 67, 95) on compact plants 1½ ft. tall and wide. 'Black-Eyed Stella' has gold flowers with a dark reddish eye and grows 1½ ft. tall and wide (pp. 60, 62). Both Stellas bloom for months. 'Lavender Bonanza' (p. **83**) have pastel colored flowers. 'Texas Sunlight' has larger gold flowers and grows 2 ft. tall and wide (p. 107).

'Russian Rhapsody' (p. 99) has large purple flowers. All daylilies prefer full sun and well-drained soil. Water regularly during bloom. Pinch off spent flowers, and then cut off flower stalks after blooming is finished. Divide in fall or late winter if you wish to propagate more plants. When planting, space shorter daylilies about 1 ft. apart and taller kinds 2 ft. apart. They will gradually fill in. Daylilies can occasionally be plagued with aphids in the spring and rust disease during humid summers.

Hesperaloe parviflora

RED YUCCA. This native Texas shrub grows in clumps of spiky gray-green succulent foliage. Attractive coral-pink trumpet flowers line graceful 3 ft. stalks from late spring to frost. Very heat and drought tolerant, red yucca is adapted to any well-drained soil in full sun. Generally requires no supplemental watering and attracts very few pests. Pages: 38, 41, 57, 75, 88.

Heuchera

CORABELLS, HEUCHERA. Perennials that form low clumps of almost-evergreen foliage and bloom spring into summer, bearing clouds of tiny red, coral, pink, or white flowers on slender stalks about 18 in. tall. They're fine accent plants or small-scale ground covers. Often sold as *H. x brizoides* or *H. sanguinea*; there are a number of other species and a variety of hybrids. All heucheras prefer full to partial sun, well-drained soil, and some summer water. Remove flower stalks as the blossoms fade. Divide every few years, replanting the divisions an inch or two deeper than the original planting. Page: 93.

Hibiscus coccineus

TEXAS STAR HIBISCUS. A tall, striking native perennial that bears large, brilliant red, star-shaped flowers above leafy stalks from early summer to frost. Foliage is medium green and deeply lobed. Plant can reach 6 ft. tall and 4 ft. wide with the right conditions. Prefers full sun and regular watering. Cut back after bloom cycle to promote bushy plants. It has no common insect or disease problems. Pages: 84, 113.

Hibiscus syriacus

ALTHEA. Also known as rose of Sharon, this is a showy deciduous shrub when in full summer-to-fall bloom. Flowers may be white, pink, or lavender, and single or double. Medium-size leaves are dull green and slightly lobed. 'Diana' (pp. 70, **73**) has large single white flowers. Altheas (p. 32, **32**) grow 6 to 8 ft. tall and 3 to 4 ft. wide. They need full sun and well-drained soil. They have few pest problems but are subject to cotton root rot in alkaline areas. Prune in early spring to give desired shape and size.

Hydrangea macrophylla

BIGLEAF HYDRANGEA. A medium-size deciduous shrub with large round leaves and papery-textured blue, pink, or white flowers in summer. Grows 6 to 10 ft. tall and equally wide. There are many varieties. Hydrangeas are usually grown in partial shade but can be planted in full sun near the coast. Needs fertile, moist, well-drained soil. Stalks grow one year, bloom the next year. In fall, cut to the ground stalks that have bloomed. Plants may require application of aluminum sulfate to produce blue flowers. Page: 99.

Hypericum calycinum

ST.-JOHN'S-WORT. A semievergreen mounding shrub that grows 2 ft. tall and wide. Its small oval leaves are green all year in mild climates and reddish purple to bronze where winters are cold. Bears five-petaled golden yellow flowers with long stamens in summer. Grows well in full sun to partial shade and prefers well-drained soils. It has few insect or disease problems and only requires watering during dry periods. Cut all stems by two-thirds in early spring. If you want to keep the plants shorter and more compact, prune all new shoots by half again in June. Pages: 46, 54, 71, 94.

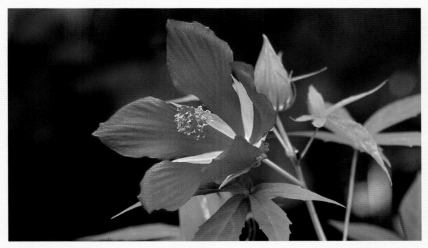

Hibiscus coccineus
TEXAS STAR HIBISCUS

Hibiscus syriacus
ALTHEA

Hypericum calycinum
ST.-JOHN'S-WORT

Recommended hollies

Ilex cornuta 'Burfordii', Burford holly

A large evergreen shrub that generally grows about 10 ft. tall and wide if left unpruned. It has shiny green foliage with a single spine at the leaf tip and attractive clusters of large red berries. Pages: 21, **23**, 76, **77**.

I. cornuta 'Burfordii Nana', Dwarf Burford holly

This smaller cultivar grows a 5 ft. tall and 3 ft. wide. It has small leaves and berries. Pages: 33, 35.

I. decidua, Possumhaw holly

A small Texas native deciduous tree with lustrous dark-green leaves. Berries are very showy after the leaves fall. They can be yellow, orange, or red depending on the cultivar. Designated a **Texas Superstar®**. Pages: 21, **23**, 114.

I. decidua 'Warren's Red'

This possumhaw cultivar has small, bright-red berries and an upright habit to 15 ft. tall and 6 ft. wide. Pages: 21, 23.

Ilex decidua
POSSUMHAW HOLLY

I. vomitoria 'Nana', Dwarf yaupon holly

A dwarf version that reaches only 3 ft. tall and wide. Commonly used as a substitute for boxwood in Texas and the South. Pages: 22, 31, 43, **43**, 44, 115.

Ilex vomitoria 'Nana'
DWARF YAUPON HOLLY

Ilex

HOLLY. An extremely versatile group of shrubs and trees, hollies are used for foundation plantings, hedges, and specimens. The attractive leaves can be small or large, smooth or spiny, dull or glossy. Holly plants are either male or female. If a suitable male is planted within a few hundred yards, females bear heavy crops of small round berries that ripen in fall and last through the next spring. All tolerate sun and partial shade and almost any well-drained garden soil. Hollies are generally pest free. Prune or shear at any season to keep them at the desired size. See "Recommended hollies," left, for more information about specific hollies.

Iris x *germanica*

BEARDED IRIS. This popular perennial blooms in early spring, with large elegant flowers in shades of blue, lavender, pink, yellow, or white, on stalks 2 ft. tall. Flowers open above an attractive clump of stiff, bladelike, gray-green leaves. Bearded iris needs full sun and extremely well-drained soil and grows best with little to no irrigation. If you live close to the coast, plant heirloom and species types; they perform better because they are less likely to suffer root rot. Pages: 60, 69, 77.

Iris x **Louisiana hybrids**

LOUISIANA IRIS. This cool-season perennial forms a clump of straplike foliage 2 ft. tall and 3 ft. wide. Large delicate flowers rise on 3 ft. stalks in early spring. Cultivars come in almost every color of the rainbow. Tolerates wet soil or a well-drained soil with winter and spring moisture. Louisiana iris has few, if any, pests. Goes somewhat dormant in summer. Pages: 54, 113, **115**.

Ixora 'Thai Dwarf'

'THAI DWARF' IXORA. Ixoras are frost-tender evergreen shrubs grown for their showy clusters of brightly colored and highly perfumed flowers atop lustrous rounded leaves. Cultivars come in many sizes. 'Thai Dwarf' reaches 4 t. tall and wide and bears multicolored flower clusters in shades of red, orange, gold, pink, and yellow. Ixoras require full sun, acid soil, and regular watering. Page: 65.

Jasminum sambac

ARABIAN JASMINE. This tropical evergreen vining shrub bears deep-green, glossy leaves and intensely fragrant small white flowers in summer.

Iris x *germanica*
BEARDED IRIS

Iris x Louisiana hybrids
LOUISIANA IRIS

Grown as a vine, it will reach 10 ft. tall and at least as wide if tied to a trellis for support. Grows well in full sun. Water regularly. Does best where winters are mild. Page: 65.

Juniperus

JUNIPER. These needle-leafed evergreens are tough, hardy shrubs for exposed sites. 'Blue Pacific' shore juniper (*J. conferta* 'Blue Pacific', pp. 95, **97**) makes a good ground cover, staying around 1 ft. tall and spreading 5 to 6 ft. wide. It has short, soft, blue-green needles. Dwarf Japanese garden juniper (*J. procumbens* 'Nana', p. 97, **97**) grows 1 to 2 ft. high, spreads 5 to 6 ft. wide, and has blue-green foliage. Junipers prefer full sun and excellent drainage. They suffer blighted foliage from excess watering. Limit pruning to maintain a natural shape and to avoid brown-tipped foliage.

Lagerstroemia

CRAPEMYRTLE. An extremely popular deciduous shrub or small tree usually grown with multiple trunks. It blooms for several months in the heat of summer, with large clusters of papery red, pink, purple, lavender, or white flowers at the end of each stem. Leaves typically turn red, orange, or yellow in the fall. Exfoliating bark reveals wonderful, smooth mottled trunks in winter. There are many cultivars to choose from, ranging from dwarf types that grow 3 ft. tall to tree types that reach 30 ft. Look for the powdery mildew-resistant cultivars that are named for American Indian tribes. The showy 'Catawba' (*L. indica*, pp. 25, **26**) is a purple-flowered cultivar that grows a standard 12 ft. tall and 6 ft. wide. It has excellent fall color and resists mildew. 'Natchez' (*L.* x *fauriei*, pp. 22, **23**) is a vigorous tree-type cultivar that reaches 25 ft. tall and 15 ft. wide. It has fragrant white flowers, spectacular tan and cinnamon bark, and

is especially resistant to powdery mildew. 'Tonto' (*L.* x *fauriei*, pp. 48, **50**) is a semidwarf cultivar that stays less than 10 ft. tall and 5 ft. wide and has watermelon pink flowers. All crapemyrtles need full sun, well-drained soil, and a modest amount of irrigation during severe droughts. Prune them in late winter if at all, removing dead branches and basal suckers only. We discourage the common practice of topping crapemyrtles because it ruins their naturally beautiful shape, scars their trunks, causes them to flop over when blooming, and leads to basal suckering.

Lantana

LANTANA. These tough colorful plants are usually grown as tender perennials or summer annuals. Clusters of small flowers, each one a magnet for butterflies, top the plants from late spring until frost. Cultivars come in white, yellow, pink, orange, red, and purple flowers. Depending on the selection, they grow 1 to 3 ft. tall and spread 2 to 5 ft. wide. Lantanas make great bedding plants, container plants, or ground covers. They are exceptional choices for hot sites and poor soils, requiring full sun and little water. Shear after bloom cycles to keep them compact and encourage more flowers. See "Recommended lantanas" on p. 134 for information on specific kinds.

Lavandula

LAVENDER. Choice evergreen shrubs ideal for dry-summer climates. They form busy mounds of fragrant gray-green foliage topped in early summer with long-stalked spikes of very fragrant flowers. *L.* 'Goodwin Creek Gray' (pp. 28, 93) has gray foliage and deep-blue blooms from early summer into fall, or longer where summers are mild. Grows 2 to 3 ft. tall and wide. Lavenders need full sun, well-drained soil, and little water.

Recommended lantanas

Lantana camara 'Dallas Red'
This bush-type cultivar has striking orange-red flowers. It grows 2 ft. tall and 3 ft. wide. Pages: 88, **90**.

L. camara 'Confetti'
Another bush-type lantana, this one has eye-catching pink-and-yellow flowers and grows 2½ ft. tall and wide. Pages: 32, 76, 81.

L. camara 'Radiation'
This bush lantana has orange and yellow flowers and grows 2½ ft. tall and wide. Pages: 41, 66, 113.

L. x hybrida 'Lemon Drop'
This vigorous cultivar of spreading lantana has creamy yellow flowers and grows 3 to 4 ft. wide. It sets little fruit, which contributes to increased flower production. Page: 89.

L. x hybrida 'New Gold'
The most popular of all spreading lantanas, 'New Gold' has golden-yellow flowers on vigorous plants that reach

2 ft. tall and spread 3 to 4 ft. It sets little fruit so it doesn't need deadheading. It is designated a **Texas Superstar**®. Pages: 41, 57, 84.

L. montevidensis 'Trailing Lavender'
A low-growing, trailing species that stays under 1 ft. tall and spreads 5 ft. or more. It drapes a profusion of fragrant lavender flowers over steps and containers from spring through the first hard freeze. Not uncommon for it to bloom year-round in coastal areas and during mild winters. It sets no fruit, so it doesn't require deadheading. Designated a **Texas Superstar**®. Pages: 35, 37, **38**, 71, 91.

L. montevidensis 'Weeping White'
This vigorous trailing selection spreads 5 to 6 ft. wide and has pure white flowers. It blooms almost year-round and needs no deadheading. Designated a **Texas Superstar**®. Pages: 46, **47**.

Lantana x *hybrida* 'Lemon Drop'

Lantana x *hybrida* 'New Gold'

Lantana camara 'Confetti'

Lantana camara 'Radiation'

Lantana montevidensis 'Trailing Lavender'

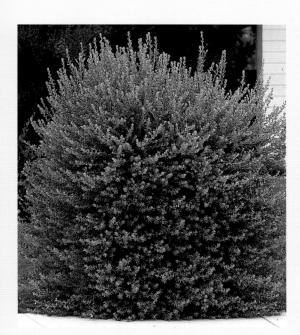

Leucophyllum frutescens 'Compactum'
COMPACT TEXAS SAGE

Liriope muscari
LILYTURF

Lonicera sempervirens
CORAL HONEYSUCKLE

Leucophyllum frutescens 'Compactum'

COMPACT TEXAS SAGE. A dwarf cultivar of the striking, silver-leaved, drought-tolerant Texas native shrub. It has a dense, slightly irregular shape and reaches 3 to 4 ft. tall and wide. Following summer rains, it becomes flushed with orchid-pink flowers. Texas sage demands full sun and excellent drainage and requires little, if any, supplemental watering. Expect few if any insect or disease problems. Does not grow well in East Texas; 'Old Blush' China rose (*Rosa chinensis* 'Old Blush') makes a good flowering substitute there. Pages: 52, 57, 76, 91, 96.

Liriope muscari

LILYTURF. This perennial ground cover forms dense tufts of dark-green grasslike leaves that stay green throughout the year. Clusters of slender lavender flower spikes bloom among the foliage in summer. Lilyturf makes a fine small-scale ground cover near walks and patios and is frequently used as an edging around borders or as a lawn substitute (p. 43, **43**). 'Big Blue' (pp. 48, 59, 63, 71, 95) has larger flowers and foliage than the species and grows about 1 ft. tall and wide. 'Majestic' (p. 79) is similar but bears purple flowers. 'Evergreen Giant' (pp. **38**, 39) is the largest cultivar. It grows 2 ft. tall and wide and is often used as a specimen clump. Variegated lilyturf ('Variegata', p. 23, **23**) has attractive striped foliage in creamy white and green and normally grows 1 ft. tall and wide. 'Silvery Sunproof' is very similar to 'Variegata,' and may be the same plant. Lilyturf can tolerate sun or shade, has few pest problems, and requires water only during dry summers. Mow or shear off old foliage in early spring.

Lonicera sempervirens

CORAL HONEYSUCKLE. This native Texas evergreen vine twines around any support, climbing 10 to 15 ft. or higher. The smooth, oval, blue-green leaves are arranged in neat pairs on the stems. Blooms heavily in early summer and continues off and on until fall. The slender, tubular red-orange flowers are scentless but attractive to hummingbirds. Songbirds eat the bright-red berries that follow the flowers. Grows in shade but blooms best when planted in full or partial sun. Prune in winter if at all, thinning out some of the older stems. Unlike Japanese honeysuckle (*L. japonica*), this species is not aggressive or invasive. Pages: 66, 84, 115.

Recommended Japanese maiden grasses

Miscanthis sinensis 'Adagio'

This dwarf grass has gray-green foliage and grows 2 ft. tall and wide. Blooms reach 3 ft. Pages: 84, 91, 107.

M. sinensis 'Gracillimus'

The most common miscanthus cultivar, 'Gracillimus' has narrow gray-green foliage and grows 3 ft. tall and wide. Blooms rise to 4 ft. Pages: 52, **54**, 66, 94

M. sinensis 'Morning Light'

This selection has very slender, white-striped leaves that look silvery from a distance. It forms a clump 3 ft. tall. Blooms reach 4 ft. Pages: 23, 73, 101.

M. sinensis 'Strictus'

Commonly called "porcupine grass," this striking cultivar has wide green leaves with yellow horizontal banding. Grows 4 ft. tall and wide. Blooms reach 5 ft. Pages: 21, **23**

Miscanthis sinensis 'Gracillimus'

Miscanthis sinensis 'Morning Light'

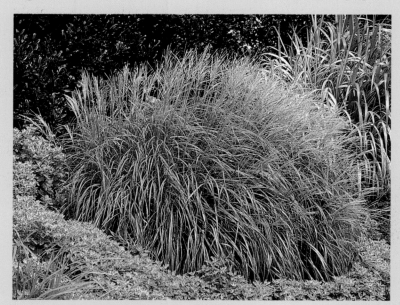

Miscanthis sinensis 'Adagio'

Loropetalum chinense rubrum

CHINESE FRINGE FLOWER . This is a popular large evergreen shrub or small tree for a woodland garden or shrub border. It bears lovely, bright-pink, fringe-like flowers among layers of small purple-tinged leaves. Blossoms occur during the spring and again in the fall. Doesn't do well where soils are extremely alkaline; a good substitute is American beautyberry. Page: 54.

Malvaviscus arboreus drummondii

TURK'S CAP. One of the easiest perennials for Texas gardens, Turk's cap performs well in sun or shade, acidic or alkaline soils, and in wet or dry situations. Plants grow a bushy 2 ft. tall and 3 ft. wide in shade but can reach 5 ft. tall in full sun. The fairly coarse-textured foliage is medium green and slightly lobed. Small red Turk's turban flowers keep on coming from summer until frost, attracting a stream of sulfur butterflies and hummingbirds, especially in the fall. Turk's cap has few pest problems and requires little water. Shear throughout the growing season to keep tidy and cut to the ground after the first frost. Pages: 37, 43, 82, 84, 89, 103, 113.

Malvaviscus arboreus drummondii
TURK'S CAP

Myrica cerifera
WAX MYRTLE

Nandina domestica 'Gulf Stream'
HEAVENLY BAMBOO

Miscanthus sinensis

JAPANESE MAIDEN GRASS. This showy grass forms a vase-shaped clump of long, arching, light-green leaves. Silvery blooms rise above the foliage in late summer or fall and last through winter. For best flowering results, plant in bright sunny spots. Japanese maiden grass has very few insect or disease pests. Water regularly during periods of drought. Cut old leaves and stalks close to the ground in late winter or early spring before the new growth emerges. Page: 25.

Myrica cerifera

WAX MYRTLE. A Texas native evergreen shrub that naturally maintains an upright and bushy profile. It can also be pruned into a small tree. The slender twigs are densely covered with glossy leaves that have a delicious spicy aroma. Historically, the leaves were used as a flavorful subtitute for bay leaf. In fall and winter, clusters of small gray berries line the stems of female plants. Wax myrtle needs full or partial sun and tolerates most soil conditions, including fairly wet ones. It has few pest problems. Water only during periods of drought. It grows quickly and can reach up to 20 ft. tall if left alone. Prune in winter if you want to keep it small or control its shape. Pages: 46, 86, 94.

Nandina domestica

HEAVENLY BAMBOO. This versatile evergreen shrub forms a clump of slender erect stems and fine-textured compound leaves that change color with the seasons, from bronze to green to red. Common nandina (pp. 25, **26**) grows 4 to 5 ft. tall and 3 ft. wide. It bears fluffy clusters of white flowers in summer and sporadically throughout the year, followed by long-lasting red berries. Cultivars are available in smaller sizes. 'Royal Princess' (p. 99) grows 3 to 4 ft. tall and 2 to 3 ft. wide. 'Harbour Dwarf' (p. 115, **115**) makes a bushy mound 2 ft. tall and wide but produces few fruit. 'Gulf Stream' (pp. 21, 42, 107, 115) is an outstanding dwarf form, 3 ft. tall and 2 ft. wide, which turns beautiful shades of orange and red during the winter months. It rarely produces fruit. All nandinas do well in shade or full sun, have virtually no pest problems, and require only sporadic irrigation during the summer months. In spring, prune to remove old, weak, or winter-damaged stems. To keep the plant full, cut some of the stems to the ground each year. This will encourage new growth from the base.

Nerium oleander 'Petite Salmon'

'PETITE SALMON' OLEANDER. A dwarf variety of a tough evergreen shrub bearing slender leaves and clusters of showy flowers. Grows 3 to 4 ft. tall and wide. Salmon-pink flowers bloom from spring to frost. Performs best in full sun and tolerates most soil conditions. Water only when severely dry. It has few pest problems. In early spring, cut out dead wood and shape into desired form. In northern areas, consider replacing it with a more cold-hardy shrub such as althea. Page: 38, **38**.

Nolina recurvata

BOTTLE PALM. A curious-looking small evergreen tree with a large swollen base, one or more tapering trunks, and drooping clusters of bright-green leaves. Bottle palm grows slowly and may eventually reach 12 to 15 ft. high. It needs full sun and well-drained soil. Does best where frosts are light or nonexistent. Page: 65.

Ophiopogon planiscapus
'Ebony Knight'
BLACK MONDO GRASS

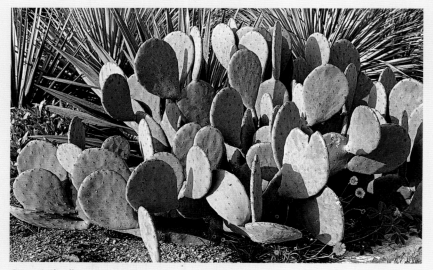

Opuntia lindheimeri
SPINELESS PRICKLY PEAR

Ophiopogon japonicus
MONDO GRASS

Ophiopogon japonicus

MONDO GRASS. This perennial ground cover resembles unmown grass. It grows in clumps of narrow, shiny, dark-green leaves 1 ft. tall and wide. Flowers are inconspicuous. The miniature 'Kyoto Dwarf' (pp. **62**, 63) grows only 4 in. tall and 6 in. wide. Black mondo grass (*O. planiscapus* 'Ebony Knight', pp. 51, **54**, 54, 63) has purple-black foliage and grows 1 ft. tall and wide. Both do best in full to partial shade; foliage can burn in the hot sun. Start with a number of small plants instead of a few large ones. They'll grow more quickly to fill a spot. Mow or shear off the top of old foliage in early spring before new growth appears. The new leaves will look fresh the rest of the year. Pages: 21, 59, **59**, 71.

Opuntia lindheimeri

SPINELESS PRICKLY PEAR. This popular cactus has smooth, succulent, gray-green leaf pads. Called "spineless," the leaves actually have tiny hidden spines, so wear gloves when handling them. The plant grows to 4 ft. tall and wide over time, on occasion producing showy yellow flowers in spring, followed by purple fruit in fall. Spineless prickly pear rarely needs water and has no major insect or disease problems. It makes a great living sculpture in the garden. Page: 57.

Pachypodium lamerei

MADAGASCAR PALM. This palmlike succulent shrub makes an exotic specimen in a pot or planted in the ground in frost-free areas. The plump spiny trunk is topped with long, strap-shaped, dull-green leaves. In summer, mature plants bear fragrant, white crepe-papery flowers with yellow centers, followed by seedpods that resemble long gourds. Grows slowly up to 8 ft. tall. Adapted to full sun or partial shade. A carefree exotic. Pages: 35, 65.

Parthenocissus quinquefolia

VIRGINIA CREEPER. This native woody vine is a great climber, growing up to 30 ft. or more. The deciduous leaves are dark green in summer and vivid orange or red in autumn. The plant adapts to sun or shade and has few pest or disease problems. Water only in periods of drought. Once established, prune as needed to control its size. Page: 103, **103**.

Penstemon gloxinioides

GARDEN OR BORDER PENSTEMON. Late-spring- and summer-flowering perennial with showy tubular flowers spikes in shades of white, pink, red, and purple. Grown as an annual in cold-winter areas. Forms erect clumps about 3 ft. tall. Many varieties available. Needs full or partial sun. Looks best with regular water, but plants must have excellent drainage or they die quickly. Cut down spent flower stalks to encourage second bloom. In colder, high elevations, *P. barbatus* is a good substitute. It bears red flowers from spring into summer. Also check nurseries for locally native species. Page: 28.

Perovskia atriplicifolia

RUSSIAN SAGE. A shrubby perennial with an open, vase-shaped habit. Straight, fairly stiff stems are lined with sparse silver-gray foliage and tiny, but abundant, powdery blue flowers for many weeks in the summer. Grow in full sun and well-drained soil. It needs little water and is rarely bothered by insects or disease. Cut old stems down to the ground in spring. The plant will reach 3 ft. tall and 2 ft. wide by fall. To control its size, cut stems back by one-third in early summer. Pages: 37, 66, 75, 78, 101.

Phlox paniculata 'John Fanick'

'JOHN FANICK' GARDEN PHLOX. This is a beautiful and dependable pink-flowering perennial. It grows into a tidy 2-ft. clump of leafy flower stalks that produce dense clusters of fragrant pale-pink flowers with dark-pink eyes starting in early summer and continuing until frost. Garden phlox needs full or partial sun and adapts to most ordinary garden soil. Water regularly during dry conditions. To promote continuous bloom, cut off the flowers after they fade. Named for the late San Antonio nurseryman John Fanick. Designated a **Texas Superstar**®. Pages: 77, **77**, 101.

Phormium tenax

NEW ZEALAND FLAX. A perennial prized for its bold evergreen foliage. Stiff, straplike leaves form a fan-like clump about 5 ft. tall and at least as wide. Stalks bearing red or yellow flowers rise high above the leaves. Many varieties with colorful foliage are available. 'Atropurpureum' (p. 78) has reddish purple leaves. A smaller variety, better suited to gardens, 'Yellow Wave' (p. 104) has yellow leaves. Plant New Zealand flax in full sun. Needs little water. Excellent accent plant, but large types need lots of room. In cold foothill areas, substitute an ornamental grass.

Photinia x fraseri

FRASER PHOTINIA. Evergreen shrub with dark-green leaves and white spring flowers. New leaves are bronzy red and appear all summer. (Shearing encourages new growth.) Grows 10 to 15 ft. tall and wide. Plant in full sun. Needs to be watered regularly. Page: 98.

Phyllostachys aurea

GOLDEN BAMBOO. An evergreen bamboo with bright-green leaves rising from golden canes. Grows 8 ft. tall and spreads by running rhizomes. Plant in full sun to partial shade. Golden bamboo can be very invasive. To control its spread, plant in heavy clay soil and prune the rhizomes each year, or surround the planting with a barrier 2 to 3 ft. deep. Make sure the barrier extends 2 to 3 in. above the soil to keep the rhizomes from growing over it. To thin the planting, cut some culms to the ground each spring. Page: **62**, 62

Pittosporum tobira 'Wheeler's Dwarf'

'WHEELER'S DWARF' PITTOSPORUM. This is a compact evergreen shrub with tufts of glossy leaves and fragrant white flowers in spring. It rarely exceeds 2 ft. in height and 3 ft. in width. It adapts to sun or shade and only needs occasional watering. Prune anytime, though it rarely needs it. In northern areas, consider choosing a more cold-hardy species like dwarf yaupon holly. Pages: **26**, 27.

Plumbago auriculata

TROPICAL PLUMBAGO. A tropical ever-blooming shrub that is often grown as a tender perennial in Texas. Plumbago mounds to 2 ft. tall and 2 to 3 ft. wide or can be grown as a climber. It is smothered with baby-blue flowers from summer to frost. Rarely plagued by insects or disease. Only needs occasional watering during dry spells. Cut to the ground after the first hard freeze and mulch well. In northern areas, use it as a summer annual for a long season of blue flowers, or consider replacing it with a cold-hardy substitute such as daylily. Pages: 31, 48, 73, 87, 97.

Perovskia atriplicifolia
RUSSIAN SAGE

Phlox paniculata
'John Fanick'
'JOHN FANICK' GARDEN PHLOX

Plumbago auriculata
TROPICAL PLUMBAGO

Quercus buckleyi
TEXAS RED OAK

Prunus caroliniana
'Compacta'
COMPACT CAROLINA
CHERRY LAUREL

Prunus caroliniana 'Compacta'

COMPACT CAROLINA CHERRY LAUREL. A very useful shrub for hedge or screen. Glossy green leaves look fresh all year. Small spikes of lightly scented white flowers appear in spring, followed by black berries in summer. Berries can be messy if the shrub is planted near a patio or walk. Although cherry laurel will grow larger, it is often pruned to about 10 ft. tall and 8 ft. wide. It does best in full sun but can take partial shade. Prefers moist well-drained soil but tolerates dry sites. Shear anytime to desired size and shape. Pages: 70, 102.

Polygala x *dalmaisiana*

SWEET-PEA SHRUB. Evergreen shrub with small narrow leaves and a long season of purplish pink, pea-shaped flowers. Grows 5 ft. tall, with a spreading habit, often bare near the ground. Plant in full sun or partial shade. Water regularly. Shear to keep full-foliaged. Page: 28.

Punica granatum

POMEGRANATE. This is a very ornamental deciduous fruiting shrub. Bronze new growth turns green in summer, and bright yellow in fall. Vibrant-orange flowers are held among the shiny leaves in spring. The widely grown cultivar 'Wonderful' (pp. 60, 107) has a fountainlike shape and reaches 6 to 8 ft. tall. Its flowers are followed by large, bright-red, edible fruit. Compact pomegranate (*P. granatum* 'Nana', pp. 84, **86**) makes an excellent container plant. It grows 3 ft. tall and 2 ft. wide and bears small inedible fruit. Plant pomegranates in full sun and well-drained soil. They need little water once established and are generally pest free. They can be sheared at any time to a desired shape.

Quercus

OAK. Among the most majestic and long-lived shade trees in Texas landscapes. The state is home to many deciduous and evergreen species. Texas red oak (*Q. buckleyi*, p. 21) is a small deciduous oak native to the Hill Country and adapted throughout Texas. It normally grows a modest 20 to 30 ft. tall and wide. Its pointed multilobed leaves turn shades of brilliant red and orange in the fall. Often available in both single and multitrunked forms.

Live oak (*Q. virginiana*, p. 90) is a slow-growing evergreen oak that achieves a height of 25 ft. and a width of 30 ft. in a person's lifetime but is capable of reaching immense proportions over the centuries. It has gnarled branches and small, hollylike deep olive-green leaves that don't drop until the new leaves emerge in the spring. This oak casts dense shade, making it difficult to grow turfgrass underneath. Ground covers are a better option.

When buying oaks, ask where the trees were grown. Texas red oaks and live oaks native to central Texas are smaller, more alkaline tolerant, and more drought tolerant than their cousins in east and southeast Texas.

All Texas oaks grow best in full sun and well-drained soils. They require supplemental watering only during periods of drought. They have few serious insect or disease problems. In areas of central Texas where oak wilt disease is a problem, prune the trees only during the dormant period of winter to avoid attracting disease-spreading insects to the fresh cut wounds. Applying a pruning paint is also recommended.

Rhaphiolepis indica

INDIAN HAWTHORN. A low, spreading, evergreen shrub bearing thick dull-green leaves, small pink or white flowers in spring, and purple-black berries that last through the summer and fall. It grows 2 to 4 ft. tall and wide. There are many fine cultivars from which to choose, including larger forms and those with single or double flowers. 'Majestic Beauty' (p. 98) is a large cultivar, growing 20 to 25 ft. tall and bearing light-pink flowers in clusters up

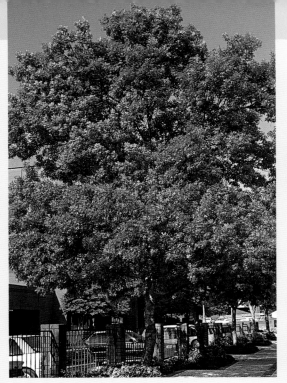

Quercus buckleyi
TEXAS RED OAK

Quercus virginiana
LIVE OAK

to 10 in. wide. Indian hawthorn needs full sun and good drainage. Requires minimal pruning or care and has few pest problems. Fungal leaf spot may occur in shady, humid sites. Pages: 48, **50**.

Rhododendron x 'Gumpo White'

'GUMPO WHITE' DWARF EVERGREEN AZALEA. A low-growing evergreen shrub with very showy white flowers in spring. Small elliptic leaves are borne on a compact plant 2 ft. tall and wide. All azaleas do best with partial shade and need fertile, moist, well-drained, acidic soil. When planting, mix ample amounts of sphagnum peat moss into the planting bed. Be sure not to plant too deep. The top of the root-ball should be level with, or a little higher than, the surrounding soil. Azaleas are shallow rooted, so cover with a layer of mulch to keep the soil cool and damp. Water regularly in summer. Prune and apply an acid azalea fertilizer after the plant finishes blooming. Azaleas are most adapted to the acid soils of east Texas. In other areas, plant in raised beds of a peat, pinebark, and sand mixture or consider an alternative such as dwarf nandina, boxwood, or dwarf yaupon holly. For pink azaleas, try 'Gumbo Pink'. Pages: 26, **26**, 99.

Rosa

ROSE. Texans love roses. Most of the roses that do well in Texas are evergreen shrubs with glossy compound leaves, somewhat thorny stems or canes, and showy, sometimes fragrant, flowers. The classes that perform best include teas, Chinas, polyanthas, and the old-fashioned ramblers. All of these roses are often referred to as "antique roses" in the nursery. They are grown and sold in containers and can be planted year-round.

All roses grow best in full sun and well-drained soil topped with a few inches of mulch. Once established, the roses recommended in this book require no more care than many other shrubs. Prune them lightly once a year in early spring, before new growth starts. (See p. 207 for more on pruning.) Apply a light application of lawn fertilizer, manure, or compost after pruning. The roses we've selected (p. 142) have good resistance to various fungal diseases. They may have problems during years that are especially moist, but each has shown that it will survive and recover without chemical sprays. Aphids, soft-bodied insects the size of a pinhead, may attack new growth, especially in the spring. Wash them away with a blast from the water hose or shear off the infected new growth. Deer eat rosebushes, despite the thorns. Where deer are a problem, consider planting oleander, Texas sage, or pomegranate instead of roses.

The Texas Cooperative Extension program (a branch of Texas A&M University) has conducted extensive research to identify the roses that perform best in Texas without pesticides. Those that pass the test are designated **Earth-Kind** roses.

Recommended roses

Rosa chinensis 'Climbing Old Blush'

The climbing form of the wonderful old China rose, 'Old Blush'. It has a heavy flush of loose double-pink blooms in spring and then a scattering of repeat blooms until fall. Grows vigorously up to 15 ft. tall and wide. There are legendary 'Old Blush' roses in front of the Admiral Nimitz Hotel in Fredericksburg. Pages: 68, **69**.

R. chinensis 'Martha Gonzales'

This dwarf China rose has brilliant red semi-double blooms all season. It grows about 3 ft. tall and 2 ft. wide and occasionally larger. The new growth in spring is a brilliant plum color. Named for the late Martha Gonzales of Navasota. Page: 69, **69**.

R. chinensis 'Mutabilis', Butterfly rose

This popular landscape rose produces showy single flowers all season in everchanging shades of yellow, orange, and pink. Flowers resemble a swarm of butterflies hovering about the bush.

Rosa chinensis 'Mutabilis' BUTTERFLY ROSE

Rosa x 'Belinda's Dream'

Grows to a generous 5 ft. tall and wide, and occasionally larger. New growth is plum colored. Designated an **Earth-Kind** rose. Pages: 72, 90.

R. x 'Belinda's Dream'

This showy shrub rose produces large, double, pink flowers all season. Generally grows around 4 ft. tall and 3 ft. wide. The fragrant flowers are great for floral arrangements. Designated a **Texas Superstar**® and an **Earth-Kind** rose. Pages: 32, 81, **83**.

R. x 'Flower Carpet Pink'

A low, spreading rose that forms a mat of dark-green leaves topped with pink flowers. Grows 2 ft. high by 3 ft. wide. Page 65.

R. x odorata 'Gilbert Nabonnand'

This healthy tea rose makes a profusion of loosely double pink blooms all season, with the heaviest bloom in spring and fall. It grows 4 ft. tall and wide and has thornless stems. If you can't find it, try 'Belinda's Dream'. Pages: 68, 69.

R. x polyantha 'Climbing Pinkie'

This is the climbing form of the polyantha, 'Pinkie'. It can be grown as a loose shrub or as a climber to 8 ft. Pink semidouble blooms smother the canes in spring and repeat the performance in fall. The stems are mostly thornless. Designated an **Earth-Kind** rose. Pages: 22, **23**.

R. x polyantha 'Marie Daly'

This is the pink sport of the popular polyantha, 'Marie Pavie'. It produces a profusion of very fragrant light-pink, semidouble flowers all season. Grows 3 ft. tall and 2 ft. wide, on mostly thornless stems. Named for the late Marie Daly of Longview. Designated both a **Texas Superstar**® and an **Earth-Kind** rose. Pages: **86**, 87.

R. x polyantha 'Marie Pavie'

This dwarf shrub rose produces small white blooms all season. It grows 3 ft. tall and 2 ft. wide. If you can't find it, another polyantha, such as 'White Pet' or 'Marie Daly', makes a good substitute. Pages: 70, **73**, 87.

Rosa x *polyantha* 'Marie Pavie'

Rosmarinus officinalis

ROSEMARY. This classic Mediterranean evergreen is a tough and attractive herbal shrub. The gray-green needlelike leaves combine a lovely fragrance with a tasty flavor. Small blue flowers bloom in late winter and early spring and sporadically throughout the year. Most rosemary species grow upright to a dense 3 ft. tall and wide (pp. 25, 32). 'Tuscan Blue' (pp. 93, 104) is upright to 6 ft., has deep blue flowers, and can be grown as a low hedge. 'Majorca Pink' (p. 111) is upright to 2 to 4 ft. but has lavender-pink blooms. 'Hill's Hardy' (pp. 44, 57, 101, 107) is a cold-hardy selection named for Texas herb expert Madeline Hill. Trailing rosemary (the low-growing *R. officinalis* 'Prostratus') has curved stems and grows 1 ft. tall and 3 ft. wide (pp. 39, 75, 97). Rosemaries do best in full sun and very well-drained soil. They need little water once established and can be pruned or sheared lightly during any season, though they suffer if cut back hard.

Rudbeckia fulgida 'Goldsturm'

'GOLDSTURM' BLACK-EYED SUSAN. This is a popular perennial that bears daisylike flowers with bright-gold petals and prominent brown conical centers in early summer. It forms a robust clump 2 ft. tall and wide, with dark-green leaves at the base and stiff, erect, branching flower stalks. Plant in full sun or partial shade in a fairly well-drained soil. It looks best with regular watering. Remove spent flowers and cut down all the flower stalks in fall or early spring. Pages: 25, 43, 66, 81, 84, 113.

Rosmarinus officinalis ROSEMARY

Rosmarinus officinalis 'Hill's Hardy'

Rudbeckia fulgida 'Goldsturm' BLACK-EYED SUSAN

Rosmarinus officinalis 'Prostratus'

Ruellia brittoniana 'Katie'
DWARF MEXICAN PETUNIA

Salvia farinacea
MEALYCUP SAGE

Ruellia brittoniana 'Katie'

DWARF MEXICAN PETUNIA. An extremely durable and attractive perennial ground cover with narrow dark green leaves. Grows in low dense clumps 1 ft. tall and wide and offers a profusion of small light-purple petunialike flowers from spring until frost. Grows in full sun or partial shade and tolerates most soil types. It is also quite tolerant of both drought and excess moisture. It has few if any pest problems. It self-seeds; pull out unwanted seedlings. Cut to the ground after the first frost. Designated a **Texas Superstar**® because of its beauty and low-maintenance requirements. Pages: 27, 31, 54, 71, 83, 109.

Salvia chamaedryoides

GERMANDER SAGE. This shrubby perennial is grown for its long bloom season (late spring into fall) and tough constitution. It forms a spreading mound of silvery leaves about 2 ft. tall covered with short spikes of beautiful light-blue flowers. Prefers full sun but can take a little shade in inland areas. Lightly shear in late fall. Page: 79.

Salvia farinacea

MEALYCUP SAGE. A popular native Texas perennial. Clusters of medium-blue flower spikes are borne on upright plants that grow vigorously to 3 ft. tall and wide. Flowers top the gray-green foliage in spring and continue until frost. Improved cultivars are purple, blue, or white and grow to a compact

1½ ft. tall and wide. Requires little water and is generally pest free. Shear off old blooms to stimulate new ones and to keep the plants tidy. Pages: 37, 43, 57, 60, 67, 94.

Salvia greggii

AUTUMN SAGE. This shrubby perennial is native to Texas and Mexico. It produces small, oval, sage-scented leaves and a profusion of two-lipped flowers, especially in spring and fall. Flowers are white, pink, red, and other colors, depending on the cultivar. 'Alba' (pp. 52, **54**) has pure white flowers. 'Pink' (pp. 48, **50**, 57, 101) is a large and dependable vivid-pink cultivar, one of many pink ones available. 'Cherry Chief' (p. 44) offers bright-red flowers. Autumn sage generally grows 2½ ft. tall and wide, has few pests, and is very tolerant of dry spells, requiring supplemental watering only during prolonged droughts. Plant autumn sage in full sun and well-drained soil and shear between flower cycles to keep the plants full and blooming. Pages: 60, 75, 78, 89, 97, 104.

Salvia greggii
AUTUMN SAGE

Salvia greggii 'Cherry Chief'
AUTUMN SAGE

Salvia leucantha
MEXICAN BUSH SAGE

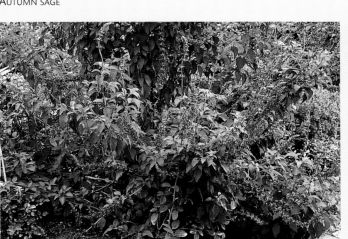

Salvia x 'Indigo Spires'
'INDIGO SPIRES' SALVIA

Santolina chamaecyparissus
GRAY SANTOLINA

Salvia leucantha

MEXICAN BUSH SAGE. This perennial blooms in the fall with hundreds of spikes of purple and white flowers above handsome gray-green foliage. Grows upright to 4 ft. tall and wide. For a bushier plant with more flower spikes, cut the stems back by half several times during the growing season. Requires full sun and good drainage. It has very few pests and needs little watering. Cut to the ground after the first frost. Designated a **Texas Superstar**®. Pages: 21, 28, 41, **43**, 52, 57, 69, 78, 81, 104.

Salvia x 'Indigo Spires'

'INDIGO SPIRES' SALVIA. A vigorous perennial that grows a bushy 5 ft. tall and 3 ft. wide. It puts out a plethora of long, deep blue-purple spikes all season. See mealycup sage (*S. farinacea*, p. 52) for growing requirements and care. Pages: 76, 87.

Santolina chamaecyparissus

GRAY SANTOLINA. A bushy little shrub grown for its soft, fragrant, fine-textured, silver-gray foliage. Often sheared to make an edging or a formal specimen, it is also useful as a ground cover. If left unsheared, it bears round yellow flowers in summer. Santolina needs full sun and well-drained, dry soil. Prune every year in early spring, before new growth starts, cutting the old stems back by half. It generally grows a little more than a foot tall and wide. Pages: 39, 44, 60, 73, 75, **77**.

Sedum 'Autumn Joy'
'AUTUMN JOY' SEDUM

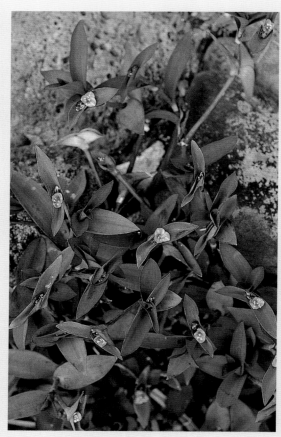

Setcreasea pallida 'Purple Heart'
PURPLE HEART

Scabiosa caucasica

PINCUSHION FLOWER. A perennial that forms a clump of gray-green leaves. Stalks about 2 ft. tall bear clusters of usually blue but sometimes white flowers from late spring through fall. Plant in full sun and water regularly. Remove spent flowers. Cut back in fall to promote additional bloom. Page: 28.

Sedum 'Autumn Joy'

'AUTUMN JOY' SEDUM. This hardy perennial forms clumps of succulent foliage on thick stems topped with flat clusters of tiny flowers in the fall. 'Autumn Joy' grows 18 in. tall and wide, with erect stems and gray-green foliage. The flowers change color from pale to deep salmon pink to rusty red over a span of many weeks in late summer and fall as they open, mature, and go to seed. Most sedums, including 'Autumn Joy', need full sun. They have few pest problems and only require occasional watering in periods of drought. Cut down the old stalks in winter or early spring. Pages: 25, 43, 107.

Setcreasea pallida 'Purple Heart'

PURPLE HEART. This Mexican perennial is among the easiest of all plants to grow. The thick succulent stems sport showy purple foliage from spring to frost. Small pink flowers throughout the growing season are an added bonus. Purple heart has no insect or disease problems and requires little to no watering. It will grow in sun or shade but has better coloration in full sun. Tolerates almost any soil. It is sometimes sold as purple Jew or *Tradescantia pallida*. Pages: 27, 54, 73, 109, **109**.

Sophora secundiflora

TEXAS MOUNTAIN LAUREL. This native shrub or small tree boasts beautiful blossoms as well as shiny evergreen foliage. It generally grows 10 ft. tall or better and 7 ft. wide. The fragrant flowers hang like clusters of purple wisteria each spring. Requires full sun and good drainage. It may occasionally suffer attack from leaf-eating caterpillars but generally recovers. It requires little to no supplemental irrigation or pruning. Do not prune during the winter when flower buds are present. Pages: 37, 48, 101.

Spiraea x bumalda

JAPANESE SPIREA. A deciduous shrub, it creates a low mound of thin, graceful, arching stems that bear sharply toothed leaves and, from late spring into summer, round flat clusters of tiny flowers. 'Anthony Waterer' (pp. 46, **47**) has carmine-pink flowers. 'Goldflame' (pp. 113, **115**) has bright-gold leaves that are tinged with orange in spring and turn red in fall. Flowers are pink. Both cultivars grow about 2 to 3 ft. tall and wide. Plant them in full or partial sun. Prune every year after bloom, removing some of the older stems at ground level and cutting the others back partway. In summer, shear off faded flowers to promote possible reblooming. Water during periods of drought. Rarely suffers from insects or disease.

Sterlitzia reginae

BIRD-OF-PARADISE. Beloved tropical-looking evergreen plant with large, eye-catching flowers that look like the head of a bird. Flowers, mostly orange but touched with blue and white, are concentrated in early spring, but some bloom year-round. Large leathery leaves form a dense clump about 5 ft. tall. Best adapted to frost-free areas. Needs protection elsewhere. Or plant in pots and move to a covered spot in winter. Best in full sun. Water and fertilize regularly. Remove spent flowers. Page: 65.

Tagetes lemmonii

COPPER CANYON DAISY. A shrublike perennial with small finely divided, dull-green aromatic leaves and bright orange-yellow, marigold-type flowers in fall. It grows 2 to 3 ft. tall and wide. Trim back by one-third several times during the growing season to maintain a compact habit and to prevent sprawling in bloom. Plant in full sun. Rarely needs water and has no pest problems. Late blooms can be damaged by a hard frost. Page: 37.

Tagetes lucida

MEXICAN MINT MARIGOLD. This Mexican perennial has aromatic foliage and clusters of small golden yellow marigold-like flowers in the fall. The scented foliage (tasting of licorice or anise) can be used as a culinary substitute for French tarragon. Generally grows 1½ ft. tall and wide and requires full to partial sun. Shear the plants back by one-third several times during the growing season to maintain a compact habit and to promote heavier bloom. It has few pests and requires watering only during dry periods. Pages: 52, 84, **86**, 101.

Sophora secundiflora
TEXAS MOUNTAIN LAUREL

Tagetes lemmonii
COPPER CANYON DAISY

Tecoma stans 'Gold Star'
'GOLD STAR' ESPERANZA

Trachelospermum asiaticum
ASIAN JASMINE

Trachelospermum jasminoides
STAR JASMINE

Tecoma stans 'Gold Star'

'GOLD STAR' ESPERANZA. This showy Texas native can be grown as a deciduous shrub in the lower third of the state. In the middle section, it may be grown as a perennial, pruned to the ground after the first hard freeze. In the northern third, it may be grown as an annual. It bears shiny bright-green pecanlike leaves, extremely showy clusters of yellow bell-shaped flowers from summer until frost, and green bean pods after the flowers fade. Generally grows to a bushy 5 ft. tall and wide. Esperanza requires full hot sun and only occasional watering during the summer. It has no major insect or disease problems. Cut off bean pods or shear plants to encourage repeat bloom. Plant it in a protected area or mulch heavily to protect it from freezing. In the northern half of the state, consider using it as an annual or potted specimen, or use a more cold-hardy substitute like the butterfly rose. Designated a **Texas Superstar**®. Pages: 25, 72, 81.

Thymus praecox ssp. arcticus

CREEPING THYME. A creeping perennial that forms low mats of wiry stems and tiny semievergreen leaves. Tolerates light foot traffic and smells good when you step on it. Clusters of pink, lavender, or white flowers bloom over a long season in midsummer. Grows 4 to 6 in. tall, 1 to 2 ft. wide. Look in the herb department of a nursery to find this plant. There are several other kinds of creeping thymes. 'Argenteus' and 'Aureus' varigated lemon thymes have lemon-scented, silver- and yellow-variegated leaves, respectively. All make attractive, fragrant, tough ground covers for sites with full sun and well-drained soil. They need little water once established. Shear old stems close to the ground in fall to early spring. Plants may self-sow and pop up in cracks of pavement, in gravel walks, or even in the lawn, but aren't weedy. Page: 93.

Tipuana tipu

TIPU TREE. This large semievergreen or deciduous tree makes a useful lawn or shade tree. It grows 25 to 35 ft. tall and spreads twice as wide. Light-green, finely divided leaves are topped with long clusters of yellow to apricot pealike flowers from late spring to early summer, followed by large seedpods. Best grown where summers are warm and winters are mild. Foliage is damaged at 25°F. Page: 64.

Trachelospermum asiaticum

ASIAN JASMINE. This common ground cover is dense and low growing, forming a thick mat of small, shiny evergreen leaves. It grows less than 1 ft. tall and spreads to about 3 ft. Asian jasmine has few pest problems and only requires watering when it's dry and the leaves turn dull green. Shear as needed to keep tidy or mow each spring with the mower on the highest setting. Pages: 21, 99.

Trachelospermum jasminoides

STAR JASMINE. This is an evergreen vine with woody, twining stems lined with pairs of small, glossy-green, oval leaves. It bears dangling clusters of sweetly scented creamy white flowers in spring. It can climb 10 to 15 ft. if given a pillar or fence for support but is also useful as a sprawling ground cover, 1 to 2 ft. tall. Prune anytime to keep within bounds. If used as a ground cover, shear as needed to keep it compact. Plant in full sun or partial shade and water during periods of drought. Also sold as star jasmine. Pages: 51, 60, 88.

Trachycarpus fortunei

WINDMILL PALM. This is one of the more cold-hardy palms. It forms a small tree with somewhat drooping, dark-green palm-shaped leaves and a matted burlaplike trunk. It commonly grows 8 to 10 ft. tall and 4 to 5 ft. wide. It has no insect or disease problems and needs watering only during dry spells. Pages: 59, 72.

Verbena bonariensis

PURPLE VERBENA. This perennial forms a low mound of basal foliage topped by a thicket of stiff, erect, much-branched but almost leafless flower stalks. They bear countless little clusters of lavender-purple flowers throughout the season. The heaviest bloom comes before the heat of summer, beckoning butterflies and floral arrangers. Purple verbena needs full sun and tolerates most soil conditions. Shear as needed during the growing season to promote new bloom stalks. It may occasionally be attacked by flea hoppers. Generally self-sows but isn't weedy. Pages: 48, 71, 91.

Verbena x hybrida

VERBENA. These are sprawling perennials with evergreen leaves and round clusters of showy flowers. 'Blue Princess' (pp. 23, 25, 52, 87, 97, 107) has lightly fragrant lavender-blue flowers and is designated a **Texas Superstar®**. 'Homestead Purple' (pp. 32, 41, 45, 77, 81, 91, 95) has vibrant purple flowers. Plant them in full sun and they will bloom nonstop from early spring until hard frost if regularly deadheaded. Plants generally grow about 1 ft. tall and spread 3 ft. or wider. Prune any damaged or frosted shoots in early spring, and shear throughout the growing season to keep tidy. Water regularly during hot spells. Plants may suffer attack from flea hoppers during summer heat.

Trachycarpus fortunei WINDMILL PALM

Verbena x *hybrida* 'Blue Princess' VERBENA

Verbena bonariensis PURPLE VERBENA

Verbena x *hybrida* 'Homestead Purple' VERBENA

Viburnum tinus 'Spring Bouquet'
VIBURNUM

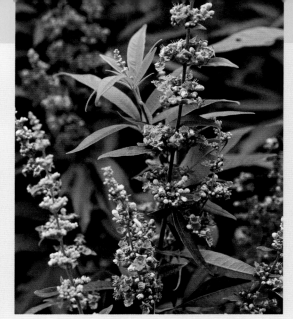

Vitex agnus-castus
CHASTE TREE

Viburnum tinus 'Spring Bouquet'

'SPRING BOUQUET' VIBURNUM. A compact evergreen shrub with dark-green leaves borne on reddish stems. It produces clusters of fragrant white flowers in spring and metallic-blue berries in late summer. Generally grows 5 ft. tall and about 4 ft. wide and has few pest problems. Water well during periods of drought. Shear anytime after blooming to maintain desired shape, but do not prune in the late fall or winter, because flower buds will be present. Pages: 32, 86, 113.

Vinca major

PERIWINKLE. A spreading evergreen ground cover with medium-green heart-shaped leaves and five-petaled lavender-purple flowers in the spring. The plants normally grow about 1 ft. tall and 2 to 3 ft. wide before rooting to form new plants. Periwinkle performs best in shady situations and well-drained soil. Water regularly during periods of drought or when the leaves turn dull green. It may suffer occasional attacks from leaf feeding insects but almost always recovers. Page: 38, **38**.

Vitex agnus-castus

CHASTE TREE. This is a tough deciduous shrub or small tree that can reach up to 20 ft. and more with age. It generally grows with multiple trunks and has an open habit. The aromatic, narrowly palmate leaves are dull green on top and grayish underneath. Showy flower spikes bear small, tubular, lavender-blue flowers. They bloom in summer and attract many butterflies. Plant in full sun and well-drained soil. Chaste tree isn't bothered by pests and is able to survive dry periods. Cut off lower limbs in winter if you want to develop a tree shape; otherwise it will be shrubby and dense. To keep it small, cut it back to 1 to 2 ft. in early spring, when new growth starts. Then shear with hedge clippers or power shears between bloom cycles to prevent seed set and promote new blooms. Pages: 38, 75, 81.

Water plants

Many garden centers offer a limited selection of water plants. Specialty nurseries and mail-order water-garden specialists often offer dozens of kinds. Most water plants are fast-growing, sometimes even weedy, so you need only one of each to start. Some water plants are tender to frost, but you can overwinter them indoors in a pot or aquarium. There are three main groups of water plants: marginal, floating, and oxygenating. Choose one or more of each for an interesting and balanced effect.

Marginal plants grow well on the edge of the pond or in containers covered with 2 in. or more of water. Their leaves and flower stalks stand above

Nymphaea x 'Charlene Strawn'
CHARLENE STRAWN

the water surface while their roots stay submerged. Louisiana iris (see *Iris* x Louisiana hybrids, p. 95) and umbrella sedge (see *Cyperus alternifolius*, p. 59) are two common examples.

Floating plants have leaves that rest on the water and roots that dangle into it. Water lettuce (*Pistia* species) is a floater that forms saucer-size rosettes of iridescent pale-green leaves.

Oxygenating, or submerged, plants grow completely under water. They help keep the water clear and provide oxygen, food, and shelter for fish. Anacharis (*Elodea* species) is a popular oxygenator with tiny, dark-green leaves.

Water lilies (*Nymphaea* species, pp. 95, **97**) are the most popular plants for pools and ponds. There are two main groups of water lilies. Hardy water lilies survive outdoors from year to year and bloom in midsummer. They are usually the easiest to grow. Tropical water lilies, such as Dauben water lily (*N.* x *daubenyana*, p. 73, **73**), need warm water and bloom over a longer season from summer through fall but are cold tender and often treated as annuals. Both kinds are available in dwarf-size plants, suitable for small pools, with fragrant or scentless flowers in shades of white, yellow, and pink. Tropicals also come in shades of blue and purple. All water lilies need full sun. Plant the roots in a container of heavy, rich, garden soil, and set the container in the pool, making sure that about 6 in. of water covers the soil. (See p. 199 for more on planting.)

Wisteria sinensis

This is a vigorous woody vine with deciduous compound leaves that turn yellow in fall. Dangling clusters of very fragrant lavender-purple flowers appear in early spring. The vine climbs by twining around a trellis, tree, or other support and may exceed 30 ft. if not controlled. To flower well, it needs full sun along with well-drained soil. A young plant may not bloom for several years after you plant it, but it should bloom as the new growth matures. Wisteria has few pest problems and only requires irrigation during dry summers. To keep it in bounds, prune the long vining shoots during summer. Major pruning should be done immediately following bloom. Do not prune during winter, when flower buds are present. Wisteria can be invasive in East Texas. Pages: 48, **50**, 93.

Yucca

YUCCA. These are bold architectural plants with pointed swordlike leaves and tall stalks of showy creamy white flowers. *Y. filamentosa* (pp. 37, **38**) has narrow leaves with hairy filaments along the margins and generally grows 3 ft. tall and wide. Soft-tip yucca (*Y. gloriosa*, pp. 52, **54**, 73, 75) has somewhat flexible gray-green leaves and grows 4 to 5 ft. tall and 3 ft. wide. Yuccas require full sun and good drainage and no supplemental irrigation. Maintenance is limited to removing dead leaves at their base and cutting down dead flower stalks. Yuccas have few if any pest problems.

Guide *to* Installation

Landscaping is rewarding, but it does require hard work in order to reap its benefits. There are various necessary tasks that come with installing any of the designs in this book, and you will find all of those projects here. To keep things simple, we've organized the jobs in the order in which you'd most likely tackle them. In addition to the instructions, we've included numerous illustrations to help you learn how to plan the job; clear the site; construct paths, patios, ponds, fences, arbors, and trellises; prepare the planting beds; and install and maintain the plantings.

So, are you ready to roll up your sleeves and dig in? If you are, all it takes is just a few weekends to create a landscape feature that will provide years of enjoyment while adding outdoor appeal and value to your home.

Organizing Your Project

If your gardening experience is limited to mowing the lawn, pruning the bushes, and growing some flowers and vegetables, the thought of starting from scratch and installing a whole new landscape feature might be intimidating. But in fact, adding one of the designs in this book to your property is completely within reach, if you approach it the right way. The key is to divide the project into a series of

steps and take them one at a time. This is how professional landscapers work. It's efficient and orderly, and it makes even big jobs seem manageable.

On this and the facing page, we'll explain how to think your way through a landscaping project and anticipate the various steps. Subsequent topics in this section describe how to do each part of the job. Detailed instructions and illustrations cover all the techniques you'll need to install any design from start to finish.

The step-by-step approach
Choose a design and adapt it to your site. The designs in this book address parts of the home landscape. In the most attractive and effective home landscapes, all the various parts work together. Don't be afraid to change the shape of beds; alter the number, kinds, and positions of plants; or revise paths and structures to bring them into harmony with their surroundings.

To see the relationships with your existing landscape, you can draw the design on a scaled plan of your property. Or you can work on the site itself, placing wooden stakes, pots, or whatever is handy to represent plants and structures.

Lay out the design on site. Once you've decided what you want to do, you'll need to lay out the paths and structures and outline the beds. Some people are comfortable pacing off distances and relying on their eye to judge sizes and relative positions. Others prefer to transfer the grid from the plan full size onto the site using garden lime (a white powder available at nurseries), as you would chalk on a blackboard, to draw a grid or outlines of planting beds.

Clear the site. (See pp. 156–157.) Sometimes you have to work around existing features—a nice big tree, a building or fence, a sidewalk—but it's usually easiest to start a new landscaping project by removing unwanted structures or pavement and killing, cutting down, or uprooting all the plants. This can generate a

DIGGING POSTHOLES

AMENDING SOIL

lot of debris for disposal, but it's worth the trouble to make a fresh start.

Make provisions for water. (See pp. 158–159.) In Texas, most landscape plants require more water than nature provides. A well-planned irrigation strategy and system can help you make the most of this increasingly precious natural resource. Keep in mind that some permanent parts of most watering systems need to be installed before the other landscape features. Additional parts are installed after the soil is prepared. And the final components are normally placed after planting.

Construct the "hardscape." (See pp. 160–193.) Hardscape includes landscape structures, such as fences, trellises, arbors, retaining walls, walkways, edging, and outdoor lighting. Install these elements before you start any planting.

Prepare the soil. (See pp. 194–197.) On most properties, it's uncommon to find soil that's as good as it should be for growing plants. Typically, the soil around a new house is shallow, compacted, and infertile. Some plants tolerate such poor conditions, but they don't thrive. To grow healthy, attractive plants, you need to improve the quality of the soil throughout the entire area that you're planning to plant.

Do the planting and add mulch. (See pp. 198–203.) Putting plants in the ground usually goes quite quickly and gives instant gratification. Mulching the soil makes the area look neat even while the plants are still small.

Maintain your plantings. (See pp. 203–213.) Most plantings need regular watering and occasional weeding for the first year or two. After that, depending on the design you've chosen, you'll have to do some routine maintenance—watering, pruning, shaping, cutting back, and cleaning up—to keep the plants looking their best. This may take as little as a few hours a year or as much as an hour or two every week throughout the growing season.

TRANSPLANTING

SETTING FLAGSTONES

Clearing the Site

The site you've chosen for a landscaping project may or may not need to be cleared of fences, old pavement, construction debris, and other objects. Unless your house is newly built, the site will almost certainly be covered with plants.

Before you start removing them, try to find someone to identify them for you. As you walk around together, make a sketch that shows what plants are where, and attach labels to them, too. Determine if there are any desirable plants worth saving—mature shade trees that you should work around, shapely shrubs that aren't too big to dig up and relocate or give away, worthwhile perennials and ground covers that you could divide and replant, or healthy sod that you could lay elsewhere. Likewise, decide which plants need to go—diseased or crooked trees, straggly or overgrown shrubs, weedy brush, invasive ground covers, or a tattered lawn.

You can clear small areas yourself, bundling the brush for pickup and tossing soft-stemmed plants on the compost pile. But if you have lots of woody brush or any trees to remove, you might want to hire someone else to do the job. A crew armed with power tools can turn a thicket into a pile of wood chips in just a few hours. Have them pull out the roots and grind the stumps, too. Save the chips; they're good for surfacing paths, or you can use them as mulch.

Working around a tree

If there are any large, healthy trees on your site, be careful as you work around them. It's okay to prune off some of a tree's limbs, as shown on the facing page, but respect its trunk and its roots. Keep heavy equipment from beneath the tree's canopy, and don't raise or lower the level of the soil there. Try never to cut or wound the bark on the trunk (don't nail things to a tree), because that exposes the tree to disease organisms. Planting beneath existing Texas natives such as post oaks can endanger their health. Consult a certified arborist on ways to integrate these handsome, but sensitive, trees into your landscape and care for them properly.

Killing perennial weeds

Some common weeds that sprout back from perennial roots or runners are bindweed, Bermuda grass, Johnson grass, nutsedge, smilax, and Carolina snailseed. Garden plants that can become weedy include bamboo, Mexican petunia, mint, and *Liriope spicata*. Once they get established, perennial weeds are hard to

Smothering weeds

Mow or cut the tops of the weeds close to the ground ❶. Then cover the area with overlapped sections of newspaper ❷ or flat cardboard and top with a layer of mulch spread several inches deep ❸.

Smothering works by excluding light, which stops photosynthesis. If any shoots reach up through the covering and produce green leaves, pull them out immediately. Wait a few months, until you're sure the weeds are dead, before you dig into the smothered area and plant there.

In Texas, you can also kill weeds through a process called "solarization." Till the weeds into the soil and moisten the area. Then cover the soil with a thick sheet of clear plastic, sealing its edges by burying them in a shallow trench. The heat generated underneath the plastic kills the weeds.

SMOTHERING WEEDS

❶ Smothering kills weeds by depriving them of light. Cut off the tops close to the ground.

❷ Cover with thick newspaper or cardboard.

❸ Top with several inches of mulch. Wait a few months to be sure weeds are dead; then till rotted newspaper and mulch into the soil.

eliminate. You can't cut off just the tops, because the plants keep sprouting back. You need to dig out the weeds, smother them, or kill them with an herbicide.

Digging. You can often remove a perennial weed if you dig carefully at the base of the stems, find the roots, and follow them through the soil, pulling out every bit of root that you find. Some plant roots go deeper than you can dig. Most plants will resprout from the bits that you miss, but these leftover sprouts are easy to pull.

Spraying. Herbicides are easy, fast, and effective weed killers when chosen and applied with care. Ask at the nursery for those that break down quickly into more benign substances, and make sure the weed you're trying to kill is listed on the product label. After spraying, you usually need to wait from one to four weeks for the weed to die completely. You may have to spray a second or third time.

Replacing turf

If the area where you're planning to add a landscape feature is currently part of the lawn, you have a fairly easy task ahead. How to proceed depends on the condition of the turf and on what you want to put in its place. If the turf is healthy, you can recycle it to replace, repair, or extend the lawn elsewhere.

The drawing below shows a technique for removing relatively small areas of strong healthy turf for replanting. First, using a sharp shovel, cut it into strips about 1- to 3 ft. square. (These small pieces are easy to lift) ❶. Then slice a few inches deep under each square and lift it, roots and all, the way you would lift brownies from a pan ❷. Quickly transplant the squares to a previously prepared site; water them well until the roots are established.

If you don't need the turf, or if it's straggly or weedy, leave it in place and kill the grass. Spraying with an herbicide kills most grasses within one to two weeks. Or cover it with a tarp or a sheet of black plastic for about four weeks during the heat of summer. Then dig or till the bed, shredding the turf, roots and all, and mixing it into the soil.

MOVING TURF

❶ With a sharp shovel, cut healthy turf into squares or strips of manageable size.

❷ Slice a few inches deep under each square, lift it, and place as soon as possible in a new spot.

Removing large limbs

If there are large trees on your property now, you may want to remove some of the lower limbs so light can reach your plantings. Major pruning of large trees is a job for a professional arborist, but you can remove limbs smaller than 4 in. in diameter and less than 10 ft. above the ground yourself with a simple bow saw or pole saw.

Use the three-step procedure shown below to remove large limbs safely. First, saw partway through the bottom of the limb, approximately 1 ft. out from the trunk ❶. This keeps the bark from tearing down the trunk when the limb falls. Then make a corresponding cut through the top of the limb ❷ and be prepared to get out of the way when the limb drops. Finally, remove the stub ❸. Undercut it slightly or hold it as you finish the cut, so it doesn't fall away and peel bark off the trunk. Note that the cut is not flush with the trunk but is just outside the thick area at the limb's base, called the "branch collar." Leaving the branch collar helps the wound heal quickly and naturally. Wound dressing is considered unnecessary today.

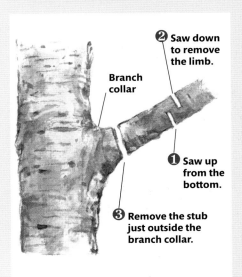

❷ Saw down to remove the limb.

Branch collar

❶ Saw up from the bottom.

❸ Remove the stub just outside the branch collar.

Water for Your Plants

Texas's long, dry summers and frequent droughts make watering a critical concern of gardeners here. Though some plants will survive long dry periods once established, almost all plants will need regular watering the first few years after planting. And most will need summer watering their entire life to look their best.

But there is more at stake than just the survival of plants. Water conservation is a daily obligation in Texas, where water is a valuable and limited resource. Outdoor landscapes use a large portion of urban water, so nothing should be wasted. During periods of drought, mandatory conservation is often strictly enforced.

So for the health of your plants and for the preservation of a valuable resource, make water conservation part of your landscape planning from the beginning. The box below outlines effective water-saving practices for home landscapes. (See p. 205 for more on when and how much to water.) You can also consult your local water department for advice about watering gardens and lawns.

Water-wise practices

Choose plants carefully. Many plants that require little water, including Texas natives, thrive in the state's dry summer climate and are increasingly available from local nurseries and garden centers.

Group plants with similar water needs. Position plants that require the most water near the house, where they can be more easily tended and watered. Use drought-tolerant plants farther from the house.

Plant in fall. This way, new plants will have the cooler, wetter winter and spring seasons to become established before facing the heat of summer.

Mulch plantings. A 2- to 3-in. layer of mulch reduces evaporation by keeping the soil cool and sheltering it from wind.

Create water-retaining basins. Use these to direct irrigation water to large plants. Make a low soil mound around the plant's perimeter, at its drip line. (Basins aren't necessary in drip-irrigated beds.)

Limit lawn size. Lawns demand lots of water. Reduce the size of your lawn by planting beds, borders, and less thirsty ground covers.

Water in the morning. Lower morning temperatures and less wind mean less water is lost to evaporation.

Adjust watering to conditions. Water less during cool weather in the spring and fall. Turn off automatic timers during the rainy season.

Install, monitor, and maintain an irrigation system. Even a simple drip system conserves water. Once it's installed, check and adjust the equipment on a regular basis. Be sure to inspect frequently for clogged emitters.

Watering systems

One of the best ways to conserve water is to use an efficient delivery system. The simplest watering systems—watering cans and handheld hoses—are also the most limited and inefficient. They can be adequate for watering new transplants or widely separated individual plants. But sprinkling plants in an entire bed with a hose and nozzle for even as long as an hour may provide less water than half an inch of rainfall. And wetting just the top few inches of soil this way encourages shallow root growth, making it necessary to water more frequently. To provide enough water to soak the soil to a depth of a foot or more, you need a system that can run untended for extended periods.

Hose-end sprinklers are easy to set up and leave to soak an area. But they're also inefficient: water is blown away by wind. It runs off sloped or paved areas. It is applied unevenly, or it falls too far away from individual plants to be of use to them. And because sprinklers soak leaves as well as soil, the damp foliage may breed fungal diseases.

Low-volume irrigation. For garden beds and landscape plantings such as those in this book, low-volume irrigation systems are the most efficient and offer the most flexibility and control. Frequently called "drip irrigation systems," they deliver water at low pressure through a network of plastic pipes, hoses, and tubing, and a variety of emitters and microsprinklers. Such systems are designed to apply water slowly and directly to the roots of targeted plants, so very little water is lost to runoff and evaporation or wasted on plants that don't need it. Because water is usually applied at soil level, the risk of foliar diseases is reduced, less soil is watered, and weeds are reduced.

Simple low-volume systems can be attached to ordinary outdoor faucets or garden hoses and controlled manually. You can set up such a system in less than an hour. Sophisticated systems include (1) their own attachment to your main water

Connection to electronic controls

Control valve with backflow prevention device

Main water supply

Filter

DRIP IRRIGATION SYSTEM

Pressure regulator

Basic components of a drip irrigation system are shown here. Individual systems will vary. Several common types of emitters are shown; systems can incorporate others.

supply, (2) a network of valves and buried pipes that allow you to divide your property into zones, and (3) an electronic control device that can automatically water each zone at preset times for preset durations. Such systems often incorporate sprinklers.

A person with modest mechanical skills and basic tools can plan and install a low-volume irrigation system. Extensive multizoned systems (particularly those with their own attachment to the main water supply) are more difficult to design and install. If you tackle one, have a professional review your plans before you start. You can buy kits or individual system components from garden centers, nurseries, or specialty suppliers. Although most manufacturers provide helpful instructions, good criteria for choosing among different local suppliers are their knowledge of system design and installation and their ability to help you with both. A supplier may charge for this service, but good advice is worth it.

Low-volume-system components. Any irrigation system connected to a domes-

tic water supply needs a **backflow prevention device** (also called an "antisiphon device") at the point of connection to the water supply to protect drinking water from contamination. Backflow devices are often mandated by city building codes, so check with local health or building officials to determine if a specific type of backflow prevention device is required.

Install a **filter** to prevent minerals and flakes that slough off metal water pipes from clogging the emitters. You'll need to clean the filter regularly. Between the filter and emitters, all hoses and tubing should be plastic, not metal.

Pressure regulators reduce the mains' water pressure to levels required by the system's low-volume emitters.

Supply lines deliver water from the source to the emitters. Some systems incorporate buried lines of rigid plastic pipe to carry water to plantings anywhere on the property. For aboveground use, you'll need flexible tubing designed specifically for low-volume irrigation.

Emitters and **soaker hoses** deliver the water to the plants. A wide range of emitters are available for different kinds of plants and garden situations. Various drip fittings, bubblers, and microsprinklers can be plugged into the flexible plastic tubing. A single emitter or a group of emitters might serve individual or groups of plants. Soaker hoses and "ooze tubes" seep or drip water along their length. Consult with your supplier about which delivery systems best meet your plants' needs. (The high calcium and salt content of many water sources in Texas can clog drip emitters, so check emitters regularly to make sure they are watering properly.)

A **timer** or **electronic controller** helps ensure efficient water use. Used in conjunction with zoned plantings, these devices provide control and flexibility to deal with the specific water needs of groups of plants or even individual specimens.

Installation. Permanent irrigation equipment should be installed early in any project. Lay underground piping that crosses paths, patios, or similar landscape features after the site is cleared but before installing any of these permanent features. Lay pipes in planting areas after you have prepared the soil. That way, you won't damage the piping when digging or rototilling. Install underground pipe in trenches dug to the appropriate depth. Then temporarily cap the ends. Hook up the aboveground tubing and position emitters after planting.

½-in. supply line

Microsprinkler

¼-in. feedline

Stake

Individual emitter

Inline emitter

Punch-in emitter

¼-in. connector

Making Paths and Walkways

Every landscape needs paths and walkways if for no other reason than to keep your feet dry as you move from one place to another. A path can also divide and define the spaces in the landscape, orchestrate the way the landscape is viewed, and even be a key element in enhancing its beauty.

Whether it is a graceful curving garden path or a utilitarian slab leading to the garage, a walk has two main functional requirements: durability and safety. It should hold up through seasonal changes and provide a well-drained surface that is easy to walk on and to maintain.

A path's function helps determine its surface and its character. In general, heavily trafficked walkways leading to a door, garage, or shed need hard, smooth (but not slick) surfaces and should take you where you want to go fairly directly. A path to a backyard play area could be a strip of soft wood bark, easy on the knees of impatient children. A relaxed stroll in the garden might require only a hopscotch collection of flat stones meandering from one prized plant to another.

Before laying out a walk or path, spend some time observing existing traffic patterns. If your path makes use of a route people already take (particularly children), it will be more likely to keep them on the path and off the lawn or flowers. Avoid areas that are slow to drain. When determining width, consider whether the path must accommodate rototillers or several strollers walking abreast, or just provide access for plant maintenance.

Dry-laid paths

You can make a path simply by laying bricks or spreading wood chips on top of bare earth. While quick and easy, this method has serious drawbacks. Laid on the surface, with no edging to contain them, loose materials are soon scattered, and solid materials are easily jostled out of place. If the earth base doesn't drain very well, the path will be a swamp after a rainstorm. In cold-winter areas of Texas, repeated expansion and contraction of the soil will heave bricks or flagstones out of alignment, making the path unsightly and dangerous.

The method we recommend—laying surface material on an excavated sand-and-gravel base—minimizes these problems. The sand and gravel improve drainage and provide a cushion against the freeze-thaw movement of the underlying soil. Excavation can place the path surface at ground level, where the surrounding soil or an installed edging can contain loose materials and prevent hard materials from shifting.

All styles, from a natural wood-bark path to a formal cut-stone entry walk, and all the materials discussed in this section, can be laid on an excavated base of gravel and sand.

Hard-surface walks

Edging

Flagstone or precast pavers

2 in. builder's sand

Bricks

4 in. coarse gravel or crushed rock

Loose-surface paths

Edging

Water-permeable landscape fabric

Pea gravel, fine crushed rock, bark, or wood chips

4 in. coarse gravel or crushed rock

Choosing a surface

Walkways and paths can be made of either hard or soft material. Your choice of material will depend on the walkway's function, your budget, and your personal preferences.

Soft materials, including bark, wood chips, pine needles, and loose gravel, are best for informal and low-traffic areas. Inexpensive and simple to install, they settle, scatter, or decompose and must be replenished or replaced every few years.

Hard materials, such as brick, flagstone, and concrete pavers, are more expensive and time-consuming to install, but they are permanent, requiring only occasional maintenance. (Compacted crushed stone can also make a hard-surface walk.) Durable and handsome, they're ideal for high-traffic, high-profile areas.

Bark, wood chips, and pine needles

Perfect for a natural look or a quick temporary path, these loose materials can be laid directly on the soil or, if drainage is poor, on a gravel bed. Bagged materials from a nursery or garden center will be cleaner, more uniform, and considerably more expensive than bulk supplies bought by the cubic yard. Check with local tree services to find the best prices on bulk material.

Gravel and crushed rock

Loose rounded gravel gives a bit underfoot, creating a soft but messy path. The angular facets of crushed stone eventually compact into a hard and tidier path that can be laid without an edging, if the surrounding soil is firm enough. Gravel and stone type and color vary from area to area. Buy materials by the ton or cubic yard.

Concrete pavers

Precast concrete pavers are versatile, readily available, and often the least expensive hard-surface material. They come in a range of colors and shapes, including interlocking patterns. Precast edgings are also available. Most home and garden centers carry a variety of precast pavers, which are sold by the piece.

HEXAGONS

RUNNING BAND

OCTAGONS AND SQUARES COMBINATION

Brick

Widely available in a range of sizes, colors, and textures, brick complements many design styles. When carefully laid on a well-prepared sand-and-gravel base, brick provides an even, safe, and long-lasting surface. Buy paving brick instead of the softer "facing" brick, which may break up after a few freeze-thaw cycles. (If you buy used brick, pick the hardest.) Avoid glazed types; the glaze traps moisture and salts, which will damage the brick.

RUNNING BOND

TWO-BRICK BASKET WEAVE

HERRINGBONE

DIAGONAL HERRINGBONE

Flagstone

"Flagstone" is a generic term for stratified stone that can be split to form pavers. Limestone and sandstone are common paving materials. The surfaces of marble and slate are usually too smooth to make safe paving. Cut into squares or rectangles, flagstone can be laid as individual stepping-stones or in interesting patterns. Flagstones come in a range of colors, textures, and sizes. Flags for walks should be at least 2 in. thick. Purchased by weight, surface area, or pallet load, flagstones are usually the most expensive paving choice.

CUT FLAGSTONE

CUT AND IRREGULAR FLAGSTONE

IRREGULAR FLAGSTONE

Drainage

Few things are worse than a path dotted with puddles or icy patches. To prevent these from forming, the soil around and beneath the path should drain well. The path's location and construction should ensure that rainwater does not collect on the surface. Before you locate a path, observe runoff and drainage on your property during and after heavy rains. Avoid routing a path through areas where water courses, collects, or is slow to drain.

While both loose and hard paving can be successfully laid directly on well-drained compacted soil, sometimes laying surface materials on a base of sand or gravel will help improve drainage and minimize frost heaving. Where rainfall is scant or drainage is good, a 4-in. base of either sand or gravel is usually sufficient. For most other situations, a 4-in. gravel bed topped with 2 in. of sand will work well. Very poorly drained soils may require more gravel, an additional layer of coarse rock beneath the gravel, or even drain tiles. If you suspect your site has serious drainage problems, consult a landscape architect or contractor.

Finally, keep water from pooling on a walk by making its surface higher in the center than at the edges. The center of a 4-ft.-wide walk should be at least ½ in. higher than its edges. If you're using a drag board to level the sand base, curve the lower edge to create this "crown." Otherwise, crown the surface by eye.

Edgings

All walk surfaces need to be contained in some fashion along their edges. Where soil is firm or tightly knit by turf, walls cut neatly out of the excavation can serve as edging. An installed edging often provides more effective containment, particularly if the walk surface is above grade. It also prevents damage to bricks or stones on the edges of paths. Walkway edgings are commonly made of 1- or 2-in.-thick lumber, thicker landscaping timbers, brick, or stone.

Wood edging

Wood should be rot-resistant redwood, cedar, or cypress, or pressure-treated for ground-contact use. If you're working in loose soils, fix a deep wooden edging to support stakes with double-headed nails. When the path is laid, pull the nails, and fill and tamp behind the edging. Then drive the stakes below grade. In firmer soils, or if the edging material is not wide enough, install it on top of the gravel base. Position the top at the height of the path. Dimensional lumber that is 1 in. thick is pliable enough to bend around gradual curves.

Treated dimensional lumber with support stakes

Landscape timbers with crossties laid on gravel base

Brick and stone edging

In firm soil, a row of bricks laid on edge and perpendicular to the length of the path adds stability. For a more substantial edging, stand bricks on end on the excavated soil surface; add the gravel base; and tamp the earth around the base of the bricks on the outside of the excavation. Stone edgings laid on end can be set in the same way. "End-up" brick or stone edgings are easy to install on curved walks.

Bricks on edge, laid on gravel base

Bricks on end, laid on soil

Preparing the base

Having decided on location and materials, you can get down to business. The initial steps of layout and base preparation are much the same for all surface materials.

Layout

Lay out straight sections with stakes and string, turning 90-degree corners with batter boards. (See illustration below.) You can plot curves with stakes and "fair" the curve with a garden hose, or outline the curve with hose alone, marking it with lime or sand ❶.

Excavation

The excavation depth depends on how much sand-and-gravel base your soil's drainage calls for, the thickness of the surface material, and its position above or below grade ❷. Mark the depth on a stake or stick, and use this to check depth as you dig. Walking surfaces are most comfortable if they are reasonably level across their width. Check the bottom of the excavation with a level as you dig. If the walk cuts across a slope, you'll need to remove soil from the high side and use it to fill the low side to produce a level surface. If you've added soil or if the subsoil is loose, compact it by tamping.

Edging installation

Some edgings can be installed immediately after excavation; others are placed on top of the gravel portion of the base ❸.

(See the sidebar, "Edgings," on the previous page.) If the soil's drainage permits, you can now lay soft materials on the excavated, tamped, and edged soil base. To control weeds, and to keep bark, chips, or pine needles from mixing with the subsoil, spread water-permeable landscape fabric over the gravel or the excavated base.

Laying the base

Now add gravel (if required); rake it level; and compact it ❹. Use gravel up to 1 in. in diameter or ¼- to ¾-in. crushed stone, which drains and compacts well. You can rent a hand tamper (a heavy metal plate on the end of a pole) or a machine compactor if you have a large area to compact.

If you're making a loose-gravel or crushed-stone walk, add the surface material on top of the base gravel. (See "Choosing a surface" page 161.) For walks of brick, stone, or pavers, add a 2-in. layer of builder's sand, not the finer sand that masons use for mixing mortar.

Rake the sand smooth with the back of a level-head rake. You can level the sand with a wooden drag board, also known as a screed ❺. Nail together two 1x4s or notch a 1x6 to place the lower edge at the desired height of the sand, and run the board along the path edging. To settle the sand, dampen it thoroughly with a hose set on fine spray. Fill any low spots; rake or drag the surface level; then dampen it again.

PREPARING THE BASE

❶ Lay out the path with stakes, string, garden hose, and lime.

❷ Dig out the path between the layout string and lime lines.

❸ Install the edging.

❹ Rake out gravel base.

Lay out free-form curved sections with garden hose and mark with lime.

Mark straight sections with 1x2 stakes and string.

Drag board

Edging

❺ Level sand base with a drag board.

Laying the surface

Whether you're laying a loose or hard material, take time to plan your work. Provide access for delivery trucks, and have material deposited as close to the worksite as possible.

Loose materials

Install water-permeable landscape fabric over the gravel base to prevent gravel from mixing with the surface material. Spread bark or wood chips 2 to 4 in. deep. For a pine-needle surface, spread 2 in. of needles on top of several inches of bark or chips. Spread loose pea gravel about 2 in. deep. For a harder, more uniform surface, add ½ in. of fine crushed stone on top of the gravel. You can let traffic compact crushed-rock surfaces, or compact them by hand or with a machine.

Bricks and precast pavers

Take time to figure out the pattern and spacing of the bricks or pavers by laying them out on the lawn or driveway, rather than disturbing your carefully prepared sand base. When you're satisfied, begin in a corner, laying the bricks or pavers gently on the sand so the base remains even ❶. Lay full bricks first; then install cut bricks to fit as needed at the edges. To produce uniform joints, space bricks with a piece of wood cut to the exact joint width. You can also maintain alignment of the bricks with a straightedge or with a string stretched across the path between nails or stakes. Move the string as you proceed with the work.

As you complete a row or section, bed the bricks or pavers into the sand base with several firm raps of a rubber mallet or a hammer on a scrap 2x4. Check with a level or straightedge to make sure the surface is even ❷. (You'll have to do this by feel or eye across the width of a crowned path.) Lift low bricks or pavers carefully and fill beneath them with sand; then reset them. Don't stand on the walk until you've filled the joints.

When you've finished a section, sweep fine, dry mason's sand into the joints, working across the surface of the path in all directions ❸. Wet thoroughly with a fine spray, and let dry; then sweep in more sand if necessary. If you want a living walk, sweep a loam-sand mixture into the joints and plant small, tough, ground-hugging plants, such as dwarf mondo grass, in them.

Rare is the brick walk that can be laid without cutting something to fit. To cut brick, mark the line of the cut with a dark pencil all around the brick. With the brick resting firmly on sand or soil, score the entire line by rapping a wide mason's chisel called a "brickset" with a heavy wooden mallet or a soft-headed steel hammer as shown on the facing page. Place the brickset in the scored line across one face and give it a sharp blow with the hammer to cut the brick.

If you have a lot of bricks to cut, or if you want greater accuracy, consider renting a masonry saw. Whether you work by hand or machine, always wear safety glasses.

LOOSE MATERIALS

Cover gravel base with water-permeable landscape fabric and add 2 to 4 in. of bark or wood chips.

BRICKS AND PRECAST PAVERS

To turn square corners, align the edging board with a carpenter's square.

❶ **Begin laying in a corner.**

❷ **Check the surface with a level or straightedge. Fill under low bricks; tamp down high ones. Use a plank to distribute your weight if you must work on the path.**

❸ **Sweep fine, dry sand into the joints to fix the bricks or pavers in place.**

Stepping-stones

A stepping-stone walk set in turf creates a charming effect and is very simple to lay. You can use cut or irregular flagstones or field-stone, which is irregular in thickness as well as in outline. Arrange the stones on the turf; then set them one by one. Cut into the turf around the stone with a sharp flat shovel or trowel, and remove the stone; then dig out the sod with the shovel. Placing stones at or below grade will keep them away from mower blades. Fill low spots beneath the stone with earth or sand so the stone doesn't move when stepped on.

Cut around stepping-stone with shovel or trowel.

Remove sod and soil.

Set in place, filling with sand or soil to bed stone firmly.

Cutting bricks

Wear safety glasses.

Scored line

Brickset chisel

Cutting flagstones

Wear safety glasses.

Scored line

Wood batten

Brickset

Flagstones

Install cut stones of uniform thickness as described for bricks and pavers. Working out patterns beforehand is particularly important—stones are too heavy to move around more than necessary. To produce a level surface with cut or irregular stones of varying thickness, you'll need to add or remove sand for each stone. Set the stone carefully on sand; then move it back and forth to work it into place ❶. Lay a level or straightedge over three or four stones to check the surface's evenness ❷. When a section is complete, fill the joints with sand or with sand and loam as described for bricks and pavers.

You can cut flagstone with a technique similar to that used for bricks. Score the line of the cut on the top surface with a brickset and hammer. Prop the stone on a piece of scrap wood, positioning the line of the cut slightly beyond the edge of the wood. Securing the bottom edge of the stone with your foot, place the brickset on the scored line, and strike sharply to make the cut.

FLAGSTONES

❶ Set flagstones in place carefully to avoid disturbing the sand base.

❷ Extend a straightedge over several stones to check the surface for evenness. Tap high spots to level.

Laying a Patio

You can make a simple patio using the same techniques and materials we have discussed for paths. To ensure good drainage, an even surface, and durability, lay hard surfaces such as brick, flagstone, and pavers on a well-prepared base of gravel, sand, and compacted soil. (Crushed-rock and gravel surfaces likewise benefit from a sound base.) Make sure the surface drains away from any adjacent structure (house or garage); a drop-off of ¼ in. per foot is usually adequate. If the patio isn't near a structure, make it higher in the center to avoid puddles.

Establish the outline of the patio as described for paths; then excavate the area roughly to accommodate 4 in. of gravel, 2 in.

of sand, and the thickness of the paving surface. (Check with a local nursery or landscape contractor to find out if local conditions require alterations in the type or amounts of base material.) Now grade the rough excavation to provide drainage, using a simple 4-ft. grid of wooden stakes as shown in the drawings.

Drive the first row of stakes next to the house (or in the center of a freestanding patio), leveling them with a 4-ft. builder's level or a smaller level resting on a straight 2x4. The tops of these stakes should be at the height of the top of the sand base (finish grade of the patio less the thickness of the surface material) **1**. Working from this row of stakes, establish another row about 4 to 5 ft. from the first. Make the tops of these stakes 1 in. lower than those of the first row, using a level and spacer block, as shown in the box below. Continue adding rows of stakes, making

LAYING A SIMPLE PATIO

48 in.

Level — Straightedge

6 in.

Slope = 1 in. in 48 in.

1 in.

6 in.

Attach a 1-in. block to straightedge for setting rows of stakes. — Final grade

Level the row of stakes next to the house. Place subsequent rows 4 to 5 ft. apart, each 1 in. lower.

1x2 stake

1 Excavate roughly to depth. Then set a grid of stakes (4 to 5 ft. on center) to establish the grade at the height of the sand base.

2 Using a tape measure or ruler, fine-tune the grade so the soil surface is 6 in. beneath the tops of all the stakes.

each 1 in. lower than the previous row, until the entire area is staked. Then, with a measuring tape or ruler and a shovel, fine-tune the grading by removing or adding soil until the excavated surface is 6 in. (the thickness of the gravel-sand base) below the tops of all the stakes ❷.

Use these stakes when installing the sand-and-gravel base, in order to maintain the drainage grade you've just established and produce an even surface for the paving material. If you have a good eye or a very small patio, you can do this by sight. Otherwise, you can use the stakes to install a series of 1x3 or 1x4 "leveling boards," as shown in the drawing below. (Before adding gravel, you may want to cover the soil with water-permeable landscape fabric to keep perennial weeds from growing; just cut slits to accommodate the stakes.)

Add a few inches of gravel ❸. Then set leveling boards along each row of stakes, making the boards' top edges even with the top of the stakes ❹. Drive additional stakes to sandwich the boards in place (don't use nails). Distribute the remaining inch or so of gravel and compact it by hand or machine; then add the 2 in. of sand. Dragging a straight 2x4 across two adjacent rows of leveling boards will produce a precise grade and an even surface ❺. Wet the sand and fill low spots that settle.

You can install the patio surface as previously described for paths, removing the leveling boards as the bricks or pavers reach them ❻. Disturbing the sand surface as little as possible, slide the boards out from between the stakes and drive the stakes an inch or so beneath the level of the sand. Cover the stakes and fill the gaps left by the boards with sand, tamped down carefully. Then continue laying the surface. Finally, sweep fine sand into the joints.

❸ **Add a few inches of gravel to the excavation.**

❻ **When you install the patio surface, remove leveling boards as you reach them.**

Patio paving

Gravel subbase

Leveling board

Add another stake to sandwich the boards in place without nails.

Leveling board (removed)

❹ **Set 1x3 leveling boards even with the top of the grade stakes. Then add sand.**

Drive stakes below the surface and fill gaps with sand.

❺ **Drag a straight 2x4 across the leveling boards to grade and smooth the sand base.**

For rectangular patios, equal diagonal measures will ensure square corners.

Work on plywood to avoid disturbing the sand.

Installing a Pond

It wasn't so long ago that a garden pond required yards of concrete, an expert mason, and deep pockets. Today's strong, lightweight, and long-lasting synthetic liners and rigid fiberglass shells have put garden pools in reach of every do-it-yourselfer. Installation does require some hard labor, but little expertise: just dig a hole, spread the liner or seat the shell, install edging, and plant. We'll discuss installation of a lined pond in the main text; see below for installing a smaller, fiberglass pool.

Liner notes

More and more nurseries and garden centers are carrying flexible pond liners; you can also buy them from mail-order suppliers specializing in water gardens. Synthetic rubber liners are longer lasting but more expensive than PVC liners. (Both are much cheaper than rigid fiberglass shells.) Buy only liners specifically made for garden ponds—don't use ordinary plastic sheeting. Many people feel that black liners look best; blue liners tend to make the pond look like a swimming pool.

Before you dig

First, make sure you comply with any rules your town may have about water features. Then keep the following ideas in mind when locating your pond. Avoid areas with shady trees that keep sun-loving water plants from thriving. A tree's roots make digging a chore and its flowers, leaves, and seeds clog the water, making it unsightly and inhospitable to plants or fish. Avoid the low spot on your property; otherwise your pond will be a catch basin for runoff. Select a level spot; the immediate vicinity of the

Small fiberglass pool

A fiberglass shell or half barrel 2 to 3 ft. in diameter and 2 to 3 ft. deep is ideal for the small pools on p. 96 and 72. Garden centers often stock pond shells in a variety of shapes. Dig a hole about 6 in. wider on all sides than the shell. Hole depth should equal that of the shell plus 1 in. for a sand base and an allowance for the mulch (p. 96) or bricks (p. 72) that surround the pool. Compact the bottom of the hole and spread the sand; then lower the shell into place. Add temporary wedges or props, if necessary, to orient and level the shell. Slowly fill the shell with water, backfilling around it with sand or sifted soil so that the fill keeps pace with the rising water level.

Mulch and juniper edging

Brick edging on sand and gravel base

Fiberglass pond shell or half barrel

Sand base, 1 in. thick

Sand/soil backfill

pond must be level, and starting out that way saves a lot of work. (Remember that you can use excavated soil to help level the site.)

Using graph paper, enlarge the outline of the pond provided on the site plan on p. 94, altering it as you wish. If you change the size or depth of the pond, or are interested in growing a wider variety of water plants or in adding fish, remember that a healthy pond must achieve a balance between the plants and fish and the volume, depth, and temperature of the water. Even if you're not making changes, consult with a knowledgeable person at a nursery or pet store.

Calculate the liner width by adding twice the maximum depth of the pool plus an additional 2 ft. to the width. Use the same formula to calculate the length. So, for instance, for a pond 2 ft. deep, 7 ft. wide, and 12 ft. long, the liner width would be 4 ft. plus 7 ft. plus 2 ft. (or 13 ft.). The length would be 4 ft. plus 12 ft. plus 2 ft. (or 18 ft.).

Water work

Unless you are a very tidy builder, the water you used to fit the liner will be too dirty to leave in the pond. (Spilled mortar can also make the water too alkaline for plants or fish.) Siphon or pump out the water; clean the liner; and refill the pond. If you're adding fish to the pond, you'll need to let the water stand for a week or so to allow any chlorine (which is deadly to fish) to dissipate. Check with local pet stores to find out if your water contains chemicals that require commercial conditioners to make the water safe for fish.

Installing the pond and plants is only the first step in water gardening. It takes patience, experimentation, and usually some consultation with experienced water gardeners to achieve a balance between plants, fish, waterborne oxygen, nutrients, and waste that will sustain all happily while keeping algae, diseases, insects, and predators at acceptable levels.

Growing pond plants

One water lily, a few upright-growing plants, and a bundle of submerged plants (which help keep the water clean) are enough for a medium-size pond. An increasing number of nurseries and garden centers stock water lilies and other water plants. For a larger selection, your nursery or garden center may be able to recommend a specialist supplier.

These plants are grown in containers filled with heavy garden soil (not potting soil, which contains ingredients that float). You can buy special containers designed for aquatic plants, or simply use plastic pails or dishpans. Line basketlike containers with burlap to keep the soil from leaking out the holes. A water lily needs at least 2 to 3 gal. of soil; the more, the better. Most other water plants, such as dwarf papyrus, need 1 to 2 gal. of soil.

After planting, add a layer of gravel on the surface to keep soil from clouding the water and to protect roots from marauding fish. Soak the plant and soil thoroughly. Then set the container in the pond, positioning it so the water over the soil is 6 to 18 in. deep for water lilies, up to 6 in. for most other plants.

For maximum bloom, push a tablet of special water-lily fertilizer into the pots once or twice a month throughout the summer. Most water plants are easy to grow and carefree, although many are tropicals that die after hard frost, so you'll have to replace them each spring.

PLANTING WATER PLANTS

Set water plants in a container of heavy garden soil. Then cover soil surface with gravel to keep soil from floating away.

Gravel

1- to 3-gal. dishpan or special container

Heavy garden soil

Excavation

If your soil isn't too compacted or rocky, a good-size pond can be excavated with a shovel or two in a weekend ❶. (Energetic teenagers are a marvelous pool-building resource.) If the site isn't level, you can grade it using a stake-and-level system such as the one described on pp. 166–167 for grading the patio.

Outline the pond's shape with garden lime, establishing the curves freehand with a garden hose or by staking out a large grid and plotting from the graph-paper plan. The pond has two levels. The broad end, at 2 ft. deep, accommodates water lilies and other plants requiring deeper water as well as fish. Make the narrow end 12 to 16 in. deep for plants requiring shallower submersion. (You can put plant pots on stacks of bricks or other platforms to vary heights as necessary.) The walls will be less likely to crumble as you dig and the liner will install more easily if you slope them inward about 3 to 4 in. for each foot of depth. Make the walls smooth, removing roots, rocks, and other sharp protrusions.

Excavate a shallow relief about 1 ft. wide around the perimeter to contain the liner overlap and stone edging. (The depth of the relief should accommodate the thickness of the edging stones.) Somewhere along the perimeter, create an overflow channel to take runoff after a heavy rain. This can simply be a 1- to 2-in. depression, 1 ft. or so wide, spanned by an edging stone. Lengths of PVC pipe placed side by side beneath the stone (as shown in the drawing opposite) will keep the liner in place. The overflow channel can open onto a lower area of lawn or garden adjacent to the pond or to a rock-filled dry well.

Fitting the liner

When the hole is complete, cushion the surfaces to protect the liner ❷. Here we show a 1-in.-thick layer of sand on the bottom

Section through pond

|← 17 ft. →|

2 ft.

12 to 16 in.

Slope bottom slightly to make draining the pond easier.

Slope in 6 to 8 in.

5 ft.

Slope in 3 to 4 in.

Slope in 3 to 4 in.

❷ **Spread sand on horizontal surfaces; cushion walls with carpet underlayment.**

INSTALLING A LINERED POND

❶ **Dig hole with sloping sides to correct depth. Make sure that the perimeter of the hole is level.**

Excavate shallow relief for edging flagstones.

surfaces and carpet underlayment on the sloping walls. Fiberglass batting insulation also works well, as does heavy landscaping fabric.

Stretch the liner across the hole, letting it sag naturally to touch the walls and bottom but keeping it taut enough so it does not bunch up. Weight its edges with bricks or stones; then fill it with water ❸. The water's weight will push the liner against the walls; the stones will prevent it from blowing around. As it fills, tuck and smooth out as many creases as you can; the weight of the water makes this difficult to do after the pond is full. If you stand in the pond to do so, take care not to damage the liner. Don't be alarmed if you can't smooth all the creases. Stop filling when the water is 2 in. below the rim of the pond, and cut the liner to fit into the overlap relief ❹. Hold it in place with a few long nails or large "staples" made from coat hangers while you install the edging.

Edging the pond

Finding and fitting flagstones so there aren't wide gaps between them is the most time-consuming part of this task. Cantilevering the stones an inch or two over the water will hide the liner somewhat.

The stones can be laid directly on the liner, as shown ❺. Add sand under the liner to level the surface where necessary so that the stones don't rock. Such treatment will withstand the occasional careful traffic of pond and plant maintenance. If you anticipate heavier traffic, you can bed the stones in 2 to 3 in. of mortar. It's prudent to consult with a landscape contractor about whether your intended use and soil require some sort of footing for mortared stones.

Elevation detail of pond overflow

Flagstone edging, 12 in. or more wide

Cover pipe with flagstone.

Pond liner

To overflow area

PVC pipe, 1- or 2-in.-dia., about 12 in. long

Garden bed or lawn

1-in. layer of sand (horizontal surfaces)

Carpet underlayment (walls)

❺ **Fit and lay flagstone edging. Add sand beneath the liner or stones where necessary to create a firm bed. Brush sand into joints when edging is complete.**

❸ **Spread liner and begin to fill with water. As water rises, tuck and smooth out as many creases as possible. Fill with water to within 2 in. of pond rim.**

To overflow area

❹ **Trim liner to fit relief for flagstone edging. Fix liner in place with long nails or bent coat-hanger "staples."**

Weigh down liner with stones.

Building a Retaining Wall

Contours and sloping terrain can add considerable interest to a home landscape. But you can have too much of a good thing. Two designs in this book employ retaining walls to alter problem slopes. The wall shown on p. 53 eliminates a small but abrupt grade change, producing two almost level surfaces and the opportunity to install attractive plantings on them. On p. 36, two low retaining walls help turn a steep slope into an outdoor showpiece.

Retaining walls can be handsome landscape features in their own right. Made of cut stone, fieldstone, brick, landscape timbers, or concrete, they can complement the materials and style of your house or nearby structures. However, making a stable, long-lasting retaining wall of these materials can require tools and skills many homeowners do not possess.

For these reasons, we've chosen retaining-wall systems made of precast concrete for designs in this book. Readily available in a range of sizes, surface finishes, and colors, these systems require few tools and no special skills to install. They have been engineered to resist the forces that soil, water, freezing, and thawing bring to bear on a retaining wall. Install these walls according to the manufacturer's specifications, and you can be confident that they will do their job for many years.

A number of systems are available in Texas through nurseries, garden centers, and local contracting suppliers. (Check the Yellow Pages or online.) But they all share basic design principles. Similar to traditional dry-stone walls, these systems rely largely on weight and friction to contain the weight of the soil. In many systems, interlocking blocks or pegs help align the courses and increase the wall's strength. In all systems, blocks must rest on a solid, level base. A freely draining backfill of crushed stone is essential to avoid buildup of water pressure in the retained soil, which can buckle even a heavy wall.

The construction steps shown here are typical of those recommended by most system manufacturers for retaining walls up to 3 to 4 ft. tall; be sure to follow the manufacturer's instructions for the system you choose.

For higher walls, walls on loose soil or heavy clay soils, and walls retaining very steep slopes, it is prudent to consult with a landscape architect or contractor. Also, check with your local building department for permits and codes.

Precast-system retaining wall

Drawing represents typical construction; dimensions and specifications will vary depending on the system.

Cap block

Topsoil, 6 to 8 in. deep

Backfill of clean crushed stone

Undisturbed soil

Batter wall by offsetting each course.

Set first course partially or completely below grade.

Base, 24-in. trench filled with 4 in. of ⅜- to ¾-in. crushed stone

Original slope

New grade level

Excavate for wall; use to level surface behind wall.

Soil

30–45° from plumb

New grade

Crushed stone

Building a wall

Installing a wall system is just about as simple as stacking up children's building blocks. The most important part of the job is establishing a firm, level base. Start by laying out the wall with string and hose (for curves) and excavating a base trench.

As the boxed drawing opposite shows, the position of the wall in relation to the base of the slope determines the height of the wall, how much soil you move, and the leveling effect on the slope. Unless the wall is very long, it is a good idea to excavate along the entire length and fine-tune the line of the wall before beginning the base trench. Remember to excavate back far enough to accommodate the stone backfill. Systems vary, but a foot of crushed-stone backfill behind the blocks is typical. (For the two-wall design, build the bottom wall first, then the top.)

Systems vary in the width and depth of trench and type of base material, but in all of them, the trench must be tamped firm and be level across its width and along its length. We've shown a 4-in. layer of ⅜- to ¾-in. crushed stone (blocks can slip sideways on rounded aggregate or pea gravel, which also don't compact as well). Depending on the system and the circumstances, a portion or all of the first course lies below grade, so the soil helps hold the blocks in place.

Add crushed stone to the trench; level it with a rake; and compact it with a hand tamper or mechanical compactor. Lay the first course of blocks carefully ❶. Check frequently to make sure the blocks are level across their width and along their length. Stagger vertical joints as you stack subsequent courses. Offset the faces of the blocks so the wall leans back into the retained soil. Some systems design this "batter" into their blocks; others allow you to choose from several possible setbacks.

As the wall rises, shovel backfill behind the blocks ❷. Clean crushed rock drains well; some systems suggest placing a barrier of landscaping fabric between the rock and the retained soil to keep soil from migrating into the fill and impeding drainage.

Thinner cap blocks finish the top of the wall ❸. Some wall systems recommend cementing these blocks in place with a weatherproof adhesive. The last 6 to 8 in. of the backfill should be topsoil, firmed into place and ready for planting.

BUILDING A WALL

❷ As you add subsequent courses, backfill behind blocks with clean crushed rock.

Stagger joints.

❸ Cap blocks complete the wall. Use topsoil for final 6 to 8 in. of backfill.

Offset courses so wall leans into retained soil.

Crushed-stone base

Level

❶ After digging and leveling the trench, spread, level, and compact the base materials; then lay the blocks. Check frequently to see that they are level across their width and length.

Wall parallel with a slope: Stepped base

Construct walls running parallel with a slope in steps, each with a level base.

Backfill so grade behind finishes level with top of wall.

Crushed-stone base

Finish grade in front of wall

Wall parallel with a slope: Stepped cap

Sometimes the top of a wall needs to step up or down to accommodate grade changes in the slope behind.

Cap block

A return corner

Where you want the slope to extend beyond the end of the wall, make a corner that cuts into the slope.

Step wall below grade to provide solid foundation.

Line of finish grade outside wall

Sloped sites

If your site slopes along the wall's length, you'll need to step the bottom of the wall, as shown at top left. Create a length of level trench along the lowest portion of the site; then work up the slope, creating steps as necessary.

The top of the wall can also step if the slope dissipates at one end. These slopes are common on sites such as the one shown on p. 36, which slopes away from the house and toward the driveway. Here the base of the wall will rest on level ground, but the slope behind the wall decreases along the wall's length. The design on p. 36 shows one solution to this dilemma—a wall of uniform height with a return corner at the street end (see bottom left), backfilled to raise the grade behind to the top of the wall. Another solution, shown at center left, is to step the wall down as the slope decreases, which saves material, produces a different look, but still works with the planting design.

Curves and corners

Wall-system blocks are designed so that curves are no more difficult to lay than straight sections. Corners may require that you cut a few blocks or use specially designed blocks, but they are otherwise uncomplicated. If your wall must fit a prescribed length between corners, consider working from the corners toward the middle (after laying a base course). Masons use this technique, which also avoids exposing cut blocks at the corners.

You can cut blocks with a mason's chisel and mallet or rent a mason's saw. Chiseling works well when the faces of the blocks are rough textured, so the cut faces blend. A saw is best for smooth-faced blocks and projects requiring lots of cutting.

Where the wall doesn't run the full length of the slope, the best-looking and most structurally sound termination is a corner constructed to cut back into the slope, as shown at bottom left.

Steps

Steps in a low retaining wall are not difficult to build, but they require forethought and careful layout. Systems differ on construction details. The drawing below shows a typical design where the blocks and stone base rest on steps cut into firm subsoil. If your soil is less stable or is recent fill, you should excavate the entire area beneath the steps to the same depth as the wall base and build a foundation of blocks, as shown in the boxed drawing.

These steps are independent of the adjacent return walls, which are vertical, not battered (stepped back). In some systems, steps and return walls are interlocked. To match a path, you can face the treads with the same stone, brick, or pavers, or you can use the system's cap blocks or special treads.

SOLID FOUNDATION: CROSS SECTION

Cap block

Return wall

Slope path away from steps.

Slope treads ¼ in. per 12 in. toward front edge to promote runoff.

Crushed-stone base

In disturbed or problematic subsoil, make a solid foundation of blocks on a level gravel base.

Stepped foundation

Width and depth of treads will depend on size of system's block.

Cap block

Return wall

Surface steps with system-provided treads or stone, pavers, or brick to match path. Set in mortar bed or weatherproof adhesive.

Increase width by adding full blocks.

Retaining wall

Path

Crushed-stone base

Wall block

In firm, undisturbed or compacted subsoil, bed blocks on steps cut in the soil.

Fences, Arbors, and Trellises

Novices who have no trouble tackling a simple flagstone path often get nervous when it comes time to erect a fence, an arbor, or even a trellis. While such projects can require more skill and resources than others in the landscape, the ones in this book have been designed with less-than-confident do-it-yourself builders in mind. The designs are simple, the materials are read-ily available, and the tools and skills will be familiar to anyone accustomed to ordinary home maintenance.

First, we'll introduce you to the materials and tools needed for the projects. Then, we'll present the small number of basic operations you'll employ when building them. Finally, we'll pro-vide drawings and comments on each of the projects.

Tools and materials

Even the least-handy homeowner is likely to have most of the tools needed for these projects: claw hammer, crosscut handsaw, brace-and-bit or electric drill, adjustable wrench, combination square, measuring tape, carpenter's level, and sawhorses. You may even have Grandpa's old posthole dig-ger. Many will have a handheld power circular saw, which makes faster (though noisier) work of cutting parts to length. A cordless drill or screwdriver is invaluable if you're substituting screws for nails. If you have more than a few holes to dig, consider renting a gas-powered posthole dig-ger. A 12-in.-diameter hole will serve for 4x4 posts; if possi-ble, get a larger-diameter digger for 6x6 posts.

Materials

Of the materials offering strength, durability, and attractive-ness in outdoor settings, wood is the easiest to work and af-fords the quickest results. While almost all commercially available lumber is strong enough for landscape structures, most decay quickly when in prolonged contact with soil and water. Cedar, cypress, and redwood, however, contain natural preservatives and are excellent for landscape use. Alternatively, a range of softwoods (such as pine, fir, and hemlock) are pressure-treated with preservatives and will last for many years. Parts of structures that do not come in contact with soil or are not continually wet can be made of ordinary construction-grade lumber, but unless they're reg-ularly painted, they will not last as long as treated or natu-rally decay-resistant material.

In addition to dimensional lumber, several of the designs incorporate lattice, which is thin wooden strips crisscrossed to form patterns of diamonds or squares. Premade lattice is widely available in sheets 4 ft. by 8 ft. and smaller. Lattice comes in decay-resistant woods as well as in treated and un-treated softwoods. Local supplies vary, and you may find lat-tice made of thicker or narrower material.

Fasteners

For millennia, even basic structures such as these would have been assembled with complicated joints. Today, with simple nailed, bolted, or screwed joints, a few hours' prac-tice swinging a hammer or wielding a cordless electric screwdriver is all the training necessary.

All these structures can be assembled using nails. But screws are stronger and, if you have a cordless screwdriver, make assembly easier. Buy common or box nails that are galvanized to prevent rust. Self-tapping screws (deck screws) require no pilot holes. For rust resistance, buy gal-vanized screws or screws treated with zinc dichromate.

Galvanized metal connectors are available to reinforce the joints used in these projects. For novice builders, con-nectors are a great help in aligning parts and making assem-bly easier. (Correctly fastened with nails or screws, the joints are strong enough without connectors.)

Finishes

Cedar, cypress, and redwood are handsome when left un-finished to weather, when treated with clear or colored stains, or when painted. Pressure-treated lumber is best painted or stained.

Outdoor stains are becoming increasingly popular. Clear or lightly tinted stains can preserve or enhance the rich red-dish browns of cedar, cypress, and redwood. Stains also come in a range of colors that can be used as you would paint. Be-cause they penetrate the wood rather than coat the surface, stains won't peel or chip the way paint does, so they are eas-ier to touch up and refinish.

When choosing a finish, take account of what plants are growing on or near the structure. It's a lot of work to remove yards of vines from a trellis or squeeze between a large shrub and a fence to repaint; consider an unfinished decay-resistant wood or an initial stain that you allow to weather.

Setting posts

All the projects are anchored by firmly set, vertical posts. In general, the taller the structure, the deeper the post should be set. For the arbors and the tallest fences, posts should be at least 3 ft. deep. Posts for fences up to 4 ft. tall can be set 2 ft. deep. To avoid post movement caused by expansion and contraction of the soil during freeze-thaw cycles, it's a good idea to set all arbor posts below the frost line. This depth is greater in colder climates; check with local building authorities.

The length of the posts you buy depends, of course, on the depth at which they will be set and their finished heights. When calculating lengths of arbor posts, remember that the tops of the posts must be level. The easiest method of achieving this is to cut the posts to length after installation. For example, buy 12-ft. posts for an arbor finishing at 8 ft. above grade and set 3 ft. in the ground. The convenience is worth the expense of the foot or so you cut off. The site and personal preference can determine whether you cut fence posts to length after installation or buy them cut to length and add or remove fill from the bottom of the hole to position them at the correct heights.

Arbor posts

Be sure to take extra care when positioning and installing arbor posts. The corners of the structure must be right angles, and the sides must be parallel with one another. Locating the corners with batter boards and string is fussy but accurate. Make the batter boards by nailing 1x2 stakes to scraps of 1x3 or 1x4, and position them about 1 ft. from the approximate location of each post as shown in the boxed drawing at right. Locate the exact post positions with string; adjust the string so the diagonal measurements are equal, which ensures that the corners of the structure will be at right angles.

At the intersections of the strings, locate the postholes by eye or with a plumb bob ❶. Remove the strings and dig the holes; then reattach the strings to position the posts exactly ❷. Plumb and brace the posts carefully. Check positions with the level and by measuring between adjacent posts and across diagonals. Diagonal braces between adjacent posts will stiffen them and help align their faces ❸. Then add concrete ❹ and let it cure for a day.

To establish the height of the posts, measure up from grade on one post; then use a level and straightedge to mark the heights of the other posts from the first one. Where joists will be bolted to the faces of the posts, you can install the joists and use their top edges as a hand-saw guide for cutting the posts to length.

SETTING ARBOR POSTS

❶ Position the posts with batter boards, taut string, and a plumb bob.

Batter board

Taut string

Plumb bob

BATTER BOARDS
Set L-shaped batter boards at each corner and stretch string to position the posts exactly.

1x2 stakes and 1x3 boards

Taut string

Taut string

18 to 24 in.

For square or rectangular post layout, diagonal measurements should be equal.

❷ Remove the string to dig the holes; then reattach it and align the outer faces of the posts with the string while you plumb and brace them.

❸ Check distances between posts at top. Add diagonal bracing between posts to fix positions.

❹ Cement posts in place.

Fence posts

Lay out and set the end or corner posts of a fence first, then add the intermediate posts. Dig the holes by hand or with a power digger ❶. To promote drainage, place several inches of gravel at the bottom of the hole for resting the post. Checking with a carpenter's level, plumb the post vertically and brace it with scrap lumber nailed to stakes ❷. Then add a few more inches of gravel around the post's base.

If your native soil compacts well, you can fix posts in place with tamped earth. Add the soil gradually, tamping it continu-ously with a heavy iron bar or 2x4. Check regularly with a level to see that the post doesn't get knocked out of plumb. This technique suits rustic or informal fences, where misalignments caused by shifting posts aren't noticeable or damaging.

For more formal fences, or where soil is loose or fence panels are buffeted by winds or snow, it's prudent to fix posts in concrete ❸. Mix enough concrete to set the two end posts; as a rule of thumb, figure one 80-lb. bag of premixed concrete per post. As you shovel it in, prod the concrete with a stick to settle it, particularly if you've added rubble to extend the mix. Build the

SETTING A FENCE POST

❷ Plumb the post, checking on adjacent faces with a level. Hold it in position with stakes and braces.

❶ Position the end or corner posts; then dig holes for them.

❸ Fill the hole with concrete and rubble.

Post

Slope top surface for drainage.

3 ft. (typical)

Concrete and rubble (shown), or tamped earth

Coarse gravel

1 ft. (typical)

concrete slightly above grade and slope it away from the post to aid drainage.

Once the end posts are set, stretch a string between the posts. (The concrete should cure for 24 hours before you nail or screw rails and panels in place, but you can safely stretch string while the concrete is still wet.) Measure along the string to position the intermediate posts; drop a plumb bob from the string at each intermediate post position to gauge the center of the hole below ❹. Once all the holes have been dug, again stretch a string between the end posts, near the top. Set the intermediate posts as described previously; align one face with the string and plumb adjacent faces with the carpenter's level ❺. Make sure to check positions of intermediate posts a final time with a measuring tape.

If the fence is placed along a slope, the top of the slats or panels can step down the slope or mirror it (as shown in the drawings below). Either way, make sure that the posts are plumb, rather than leaning with the slope.

❹ Stretch a string between the tops of the two end posts. Then locate positions of intermediate posts with a plumb bob.

❺ After digging the holes, stretch a string between the end posts to align intermediate posts. Use a level to plumb adjacent faces.

Fencing a slope

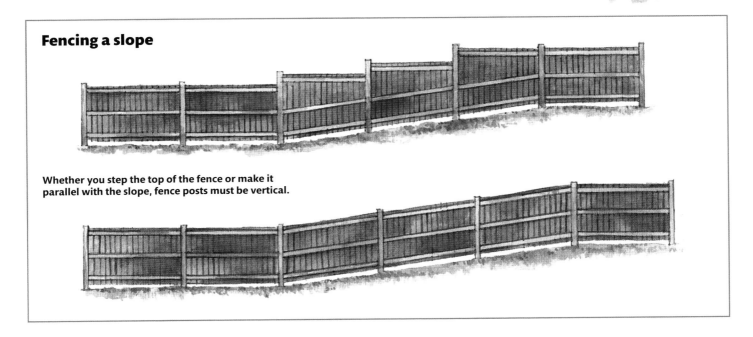

Whether you step the top of the fence or make it parallel with the slope, fence posts must be vertical.

Joints

The components of the fences, arbors, and trellises used in this book are attached to the posts and to each other with the simple joints shown below. Because all the parts are made of dimensioned lumber, the only cuts you'll need to make are to length. For strong joints, cut ends as square as you can, so the mating pieces make contact across their entire surfaces. If you have no confidence in your sawing, many lumberyards will cut pieces to length for a modest fee.

Novices often find it difficult to keep two pieces correctly positioned while trying to drive a nail into them, particularly when the nail must be driven at an angle, called "toenailing." If you have this problem, consider assembling the project using screws, which draw the pieces together, or with metal connectors, which can be nailed or screwed in place on one piece and then attached to the mating piece.

For several designs, you need to attach lattice panels to posts. The panels are made by sandwiching store-bought lattice be-

**Toenailed butt joints
(use nails or screws)**

Post

Rail

Post

Rail

**Metal connectors
for butt joints**

Joist hanger: nail through flanges to post and rail.

Angle clip

Rafter-to-joist joints

Rafter

Joist

Toenail

Rafter

Joist

Rafter tie

Joist

Rafter

tween frames of dimension lumber (construction details are given on the following pages). While the assembled panels can be toenailed to the posts, novices may find that the job goes easier using one or more types of metal connector, as shown in the drawings below. Attach the angle clips or angle brackets to the post; then position the lattice panel and fix it to the connectors. For greatest strength and ease of assembly, attach connectors using self-tapping screws driven by an electric screwdriver.

In the following pages, we'll show construction details of the fences, arbors, and trellises presented in the Portfolio of Designs. (The page number indicates the design.) Where the basic joints discussed here can be used, we have shown the parts but left the choice of fasteners to you. Typical fastenings are indicated for other joints. We have kept the constructions shown here simple and straightforward. They are not the only possibilities, and we encourage experienced builders to adapt and alter constructions as well as designs to suit differing situations and personal preferences.

Frame corner with metal connector

Nailing plate

Angled plate

Attaching framed lattice panels to posts

Post

Post

Lattice panel

Lattice panel

Toenail frame to post with nails or screws.

Angle clip

Fix angle brackets to post; then to top and bottom edges of frame.

Fix angle clips to post; then to panel frame.

Homemade lattice trellis
(pp. 60–63)

The trellis shown here supports climbing plants to make a vertical garden of a blank wall. The design can be altered to fit walls of different sizes. The three 32-in.-wide modules, hung on L-hangers, are simpler to make than a single large trellis and easy to remove when you need to paint the wall. (If you're in a hurry, you can just attach ready-made lattice to 2x2 frameworks of the same dimensions as shown here.)

Start by cutting all the pieces to length. (Here we'll call the horizontal members "rails" and the vertical members "stiles.") Working on a large flat surface, nail or screw the two outer stiles to the top and bottom rails, checking the corners with a framing square. The 2x2 rails provide ample material to house the L-hangers.

Carefully attach the three intermediate stiles, then the 1x2 rails. Cut a piece of scrap 6 in. long to use as a spacer. Fix the L-shaped hangers to 2x4 studs inside the wall. Buy hangers long enough to hold the trellis several inches away from the wall.

32 in.

2x2 top rail

Make squares 6 in. by 6 in. (inside dimensions).

6 to 8 ft.

Unless otherwise noted, all parts are made of 1x2 stock.

Outer stile

Intermediate stile

Intermediate rail

2x2 bottom rail

TRELLIS HANGER

2x2 top rail

L-hanger

Hang trellis on wall for easy removal.

Stile

2x2 bottom rail

CONSTRUCTION DETAILS

2x2 top rail

Hole for L-hanger

1x2 outer stile

Nail or screw each joint twice for rigidity.

1x2 intermediate stile

1x2 intermediate rail

Hole for L-hanger

Nail or screw through 1x2 stile into 2x2.

2x2 bottom rail

Lattice-panel screen
(pp. 22–23)

This screen serves as a decorative embellishment and vine support in the design on p. 22, but it can make an effective enclosure if you wish. The lattice is held in a frame made of 1x2s sandwiched between 1x3s and 1x4s. (The 1x4s add visual weight to the bottom of the screen.) Note how the parts overlap at the corners of the frame to form an interlocking joint.

Panels wider than 6 ft. are awkward to construct and to install. It is easiest to construct the panels on a large flat surface (a garage or basement floor). Lay out the 1x3s and 1x4 that form one face of the panel frame ❶. Then position and nail the 1x2s to them ❷. Add the lattice, then the other layer of 1x3s and 1x4 ❸. As you work, regularly check that the panel is square, its corners at right angles. (Use a framing square or measure across the diagonals to check that they are equal.) Lattice varies in thickness; if yours rattles in its groove, you can add ¾-in. quarter round as shown in the lower box to tighten the fit.

You can build the panels first and then use them to space the posts, or you can set the posts first (see pp. 176–179) and build the panels to fit. Either way, attach the panels to the posts by toe-nailing (using nails or screws) or with metal connectors along the lengths of the upright members. Add the 1x4 cap after attaching the panels to the posts. Finials in a variety of styles are available at home and garden stores.

FRONT VIEW

Finial — Lattice panel, to 6 ft. wide — 4x4 post — 1x4 cap — Lattice, 4-in. x 4-in. squares

40 in.

2-in. clearance

PANEL CONSTRUCTION

❶ Lay out one face of the panel on a flat surface, checking the corners with a framing square.

Framing square

1x3 — 1x4 bottom frame rail

CORNER DETAIL

1x2 — 1x3 — 1x4

❷ Nail the inner 1x2s in place, overlapping the joints at the corners.

1x2

1x3 — 1x4 bottom frame rail

❸ Place the lattice inside the 1x2 frame. Then nail the other face pieces in place, again overlapping the corner joints.

SCREEN CONSTRUCTION DETAIL

Finial

4x4 post

1x4 cap

1x2

1x3

¾-in. quarter round (optional)

Lattice

Patio arbor and sun screen
(pp. 88–89)

This simple structure offers relief from the sun on a portion of a backyard patio. The closely spaced 2x4 rafters form a sun screen, while allowing air circulation. Adapt rafter spacing and orientation to accommodate your site. In the design on pp. 88–89, the arbor supports a trumpet vine, which provides additional cooling shade as well as a pleasant leafy ambiance.

If you're building the patio and arbor at the same time, set the 6x6 posts (see pp. 176–179) before you lay the patio surface. If you're adding the arbor to an existing patio, you'll need to break through the paving to set the posts or pour footings to support surface attachments. Consult local building officials or a landscape contractor for advice on how best to proceed.

Once the posts are set, fix the 2x8 beams to pairs of posts using carriage bolts. Nail the 2x8s in place; then make the bolt holes by boring through the 2x8s and the post using a long electrician's bit. Fix the long 2x6 joists and the 2x4 rafters in place with metal connectors. Metal connectors fixed with screws will stand up best to the vigorous growth of the vine.

PLAN VIEW

Space rafters closer together for greater screening of sunlight. (Shown spaced 6 in. on center.)

CONSTRUCTION DETAILS

2x4 rafter

2x6 joist

Rafter tie

½ x 10 carriage bolt

2x8 beam

6x6 post

Fix joists and rafters using metal connectors.

FRONT VIEW

2x4 rafter
2x6 joist
2x8 beam
6x6 post

11 ft.

8 ft. on center

SIDE VIEW

11 ft.

8 ft.

8 ft. on center

Woodland arbor
(pp. 114–115)

Draped with honeysuckle, this shallow arbor helps establish a connection between a mixed border and an adjacent woodland. Once you have gathered the materials, you should need no more than an afternoon to build the arbor.

Set the posts first, as described on pp. 176–179. The hefty 6x6 posts shown here add presence to the arbor, but cheaper, easier-to-handle 4x4s will make an equally sturdy structure. Cut the joists and rafters to length. The 60° angles on their ends can easily be cut using a handsaw. Bolt or nail the joists in place. Then toenail the short rafters to the joists or attach them with metal connectors.

In addition to the posts, you can provide other supports for the honeysuckle to twine around. Strands of coarse rope or cord work well when stretched between the large screw eyes fixed to the rafters and the base of the posts, as shown here. The vines soon hide the rope or cord from view.

CONSTRUCTION DETAILS

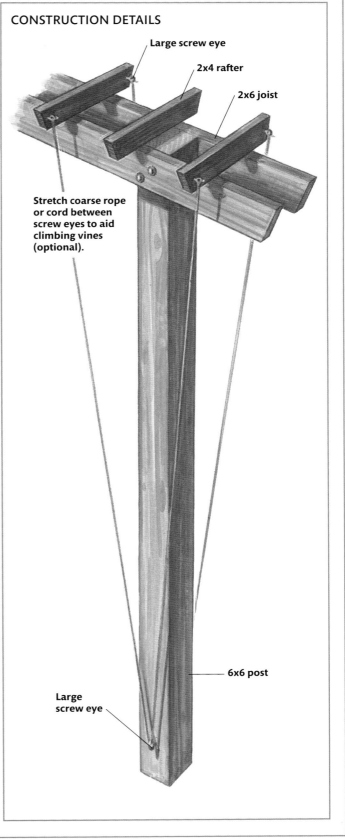

Large screw eye

2x4 rafter

2x6 joist

Stretch coarse rope or cord between screw eyes to aid climbing vines (optional).

6x6 post

Large screw eye

PLAN VIEW

10 ft.

18 in.

2x6 joist

2x4 rafter

6x6 post

FRONT VIEW

Large screw eye

Space rafters 12 in. on center.

2x4 rafter

2x6 joist

Cut ends of joists and rafters at 60° angle.

8 ft.

Coarse rope or cord aids climbing vines (optional).

6x6 post

6 ft.

Entry arbor and fence
(pp. 66–69)

This arbor makes an event of the passage from sidewalk to front door or from one part of your property to another. Two versions are shown in the Portfolio. One features the arbor alone; the other adds a picket fence.

Hefty 6x6 posts provide real presence here; the 12-footers you'll need are heavy, so engage a couple of helpers to save your back. You can toenail the 3x6 beams to the tops of the posts and the 2x4 rafters to the beams. (Or you can fix them using long spikes or lag screws, 10 in. and 8 in. long, respectively. This job is easier if you drill pilot holes, with bits slightly thinner than the spikes.) Use screws or nails to attach the 2x2 cross rafters. If you can't buy 3x6s, you can nail two 2x6s together face to face.

Sandwich lattice between 1x3s to make the side panels and fix them between posts using nails, screws, or metal connectors. Alternating the corner overlap, as shown on the drawing, makes a stronger frame.

The fence extends from both sides of the arbor. We've shown 6x6 fence posts to match the arbor. But 4x4s work just as well. Space posts farther apart than 8 ft. You can purchase ready-made lengths of picket fence, but it is easy enough to make yourself. Set the posts; then cut and fit 2x4 rails on edge between them. Space 1x3 picket slats 1½ in. apart. The drawing on the facing page shows large round wooden finials atop the fence posts; you can buy various types of ready-made finials, or you could work a heavy bevel around the top end of the posts themselves.

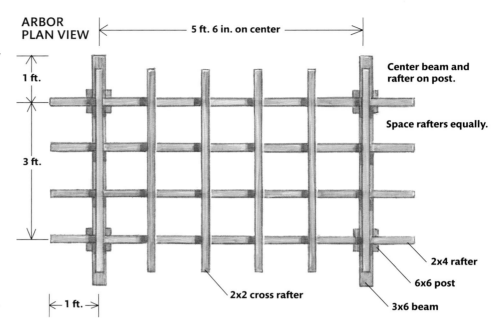

ARBOR PLAN VIEW

5 ft. 6 in. on center
1 ft.
3 ft.
1 ft.
Center beam and rafter on post.
Space rafters equally.
2x4 rafter
6x6 post
3x6 beam
2x2 cross rafter

ARBOR CONSTRUCTION DETAIL

2x2 cross rafter
2x4 rafter
3x6 beam
6x6 arbor post
1x3 frame
Lattice

Sandwich lattice between 1x3s. Note that the horizontal member of one frame overlaps the vertical member of the other.

ARBOR SIDE ELEVATION DETAIL

3½ in.

1½ in.

R = 4 in.

4 in.

2¾-in. clearance

7 ft. 6 in. to grade

FENCE PLAN VIEW

4x4 post

2x4 rail (top and bottom)

1x3 picket slat

1½ in.

¾-in. clearance (optional)

Wooden ball or other attached finial

Entry arbor and fence

6x6 entry post

Additional fence posts can be 4x4s, 8 ft. or less on center.

Lattice panel

6x6 arbor post

Wooden ball or other attached finial on 6x6 post

Picket fence

Pickets should clear ground by 2 in.

Fence, 3 ft. to grade

3 ft. on center

Frame clears ground by 2 in.

5 ft. 6 in.

Louvered screen
(pp. 38–39)

Made of vertical slats set at an angle, this 6-ft.-tall fence allows air circulation to plants and people near the patio while providing a privacy screen. Be sure to check local codes about height and setback from property lines.

The slats are supported top and bottom by 2x4 rails; a 2x6 beneath the bottom rail stiffens the entire structure, keeps the slat assembly from sagging, and adds visual weight to the design. Set the posts; then cut the rails to fit between them. Toenailed nails or screws or metal connectors are strong enough, but you can add a 2x4 nailer between the rails (as shown in the drawing at bottom right) to make positioning and assembly easier.

Position the 1x6 slats with a spacer block 1½ in. wide and angled 45° at its ends. Nailing or screwing down through the top rail is easy. Nailing up through the bottom rail is more difficult; instead, you could toenail through the edges or faces of the slats into the bottom rail.

FRONT VIEW

4 to 8 ft.

2x4 top rail

4x4 post

1x6 slats

6 ft.

2x4 bottom rail

2x6 base rail

6-in. clearance

CONSTRUCTION DETAILS

2x4 top rail

Alternative construction: Fix 2x4 to post; nail or screw rails to its ends.

4x4 post

1x6 slat

2x6 base rail

2x4 bottom rail

SLAT ASSEMBLY

1½ in.

Spacer block

45°

4x4 post

Position first slat at 45°.

Position slats with spacer block.

Toenail slats into position.

Hideaway arbor
(pp. 84–85)

This cozy enclosure shelters a bench and supports vines to shade the occupants. Once the posts are set in place, this project can be finished in a weekend.

Build the arbor before laying the pavers under it. After setting the posts (see pp. 176–179), attach the 2x10 joists using carriage bolts. (The sizes of posts and joists have been chosen for visual effect; 4x4 posts and 2x6 or 2x8 joists will work, too.) Use nails to tack the joists in place; then bore holes for the bolts through post and both joists using a long electrician's auger bit. Fix the rafters by toenailing or using rust-protected metal rafter ties. Nail or screw the rafters at each end to the posts for added stability. For more privacy, you can add lattice between the posts at each end. (See p. 183 for a method of lattice panel construction.)

Space rafters evenly

2x4 rafter, 7 ft. 6 in. long

Fix outer rafters to posts.

6x6 post

Bolt joists to post.

2x10 joist, 11 ft. 6 in. long

80 in. minimum from joist to ground.

8 ft. on center

6x6 post

4 ft. on center

POST-TO-JOIST DETAIL

2x4 rafter

Hex nut

Washer

½ x 10 carriage bolt

2x10 joist

6x6 post

Good-neighbor fence
(pp. 74–77)

A variation on the traditional picket fence, this design provides privacy and good looks to neighbors on both sides, in addition to serving as a backdrop for a perennial border.

This is a simple fence to construct. Just set the posts; cut top and bottom rails to fit between them; and attach the slats. Note that the slats overlap roughly ½ in.; a 4½-in.-wide spacer block (1 in. narrower than the actual 5½-in. width of the 1x6s) makes positioning them a snap. Use two screws or nails positioned diagonally for each slat-to-rail connection.

CONSTRUCTION DETAILS

PLAN VIEW

Slats overlap on each side ½ in.

4x4 post

2x4 top rail

4x4 post

1x6 slats

2x4 top rail

Position nails or screws diagonally.

FRONT VIEW

2x4 top rail

1x6 slats

4x4 post

4 to 6 ft.

6 in.

10 in.

6 ft.

4-in. clearance

2x4 bottom rail

Picket fence
(pp. 96–97)

This fence, a variation of the traditional picket fence, supports a profusion of vining foliage and flowers and provides a sense of enclosure to a small pond and planting. The hefty 6x6 posts are used for their visual weight; 4x4 posts are strong enough if you prefer them.

To build the fence, you can set the posts first (see pp. 178–179) and make fence sections to fit between them. Or make the sections first and set posts accordingly. The pickets are sandwiched between two sets of rails top and bottom and are fixed in place using nails or screws. If you're making fence sections to fit a pre-

SIDE VIEW

POST CAP:
1x4x4
1x6x6
1x8x8

1½ in.

40 in.

1x4 fence cap

1x3 rail

1x3x33¼ picket

6x6 post

1x4 rail

determined distance be-
tween posts, adjust the gap
between pickets to ensure
uniform spacing. When you
lay out the pickets, make
sure that there is a space
between each post and the
end picket.

You can fasten the rails
to the posts by toenailing
or using metal fasteners.
Adding a spacer between
the ends of the rails, as
shown in the detail draw-
ing, may make attachment
easier. After the fence sections are fixed to the posts,
add the cap pieces to the
top rails and to the posts.

FENCE-CONSTRUCTION DETAIL

POST CAP:
1x4x4
1x6x6
1x8x8

1x4
fence cap

1x3
rail

6x6
post

1x3
picket

1x4
rail

DETAIL: SPACER BLOCK

Fix a spacer block between pairs of rails before attaching fence section to post.

1x3 rail

6x6
post

FRONT VIEW

Picket spacing, 2½ in. (typical)

1½ in.

33¼ in.

36 in.

2-in. clearance

Patio screen
(pp. 88–91)

Draped with vines, this makes an attractive but unobtrusive privacy screen between your patio and an adjacent property.

The screen is a snap to build. After setting the posts (see pp. 176–179), add the top and bottom rails. Cut the ends of those for the angled corners at 45° and toenail or screw them to the posts. Trim the ends of the "pickets" at a 45° angle and fix them into each rail using a nail or a screw. Position the pickets before fastening them to ensure even spacing. If you want a more solid-looking screen, offset the pickets so that those on one side fill the gaps left by those on the other. You can vary the size of the screen and the materials shown here. Keep in mind that the proportions are what make this simple design look good.

4x4 post
2x8 top rail
2x2 picket
2x8 bottom rail

PLAN VIEW

2x2 picket
4x4 post
2x8 rail
→| |← **2 in. (approximate)**

FRONT ELEVATION

|← 7 ft. →|
Post cap (optional)
4x4 post
2x8 top rail
2x2 pickets
2x8 bottom rail
6 in.
2 in.
65 in.
2 in.
9 in.

SIDE VIEW
7 ft.

Privacy fence
(pp. 48–51)

This design provides privacy and an attractive backdrop for a planting. If the fence is used on a property line, be sure to check local codes for restrictions on placement and height.

This is a simple fence to construct. Assemble the panels on a flat surface, nailing or screwing the slats to the three 2x4 rails. You can lay out the arc at the top of each panel by "springing" a thin strip of wood, as shown on the facing page. Place the strip against a nail driven into a slat at the highest point of the arc in the center of the panel ❶. Enlist a couple of assistants to bend each end of the strip down to nails near each edge of the panel indicating the lowest points of the arc ❷. Pencil in the arc against the strip ❸; then cut to the line. (A handheld electric saber saw does the job quickly, but the curve is gentle enough to cut with a handsaw.)

VIEW FROM BACK OF FENCE
1x4 slat
2x4 rail
2x4 rail
2x4 rail

Set the posts (see pp. 176–179) according to the widths of the finished panels. The 6x6 posts shown here add an eye-pleasing heft to the fence, an effect emphasized by setting the face of the panel 1 in. back from the faces of the posts. (Posts made of 4x4s will work just as well.) Metal connectors are the easiest means of attaching the completed panels to the posts. To allow yourself access to the rails when mounting the metal connectors, leave the last slats at each end off when you assemble the panels. We've shown a spherical finial attached to the end of each post; you can buy finials of various types at home centers.

SPRINGING AN ARC

1 Position a thin strip of wood against nail driven into slat at top of arc.

3 Scribe arc against bent strip.

Fence panel

2 Pull ends of strip down to nails driven near low points of arc at panel edges.

FRONT VIEW

6 ft. on center

Finial

6 in.

6x6 post

1x4 slat

6 ft.

6 in.

Assemble rails and slats; then fix panel to posts.

SIDE ELEVATION

Finial

2x4 rail

6x6 post

20 in.

2x4 rail

20 in.

1x4 slat

2x4 rail

12 in.

Set slats back 1 in. behind face of post.

Preparing the Soil for Planting

The better the soil, the better the plants. Soil quality affects how fast plants grow, how big they get, how good they look, and how long they live. But on many residential lots, the soil is shallow and infertile. Unless you're lucky enough to have a better-than-average site where the soil has been cared for and amended over the years, perhaps for use as a vegetable garden or flower bed, you should plan to improve your soil before planting in it.

If you were planting just a few trees or shrubs, or planting a bed of perennials on a rocky hillside, you could prepare individual planting holes for the plants and leave the surrounding soil undisturbed. However, for nearly all the plantings in this book, digging individual holes is impractical, and it's much better for the plants if you prepare the soil throughout the entire area that will be planted. (The major exception is when you're planting under a tree, which is discussed on p. 196.)

For most of the situations shown in this book, you could prepare the soil using hand tools—a spade, digging fork, and rake. The job will go faster and mix in amendments better if you use a gas-powered rototiller. Unless you grow vegetables, you probably won't use a rototiller often enough to justify buying one yourself, but you can easily borrow or rent a rototiller or hire someone with a tiller to come and prepare your site.

Loosen the soil

After you've removed any sod or other vegetation from the designated area (see pp. 156–157), the first step is digging or tilling to loosen the soil ❶. Do this on a day when the soil is moist—not so wet that it sticks to your tools or so dry that it makes dust. Try to dig down at least 8 in., or deeper if possible. If the ground is very compacted, you'll need to make repeated passes with a tiller to reach 8 in. deep. Toss aside large rocks, roots, or debris. When you're working near a house or other building, be sure to locate buried wires, cables, and pipes. Most local governments and utility companies have a number you can call to request help locating buried utilities.

After this initial digging, the ground will likely be very rough and lumpy. Whump the clods with the back of a digging fork or make another tiller pass. Continue until you've reduced all the clumps to the size of apples.

Once you've loosened the existing soil and dug it as deeply as possible, you may need to add clean topsoil or a landscape mix to fill in low spots, refine the grade, or raise the planting area above the surrounding grade for better drainage or to make it easier to see a favorite plant. Unless you need just a small amount, order topsoil or landscape mix by the cubic yard. (Landscape mix is primarily composted pine bark, sometimes with sand, manure, and other composted materials.) Consult the staff at your local nursery to find a reputable supplier of bulk landscape materials.

In many areas of central Texas, only a thin layer of soil covers limestone bedrock, making digging or tilling impossible. In these areas, the best option is to bring in topsoil or landscape mix. Mound it to create a low berm or contain it in a raised soil bed enclosed in wood or stone.

Add organic matter

Common soil (and purchased topsoil, too) consists mainly of rock and mineral

---

Common soil amendments and fertilizers

The following materials serve different purposes. Follow soil-test recommendations or the advice of an experienced gardener in choosing amendments that would be best for your soil. If so recommended, you can apply two or three of these amendments at the same time, using the stated rate for each one.

Material	Description	Amount for 100 sq. ft.
Compost	Amendment. Decomposed or aged plant parts and animal manures.	1 cubic yard
Wood by-products	Amendment. Finely ground bark or sawdust, composted or not. Add nitrogen to noncomposted material.	1 cubic yard
All-purpose fertilizer	Synthetic fertilizer containing various amounts of nitrogen, phosphorus, and potassium.	According to label
Organic fertilizer	Derived from a variety of organic materials. Provides nutrients in slow-release form.	According to label
Composted manure	Weak nitrogen fertilizers. Bagged steer manure is common.	6–8 lb.

fragments of various size. One of the best things you can do to improve any kind of soil for landscape and garden plants is to add some organic matter.

Organic materials used in landscaping are derived from plants and animals and include ground bark, peat moss, compost, and composted manures. Organic matter can be bought in bags or in bulk at nurseries, landscape supply companies, and many municipal recycling centers. If possible, buy only composted or aged material to amend your soil. Fresh manure can burn plant roots. Fresh bark and sawdust can steal nitrogen from the soil as they decay. If you buy uncomposted materials, ask at your nursery about how best to use them. (Some require supplemental nitrogen.)

How much organic matter should you use? Compost or aged material can be spread 2 to 3 in. thick across the entire work area ❷. At this thickness, a cubic yard (about one heaping pickup-truck load) of material will cover 100 to 150 sq. ft. Composted and aged manures, such as the bagged steer manure sold at nurseries, contain higher concentrations of nitrogen and should be applied at lower rates than other composts. They are more commonly used as slow-release fertilizers than as soil-improving amendments.

Add fertilizers and mineral amendments

Organic matter improves the soil's texture and helps it retain water and nutrients, but these materials usually lack essential nutrients. To provide the nutrients that plants need, you typically need to use organic or synthetic fertilizers. It's most helpful if you mix these materials into the soil before you do any planting ❸, working them into the root zone, but you can also sprinkle them on top of the soil to maintain an established planting.

Testing a sample of soil is the most accurate way to determine how much of each nutrient is needed. (To locate a soil-testing lab, consult the Internet, the Yellow Pages, or your Cooperative Extension Service.) Less precise, but often adequate, is the advice of nursery staff. Test results or an adviser will point out any significant deficiencies. Most soil just needs a moderate, balanced dose of nutrients.

Avoid using too much of any fertilizer or mineral. Don't guess at this; measure and weigh carefully. Calculate your plot's area. Follow your soil-test results or instructions on a commercial product's package. If necessary, weigh out the appropriate amount, using a kitchen or bathroom scale. Apply the material evenly across the plot with a spreader or by hand.

PREPARING THE SOIL FOR PLANTING

❶ Use a spade, digging fork, or tiller to dig at least 8 in. deep and break the soil into rough clods. Discard rocks, roots, and debris. Watch out for underground utilities.

❷ Spread a 2- to 3-in. layer of organic matter on top of the soil.

❸ Sprinkle measured amounts of fertilizer and mineral amendments evenly across the entire area, and mix thoroughly into the soil.

Mix and smooth the soil

Finally, use a digging fork or tiller and go back and forth across the bed again until the added materials are mixed thoroughly into the soil and everything is broken into nut-size or smaller lumps ❹. Then use a rake to smooth the surface ❺.

At this point, the soil level may look too high compared with adjacent pavement or lawn, but don't worry. Once the soil gets wet, it will settle a few inches and end up close to its original level.

Working near trees

Plantings under the shade of old trees can be cool oasis, such as the one shown on pp. 72–73. But to establish the plants, you'll need to contend with the tree's roots. Contrary to popular belief, most tree roots are in the top few inches of the soil, and they extend at least as far away from the trunk as the limbs do. Always try to disturb as few roots as possible when planting beneath established trees. To do so, it's often best to dig individual planting holes, rather than tilling a bed. Avoid cutting large roots. To start ground covers and perennials, you can add up to 4 in. of loose soil or landscape mix under the canopy of many established trees. Keep the new soil and any mulch away from the trunk. Covering roots with too much soil can starve them of oxygen, damaging or killing them; soil or mulch next to the trunk can rot the adjacent bark.

Plantings beneath existing native post oaks are normally problematic because the additional water needed to maintain the planting may damage or kill these trees. If you're uncertain about whether or how to plant beneath any established tree, or if your landscape plans call for significant grade changes beneath them, consult with a certified arborist.

❹ Use a tiller or digging fork to mix everything together, again working as deep as possible.

❺ Finish by smoothing the surface using a rake.

Making neat edges

All but the most informal landscapes look best if you define and maintain neat edges between the lawn and any adjacent plantings. There are several ways to do this, varying in appearance, effectiveness, cost, and convenience. Attractive, easy-to-install edges include cut, brick or stone, and strip edgings of plastic, fiberglass, or steel. If you plan to install an edging, put it in after you prepare the soil but before you plant.

Cut edge

Lay a hose or rope on the ground to mark the line where you want to cut. Then cut along the line using a sharp spade or edging tool. Lift away any grass that was growing into the bed (or any plants that were running out into the lawn). Use a rake or hoe to smooth out a shallow trench on the bed side of the cut. Keep the trench empty; don't let it fill up with mulch.

Pros and cons: Free. Good for straight or curved edges, level or sloped sites. But you'll need to recut the edge every four to eight weeks during the growing season; you can cut 50 to 100 ft. in an hour or so. Don't cut the trench too deep; if a mower wheel slips down into it, you'll scalp the lawn. Crabgrass and other weeds may sprout in the exposed soil; if this happens, hoe or pull them out.

Brick mowing strip

Dig a trench about 8 in. wide and 4 in. deep around the edge of the bed. Fill it halfway with sand; then lay bricks on top, setting them level with the soil on the lawn side. You'll need three bricks per foot of edging.

Sweep extra sand into any cracks be-tween the bricks. In cold-winter areas, you'll probably need to reset a few frost-heaved bricks each spring. You can substitute cut stone blocks or concrete pavers for bricks.

Pros and cons: Good for straight or curved edges on level or gently sloped sites. Looks good in combi-nation with brick walkways or brick house. Fairly easy to install and maintain. Some kinds of grass and plants will grow under, between, or over the bricks.

Plastic strip edging

Garden centers and home-improvement stores sell heavy-duty plastic edging in strips 5 or 6 in. wide and 20 or 50 ft. long. To install it, use a sharp tool to cut straight down through the sod around the edge of the bed. Hold the edging so the round lip sits right at soil level, and drive the stakes through the bottom of the edging and into the undisturbed soil under the lawn. Stakes, which are supplied with the edging, should be at least 8 in. long and set about 3 ft. apart. Similar strip edging in steel or fiberglass is installed in much the same way.

Pros and cons: Good for straight or curved edges, but only on relatively level sites. Neat and carefree when well installed, but installation is a two- or three-person job. If the lip isn't set right on the ground, you're likely to hit it with the mower blade. Liable to shift or heave un-less it's very securely staked. Hard to drive stakes in rocky soil. Some kinds of grass and ground covers can grow across the top of this type of edging.

CUT EDGE

BRICK MOWING STRIP

PLASTIC STRIP EDGING

Buying Plants

Once you have chosen and planned a landscape project, make a list of the plants you want and start thinking about where to get them. You'll need to locate the kinds of plants you want, choose good-quality plants, and get enough of the plants to fill your design area.

Where and how to shop

You may already have a favorite place to shop for plants. If not, look in the Yellow Pages under the headings "Nurseries," "Nurserymen," and "Garden Centers," or on the Internet and choose a few places to visit. Take your shopping list, find a salesperson, and ask for help. The plants in this book are commonly available in most parts of Texas, but you may not find everything you want at one place. The salesperson may refer you to another nursery, offer to special-order plants, or recommend similar plants that you could use as substitutes.

If you're buying too many plants to carry in your car or truck, ask about delivery—it's usually available and sometimes free. Some nurseries offer to replace plants that fail within a limited guarantee period, so ask about that, too.

The staff at a good nursery or garden center will normally be able to answer most of the questions you have about which plants to buy and how to care for them. If you can, go shopping on a rainy weekday when business is slow so staff will have time to answer your questions.

Don't be lured by the low prices of plants for sale at supermarkets or stores that sell plants for only a few months unless you're sure you know exactly what you want and how to identify it. The staff at these stores rarely have the time or knowledge to offer you much help, and the plants are often disorganized, unlabeled, and stressed by poor care.

If you can't find a plant locally or have a retailer order it for you, you can always order it yourself from a mail-order nursery. Most mail-order nurseries produce good plants and pack them well, but if you haven't dealt with a business before, be smart and place a minimum order first. Judge the quality of the plants that arrive; then decide whether or not to order larger quantities from that firm.

Timing

It's a good idea to plan ahead and start shopping for plants before you're ready to put them in the ground. That way, if you can't find everything on your list, you'll have time to keep shopping around, place special orders, or choose substitutes. Some nurseries will let you flag an order for later pickup or delivery, and they'll take care of the plants in the meantime. Or you can bring the plants home; just remember to check the soil in the containers every day and water if needed.

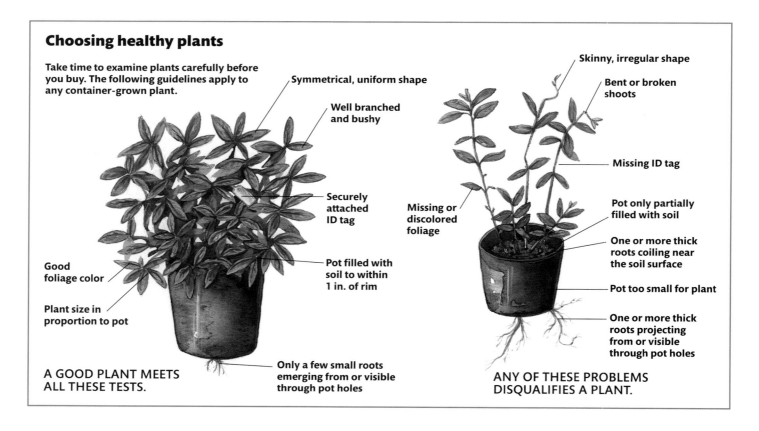

Choosing healthy plants

Take time to examine plants carefully before you buy. The following guidelines apply to any container-grown plant.

Symmetrical, uniform shape

Well branched and bushy

Securely attached ID tag

Good foliage color

Plant size in proportion to pot

Pot filled with soil to within 1 in. of rim

Only a few small roots emerging from or visible through pot holes

A GOOD PLANT MEETS ALL THESE TESTS.

Skinny, irregular shape

Bent or broken shoots

Missing ID tag

Missing or discolored foliage

Pot only partially filled with soil

One or more thick roots coiling near the soil surface

Pot too small for plant

One or more thick roots projecting from or visible through pot holes

ANY OF THESE PROBLEMS DISQUALIFIES A PLANT.

Choosing particular plants

If you need, for example, five hollies and the nursery or garden center has a whole block of them, how do you choose which five to buy? Because the sales staff may be too busy to help you decide, you may need to choose yourself.

Most plants today are grown in containers, so it's possible to lift them one at a time and examine them from all sides. Following the guidelines shown in the drawings on the opposite page, evaluate each plant's shape, size, health and vigor, and root system.

Trees and shrubs are sometimes sold "balled-and-burlapped," that is, with a ball of soil and roots wrapped tightly in burlap. For these plants, look for strong limbs with no broken shoots, an attractive profile, and healthy foliage. Then press your hands against the burlap-covered root ball to make sure that it feels firm, solid, and damp, not loose or dry. (If the ball is buried within a bed of wood chips, carefully pull the chips aside; then push them back after inspecting the plant.)

To make the final choice when you're considering a group of plants, line them up side by side and select the ones that are most closely matched in height, bushiness, and foliage color. If your design includes a hedge or mass planting where uniformity is very important, it's a good idea to buy a few extra plants as potential replacements in case of damage or loss. It's easier to plan ahead than to find a match later. Plant the extras in a spare corner so you'll have them if you need them.

Sometimes a plant will be available in two or more sizes. Which is better? That depends on how patient you are. The main reason for buying bigger plants is to make a landscape look impressive right away. If you buy smaller plants and set them out at the same spacing, the planting will look sparse at first, but it will soon catch up. A year after planting, you can't tell if a perennial came from a quart or gallon pot: they will look the same. For shrubs, the difference between one size pot and the next usually represents one year's growth.

The Planting Process

Throughout most of Texas, the cooler weather of fall or early spring makes those times best for planting. In fall, new plants have the upcoming wet season to become established before the onset of hot summer weather. However, frost-tender plants such as tropical hibiscus are best planted in spring after the threat of cold temperatures has passed. Although it's handy to plant a whole bed at once, you can divide the job, setting out some plants in fall and adding the rest in spring, or vice versa. If possible, do the actual planting on a cloudy day or evening when rain is forecast. Compared with preparing the soil, putting plants in the ground goes quite quickly. If you're well prepared, you can plant a whole bed in just an hour or two. On the following pages, we'll give an overview of the process and discuss how to handle individual plants. If you're installing an irrigation system, remember that some of the components may need to be put in place after the soil is prepared but before planting.

Try to stay off the soil

Throughout the planting process, do all you can by reaching in from outside the bed. Stepping on the newly prepared bed compacts the soil and makes it harder to dig planting holes. Use short boards or scraps of plywood as temporary steppingstones if you do need to step on the soil. As soon as you can decide where to put them, lay permanent steppingstones.

Check placement and spacing

The first step in planting is to mark the position of each plant. It's easy to arrange most of the plants themselves on the bed; use empty pots or stakes to represent plants too heavy to move easily. Follow your site plan for the design, checking the spacing with a yardstick as you place the plants.

Then step back and take a look. Should any of the plants be adjusted a little? Don't worry if the planting looks a little sparse. It *should* look that way at first. Plants almost always get bigger than you can imagine when you're first setting them out. And it's almost always better to wait for them to fill in rather than having to prune and thin a crowded planting in a few years. You might fill in with low-growing annuals. (See p. 200.)

PLANTING POINTERS

When working on top of prepared soil, kneel on a piece of plywood to distribute your weight.

Use empty pots or stakes to mark positions of plants not yet purchased or too heavy to move frequently.

Moving through the job

When you're satisfied with the arrangement, mark the position of each plant using a stake or stone, and set the plants aside, out of the way, so you won't knock them over or step on them as you proceed. Start planting in order of size. Plant the biggest plants first; then move on to the medium-size and smaller plants. If all the plants are about the same size, start at the back of the bed and work toward the front, or start in the center and work to the edges.

Position trees and shrubs to show their best side

Most trees and shrubs are slightly asymmetric. There's usually enough irregularity in their branching or shape that one side looks a little fuller or more attractive than the other sides do. After you've set a tree or shrub into its hole, step back and take a look. Then turn it partway, or try tilting or tipping it a little to one side or the other. Once you've decided which side and position looks best, start filling in the hole with soil. Stop and check again before you firm the soil into place.

The fine points of spacing

When you're planting a group of the same kind of plants, it normally looks best if you space them in slightly curved or zigzag rows. Don't arrange plants in single file unless you want to emphasize a line, such as the edge of a bed. In that case, make the row perfectly straight by sight, adjusting any plants that are out of line. (Stretch a string for long rows.) After planting, step back and evaluate the effect. If you want to adjust the placement or position of any plant, now is the time to do so.

Rake, water, and mulch

Use a garden rake to level the bed after planting. Water enough to settle the soil into place around the roots. Water each plant individually, or you can set up a sprinkler to do the whole planting at once. Mulch the entire planting area with 1 to 3 in. of bark, wood chips, or other organic matter. Mulch is indispensable for controlling weeds and regulating the moisture and temperature of the soil. If you're running out of time, you don't have to spread the mulch right away, but try to get it done within a week or so.

Using annuals as fillers

The plants in our designs have been spaced so they will not be crowded at maturity. Buying more plants and spacing them closer may fill things out faster, but in several years (for perennials; longer for shrubs) you'll need to remove plants or prune them frequently.

If you want something to fill the gaps between young plants for that first year or two, use some annuals. The best annual fillers are those that stay fairly low to the ground. These plants will hide the soil or mulch and make a colorful carpet, but won't shade or smother your permanent plantings. And don't forget to feed them. Annuals generally require more nutrients than perennials.

The following annuals are all easy to grow, readily available, and inexpensive. In Texas, different annuals perform better at different times of the year. Here, those that do best in winter are indicated by **W**; spring and fall by **SF**; and summer by **Su**. For more on annuals, see p. 118.

Begonia (SF): Red, pink, or white flowers. Good for shady sites but takes sun if planted in early spring.

Blue daze (Su): Pure blue flowers on low-growing plant. Full sun or part shade.

Dianthus (W): Red, pink, or white flowers. Full sun.

Dusty miller (SF): Silvery foliage, often lacy-textured. No flowers. Full sun or part shade.

Lantana (Su): Red, orange, yellow, pink, white, or bi-colored flowers. Full sun.

Pansy and viola (W): Multicolored flowers. Full sun or part shade.

Persian shield (Su): Shrubby plant with pink and silver variegated foliage. Shade.

Petunia (SF): Red, pink, purple, or white flowers. Full sun or part shade.

Sweet alyssum (W): Fragrant white, pink, or purple flowers. Blooms for months. Full sun.

Vinca (Su): Red, pink, or white flowers. Full sun and hot, dry conditions.

Planting Basics

Most of the plants that you buy for a landscaping project today are grown and sold in individual plastic containers. A few large shrubs and trees may be balled-and-burlapped, and some deciduous plants are sold bare-root. Ground covers are sometimes sold in flats. In any case, be careful what you do to a plant's roots. Spread them out; don't fold, coil, or cram them into a tight hole. Keep them covered; don't let the sun or air get them dry. Don't bury them too deep; set the top of the root-ball level with the surrounding soil. Make sure to regularly water the young plant so that it doesn't get dry.

Planting container-grown plants

The steps are the same for any plant, no matter what size the container. Dig a hole that's a little wider than the container but not quite as deep ❶. Check by setting the container into the hole—the top of the soil in the container should be slightly higher than the surrounding soil. Dig several holes at a time, at the positions that you've already marked out.

Remove the container ❷. With one hand, grip the plant at the base of its stems or leaves, while you tug on the pot with the other hand. If the pot doesn't slide off easily, don't pull harder on the stems. Try whacking the pot with your trowel or use a strong knife to cut or pry it off the plant.

Examine the plant's roots ❸. If there are any thick, coiled roots, unwind them and cut them off close to the root-ball, leaving short stubs. If the root-ball is a mass of fine, hairlike roots, use the knife to cut three or four slits from top to bottom, about 1 in. deep. Pry the slits apart, and tease the cut roots to loosen them. This may seem drastic, but it's actually good for the plant because it forces new roots to grow into the surrounding soil.

Work quickly. Once you've taken a plant out of its container, get it in the ground as soon as possible. If you want to prepare several plants at a time, cover them to keep the roots from drying out.

Set the root-ball into the hole ❹. Make sure that the plant is positioned right, with its best side facing out, and that the top of the root-ball is level with or slightly higher than the surface of the bed. Then add enough soil to fill in the hole, and pat it down firmly.

PLANTING CONTAINER-GROWN PLANTS

❶ Dig a hole a little wider than the container but not as deep.

❷ Remove the plant from the container.

❸ Unwind any large, coiled roots and cut them off short. Cut vertical slits through masses of fine roots.

❹ Position the plant in the hole and fill in around it with soil.

Planting a balled-and-burlapped shrub or tree

Nurseries often grow shrubs and trees in fields, and then dig them with a ball of root-filled soil and wrap a layer of burlap snugly around the ball to keep it intact. The problem is that even a small ball of soil is very heavy. A root ball that is a foot wide is a two-person job. For larger root-balls, ask the nursery to deliver and plant it. Here's how to proceed with plants that are small enough that you can handle them.

Dig a hole several inches wider than the root-ball but not quite as deep as the root-ball is high. Firm the soil so the plant won't sink. Set the plant into the hole, and lay a stick across the top of the root-ball to make sure it's at or a little higher than grade level. Be sure to cut or untie any twine that wraps around the trunk. Fold the burlap down around the sides of the ball. Don't try to pull the burlap out altogether—roots can grow out through it, and it will eventually decompose. Fill soil all around the sides of the ball and pat it down firmly. Spread only an inch of soil over the top of the ball.

The top of the ball should be level with the surrounding soil. Cut twine that wraps around the trunk. Fold down the burlap, but don't remove it.

Planting bare-root plants

Mail-order nurseries sometimes dig perennials, roses, and other plants when the plants are dormant, cut back the tops, and wash all the soil off the roots, to save space and weight when storing and shipping them. If you receive a plant in bare-root condition, unwrap it, trim away any roots that are broken or damaged, and soak the roots in a pail of water for several hours.

To plant, dig a hole large enough that you can spread the roots across the bottom without folding them. Start covering the roots with soil, then lay a stick across the top of the hole and hold the plant against it to check the planting depth, as shown in the drawing. Raise or lower the plant if needed in order to bury just the roots, not the buds. Add more soil, firming it down around the roots, and continue until the hole is full.

Dig a hole wide enough that you can spread out the roots. A stick helps position the plant at the correct depth as you fill the hole with soil.

Planting ground covers from flats

Sometimes ground covers are sold in flats of 25 or more rooted cuttings. Start at one corner, reach underneath the soil, and lift out a portion of the flat's contents. Working quickly, because the roots are exposed, tease the cuttings apart, trying not to break off any roots, and plant them individually. Then lift out the next portion and continue planting.

Remove a clump of little plants; tease their roots apart; and plant them quickly.

Planting bulbs

Plant spring-blooming bulbs in October and November. If the soil in the bed was well prepared, you can use a trowel to dig holes for planting individual bulbs; where you have room, you can dig a wider hole or trench for planting a group of bulbs all at once. The perennials, ground covers, shrubs, and trees you planted earlier in the fall or in the spring will still be small enough that you won't disturb their roots. As a rule of thumb, plant small (grape- or cherry-size) bulbs about 2 in. deep and 3 to 5 in. apart, and large (walnut- or egg-size) bulbs 4 to 6 in. deep and 6 to 10 in. apart.

Plant bulbs with the pointed end up, at a depth and spacing determined by the size of the bulb.

Basic Landscape Care

Planting on a hillside

Successful planting on a hillside depends on keeping the bare soil and young plants from blowing or washing away while they establish themselves. Here are some tips: rather than digging and amending all the soil, prepare individual planting holes. Work from the top of the slope to the bottom. Push one or more wooden shingles into the slope just below a plant to help hold it in place. Mulch with heavier materials, such as wood chips, that won't wash or blow away. If the soil is loose, spread water-permeable landscape fabric over it to help hold it in place; slit the fabric and insert plants through the openings. Water with drip irrigation, which erode less soil than sprinklers.

Confining perennials

Mexican petunia, obedient plant, mint, bee balm, and various other perennials, grasses, and ferns are described as invasive because they spread by underground runners. To confine these plants to a limited area, cut off the bottom of a 5-gal. or larger plastic pot; bury the pot so its rim is above the soil; and plant the perennial inside. You'll need to lift, divide, and replant part of the perennial every second or third year.

Position rim above soil surface.

Remove bottom of pot.

The landscape plantings in this book will grow increasingly carefree from year to year as the plants mature, but of course you'll always need to do some regular maintenance. This ongoing care may require as much as a few hours a week during the season or as little as a few hours a year. You'll need to control weeds, use mulch, water as needed, and do spring and fall cleanups. Trees, shrubs, and vines may need staking or training at first and occasional pruning or shearing afterward. Perennials, ground covers, and grasses may need to be cut back, staked, deadheaded, or divided. Performing these tasks, which are explained on the following pages, is sometimes hard work, but for many gardeners it is enjoyable labor, a chance to get outside in the fresh air. Also, spending time each week with your plants helps you identify and address problems before they become serious.

Mulches and fertilizers

Covering the soil in all planted areas with a layer of organic mulch does several jobs at once: it improves the appearance of your garden while you're waiting for the plants to grow, reduces the number of weeds that emerge, retards water loss from the soil during dry spells, moderates soil temperatures, and adds nutrients to the soil as it decomposes. Earthworms, which aerate the soil, also love it. Inorganic mulches such as landscape fabric and gravel also provide some of these benefits, but their conspicuous appearance and the difficulty of removing them if you ever want to change the landscape are serious drawbacks.

Many materials are used as mulches; the box on p. 204 presents the most common ones, with comments on their advantages and disadvantages. Consider appearance, availability, cost, and convenience when you're comparing products. Most garden centers have a few kinds of bagged mulch materials, but for mulching large areas, it's easier and cheaper to have a supplier deliver a truckload of bulk mulch. A landscape looks best if you see the same mulch throughout the entire planting area, rather than a patchwork of different mulches. You can achieve a uniform look by spreading a base layer of homemade compost, hay, or other inexpensive material and topping that with a neater-looking material such as bark chips or shredded bark.

It takes at least a 1-in. layer of mulch to suppress weeds, but there's no need to spread it more than 3 in. deep. As you're spreading it, don't put any mulch against the stems of any plants, because that can lead to disease or insect problems. Put most of the mulch between plants, not right around them. Check the mulch during your spring and fall cleanups. Be sure it's pulled back away from the plant stems. Rake the surface lightly to loosen it, and top it up with a fresh layer if the old material has decomposed.

Fertilizer

Decomposing mulch frequently supplies enough nutrients to grow healthy plants, but using fertilizer helps if you want to boost the plants—to make them grow faster, get larger, or produce more flowers. Young plants or those growing in poor soils also benefit from occasional applications of fertilizer. There are dozens of fertilizer products on the market—liquid and granular, fast-acting and slow-release, organic and synthetic. All give good results if applied as directed. And observe the following precautions: don't overfertilize, don't fertilize when the soil is dry, and don't fertilize tender plants after late summer, because they need to slow down and finish the season's growth before cold weather comes.

Mulch materials

Bark products
Bark nuggets, chipped bark, shredded bark, ground bark, and composted bark, usually from conifers, are available in bags or in bulk. All are attractive, long-lasting, medium-price mulches.

Chipped tree trimmings
The chips available from utility companies and tree services are a mixture of wood, bark, twigs, and leaves. Chips such as these cost less than pure bark products. In fact, you may be able to get a load for free. But they don't look very attractive, and you have to replace them more often because they decompose quickly.

Sawdust and shavings
These are cheap or free at sawmills and woodshops. They make good path coverings, but they aren't ideal mulches, because they tend to pack down into a dense, water-resistant surface. Sawdust can also blow around.

Hulls and shells
Ground coconut hulls, cocoa hulls, and nut shells can be picked up at food-processing plants and are sometimes sold at garden centers. They're all attractive, long-lasting mulches. Price varies from free to quite expensive, depending on where you get them.

Tree leaves
A few big trees may supply all the mulch you need, year after year. You can just rake the leaves onto a bed in fall, but it's better to chop them up with the lawn mower, pile them in compost bins for the winter, and spread them where needed in late spring. Pine needles, likewise, make good mulch, especially for camellias, azaleas, gardenias, and other acid-loving shrubs. Also, they are not messy; you can spread pine needles in fall, because they cling together and don't blow around.

Gravel
A mulch of pea gravel or crushed rock, spread 1 to 2 in. thick, helps keep the soil cool and moist. Many plants grow very well with a gravel mulch, especially succulents that thrive in dry conditions and Mediterranean herbs. However, gravel mulch is much more tiring to apply than organic materials, such as bark or leaves. It's harder to remove leaves and litter from gravel or weeds that sprout up through it. It's annoying to dig through the gravel if you want to replace or add plants later. And it's tedious to remove the gravel itself, should you ever change your mind about having it there.

Grass clippings
A 1- to 2-in. layer of dried grass clippings makes an acceptable mulch that decomposes within a single growing season. Don't pile clippings too thick, though. If you do, the top surface dries and packs into a water-resistant crust, and the bottom layer turns into nasty slime.

Hay and straw
Farmers sell hay that's unsuitable for fodder as "mulch" hay. Hay is cheap but likely to include weed seeds. Straw and coastal Bermuda grass hay are both more expensive than mulch hay but are usually free of seeds. Both hay and straw are more suitable for mulching vegetable gardens than landscape plantings because they decompose quickly and must be renewed each year. They also tend to attract rodents.

Landscape fabrics
Various types of synthetic fabrics, usually sold in rolls 3 to 4 ft. wide and 20, 50, or 100 ft. long, can be spread over the ground as a weed barrier. Unlike plastic, these fabrics allow water and air to penetrate into the soil. A topping of gravel, bark chips, or other mulch can anchor the fabric and hide it from view. If you're planting small plants, you can spread the fabric and insert the plants through X-shaped slits cut in the fabric where needed. You can plant larger plants first; then cut and snug the fabric around them. Drip irrigation is best laid on top of the fabric to make it easier to see clogs and leaks. It's also useful to lay fabric under paths, although it can be difficult to secure the fabric neatly and invisibly along the edges of adjacent planting beds. Removing fabric—if you change your mind—is a messy job. However, there are newer biodegradable fabrics that break down after a few years.

Clear or black plastic
Don't even think about using any kind of plastic sheeting as a landscape mulch. The soil underneath a sheet of plastic gets bone-dry, while water accumulates on top. Any loose mulch you spread on plastic won't stay in an even layer. No matter how you try to secure them, the edges of plastic sheeting always pull loose, appear at the surface, degrade in the sun, and shred into tatters.

Watering

Watering, as we've discussed previously (see pp. 158–159), is a necessity for most residential landscapes in Texas. To use water efficiently and effectively, it is helpful to know how to gauge when your plants need water, how much water they need, and how to ensure that your system supplies the desired amounts.

Deciding whether water is needed

Many experienced gardeners can judge whether a plant needs water simply by looking at its leaves. But drooping or dull leaves can also be caused by pests, disease, and over-watering. A surer way to decide whether you need to water is to examine the soil. If the top 3 to 4 in. is dry, most annuals, perennials, and shallow-rooted shrubs such as azaleas will need to be watered. Most trees and larger shrubs need water if the top 6 to 8 in. is dry. To check soil moisture, you can get down on your hands and knees and dig. But digging in an established planting can be awkward as well as harmful to crowded roots.

A less-invasive method of checking moisture is to use a paint stirrer or similar piece of unfinished, light-colored wood as a dipstick. Push it down through the mulch and 6 to 8 in. into the soil. Leave it there for an hour or so, and pull it out to see whether moisture has discolored the wood. If so, the soil is moist enough for plants. If not, it's time to water. Let the stick dry out before you use it again; it's handy to have several of these sticks around the garden shed.

It is also helpful to make a habit of monitoring rainfall. Set up your own rain gauge and listen to the weather reports, marking a calendar to keep track of rainfall amounts.

Pay attention to soil moisture or rainfall amounts all year long, because plants can suffer from dryness in any season, not the heat of summer. Water whenever the soil is dry. As for time of day, it's best to water early in the morning when the wind is calm, evaporation is low, and plant foliage will have plenty of time to dry off before nightfall. (Wet leaves at night can promote some foliar diseases.) Early morning (before 5 a.m.) is also when most urban and suburban neighborhoods have plenty of water pressure.

How much to water

Determining how much water to apply and how often to apply it is one of gardening's greatest challenges. Water too often, and plants drown. Water too little, and they dry out and die. For most gardeners, gauging how much water a plant or bed needs is an art more than a science. The key to watering enough but not too much is to be a good observer.

Examine your soil often; keep an eye on your plants; and make adjustments with the weather.

New plantings, even those of drought-tolerant plants, require frequent watering during the first year until the plants are established. In the heat of summer, new plantings may require water twice a week or more. Established landscape plants vary in their water needs.

It is always best to water deeply, wetting a large portion of the plant's root zone. Shallow watering encourages shallow rooting, and shallow-rooted plants dry out fast and need watering more frequently. Furthermore, a water-stressed plant is also more susceptible to disease and insect damage. As a rule of thumb, water most perennials to a depth of 12 to 18 in.; water most shrubs 2 to 3 ft. deep and most trees 3 to 4 ft. deep. (Lawns, in contrast, should be watered 6 to 8 in. deep, but they require frequent watering.)

Determining how much water will be required to penetrate to these depths depends on your soil. Water moves through different soils at different speeds. In general, 1 in. of water will soak about 4 to 5 in. deep in clay soil, 6 to 7 in. deep in loam, and 10 to 12 in. in sandy soil.

Different systems deliver water at different rates. Manufacturers often provide these rates in the product descriptions. You can determine the delivery rate for a sprinkler by setting tuna-fish cans in the area it covers and timing how long it takes to deposit an inch of water in one or more cans.

Whatever your system, you'll need to know how long it has to run for water to penetrate to the desired depth. To gauge penetration, use a wooden "dipstick," see below, after you've watered. For a rough gauge of deeper penetration, you can push a 1/4- to 1/2-in.-diameter iron bar into the soil. The bar will move easily through wet soil. When it encounters dry soil, the bar will become harder to push. Run your system, and time it as you check penetration depths.

CHECKING SOIL MOISTURE

Stick a paint stirrer or similar piece of light-colored, unfinished wood down through the mulch and into the soil. Pull it up after an hour. If the bottom of the stick looks and feels damp, the soil is moist enough for plants.

Controlling weeds

Weeds are not much of a problem in established landscapes. Once the "good" plants have grown big enough to merge together, they tend to crowd or shade out all but the most persistent undesirable plants. But weeds can be troublesome in a new landscape unless you take steps to prevent and control them.

There are two main types of weeds: those that mostly sprout as seedlings and those that keep coming back from perennial roots or runners. Try to identify and eliminate any perennial weeds before you start a landscaping project (see p. 156). Then you'll only have to deal with new seedlings later, which is a much easier job.

Annual and perennial weeds that commonly grow from seeds include Bermuda grass, bindweed, dandelions, oxalis, plantain, purslane, and spurge. Trees and shrubs such as cherry laurel, Chinese tallow, privet, cedar elm, mimosa, hackberry, and Chinaberry produce weedy seedlings, too. For any of the weeds that grow from seeds, the strategy is twofold: try to keep the weed seeds from sprouting, and eliminate any seedlings that do sprout as soon as you see them, while they are still small.

Almost any patch of soil includes weed seeds that are ready to sprout whenever that soil is disturbed. Preparing the soil for planting will probably cause an initial flush of weeds, but you won't see as many weeds again if you leave the soil undisturbed in subsequent years. You don't need to hoe, rake, or cultivate around perennial plantings. Leave the soil alone, and fewer weeds will appear. Using mulch helps even more; by shading the soil, it prevents weed seeds from sprouting. And if weed seeds blow in and land on top of the mulch, they'll be less likely to germinate there than they would on bare soil.

Pull or cut off any weeds that appear while they're young and small, just a few inches tall. Don't let them mature and go to seed. Most weed seedlings emerge in late spring and early summer. If you get rid of them then, you won't see many more seedlings for the rest of the growing season.

Using herbicides

Two kinds of herbicides can be very useful and effective in maintaining home landscapes, but only if used correctly. Choose the right product for the job and follow the directions on the label regarding dosage and timing of application exactly.

Preemergent herbicides. Sold in granular or liquid form, these herbicides are designed to prevent weed seeds, particularly crabgrass and other annual weeds, from sprouting. For annual winter weeds such as chickweed and henbit, make the first application in early fall before the first signs of rain and cooler weather. For annual summer weeds such as crabgrass

WEEDS THAT SPROUT FROM SEEDS

Simple root systems can be easily pulled while still small.

WEEDS THAT SPROUT BACK FROM PERENNIAL ROOTS OR RUNNERS

Connected by underground runners, the shoots of these weeds need to be pulled repeatedly, smothered with a thick mulch, or killed with an herbicide.

Bermuda grass

Runner

Use a disposable, sponge-type paintbrush to apply the herbicide selectively, painting only the weeds. Prepare the solution as directed for spray application. Use only enough to wet the leaves, so none drips off.

USING HERBICIDES ON PERENNIAL WEEDS

Ready-to-use spot-weeder sprays are convenient, but you must aim carefully. Try using a sheet of cardboard as a backdrop to protect desirable plants from herbicide drift.

Caring for Woody Plants

and spurge, you'll need to make another application in spring. Follow package directions to determine how long to wait between each application.

Read the label carefully, and make sure the herbicide you buy is registered for use around the kinds of plants you have. Granular forms are often used in smaller areas, liquid in larger areas. Apply them exactly as described on the product label. Wear heavy rubber gloves that are rated for use with farm chemicals, not common household rubber gloves, and follow the safety precautions on the label.

Postemergent herbicides. These chemicals are used to kill growing plants. Some kill only the aboveground parts of a plant; others are absorbed into the plant and kill it, roots and all. Postemergent herbicides are typically applied as sprays, which you can buy ready-to-use or prepare by mixing a concentrate with water. Look for those that break down quickly, and read the label carefully.

Postemergent herbicides work best if applied when the weeds are growing vigorously and the weather is dry. You usually need to apply enough to thoroughly wet the plant's leaves. Herbicides can be effective at getting rid of perennial weeds that you can't dig or pull up, but it's really better to do this before you plant a bed, as it's hard to spray herbicides in an established planting without getting some on your good plants. (Some postemergent herbicides are more selective, affecting only certain types of plants.) Aim carefully, shielding nearby plants as shown in the drawing at left, and don't spray on windy days. You can brush or sponge the herbicide on the leaves to avoid damaging adjacent plants. Using postemergent herbicides in an established planting may be the only way to get rid of a persistent perennial weed.

A well-chosen garden tree, such as those recommended in this book, grows naturally into a pleasing shape, won't get too large for its site, is resistant to pests and diseases, and doesn't drop messy pods or other litter. Once established, these trees need very little care from year to year.

Regular watering is the most important concern in getting a tree off to a good start. Don't let it suffer from drought for the first few years. To reduce competition, don't plant ground covers or other plants within 2 ft. of the tree's trunk. Arborists now dismiss other care ideas that once were common practice. According to current thinking, you don't need to fertilize a tree when you plant it (in fact, unless they show obvious signs of deficiency or grow poorly, most landscape trees never need fertilizing). Keep pruning to a minimum at planting time; remove only dead or damaged twigs, not healthy shoots. Finally, research has shown that tree trunks grow stronger when they're not staked rigidly. However, taller trees and shrubs need some support, usually for no more than a year. It is very important that the supported trunk be allowed to flex in the wind. Be sure to ask an arborist or nursery staff about proper staking for the trees you buy.

Pruning basics

Proper pruning keeps plants healthy and looking their best. There are two basic types of pruning cuts: heading and thinning. Heading cuts are made along the length of a branch or stem, between its tip and its base. These cuts induce vigorous growth in the dormant buds below the cut. Such growth is useful for filling in hedges and rejuvenating shrubs and perennials. But heading can drastically change the appearance of a plant, even destroying its natural shape. Heading can also produce weakly attached branches in trees and shrubs.

Thinning cuts remove stems and branches at their origin (the plant's crown or where the branch attaches to the trunk or a larger limb). Unlike heading, thinning does not produce vigorous growth. Instead, thinning opens

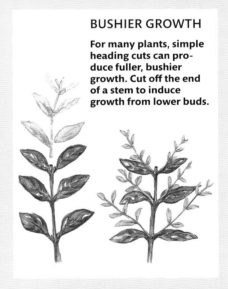

BUSHIER GROWTH

For many plants, simple heading cuts can produce fuller, bushier growth. Cut off the end of a stem to induce growth from lower buds.

the plant's interior to light and air, which improves its health. And, by reducing congested growth, thinning often enhances the natural appearance of the plant. In most cases, thinning is the preferred pruning technique, especially for trees and shrubs.

Pruning roses

Roses are vigorous, fast-growing shrubs that need regular pruning to keep them shapely and attractive. Most of this pruning is done in winter to early spring, just as the buds start to swell but before the new leaves start to unfold. Right after pruning is a good time to add fresh mulch around the plant.

Prune hybrid tea roses to keep them neat, compact, and continuously producing long-stemmed flowers. Remove skinny or weak stems, plus a few of the oldest stems (their bark is tan or gray instead of green) by cutting them off at their base. Prune off any shoots that got broken or were blackened by freezing during the winter, remove old or weak shoots and crossing or crowded stems, and trim back any asymmetric or unbalanced shoots. If you cut old stems near the graft union (the swelling at the base of the plant where the top growth was grafted to the root stock), new ones will replace them.

Hybrid tea roses bloom on new growth, so if you prune in early spring you aren't cutting off any flower buds. During the growing season, remove flowers as soon as they fade. This keeps the plant neat and makes it bloom longer and more abundantly. At least once a week, locate each faded flower, fol-

low down its stem to the first or second five-leaflet leaf, and prune just above one of those leaves. (Follow the same steps to cut roses for a bouquet.)

Climbing roses are pruned differently than hybrid teas. In late winter, remove weak, dead, or damaged shoots by cutting them back to the ground or to healthy wood. Select the healthiest stems for a main framework, and tie them securely to a support. Shorten all side shoots on these stems to two buds. Shoots growing from these buds will produce flowers.

Climbing roses need regular attention throughout the summer because their stems (also called canes) can grow a foot or more in a month. Check regularly and tie this new growth to the trellis while it's still supple and manageable. When the canes grow long enough to reach the top of the trellis or arbor, cut off their tips and tie the canes horizontally to induce production of flowering side shoots. Remove spent roses by cutting the stems back to the nearest healthy five-leaflet leaf.

Tea, China, polyantha, and other shrub roses can be pruned with hedge shears. Simply cut back one-third to one-half the growth in winter and remove diseased or damaged canes.

PRUNING A HYBRID TEA ROSE

Cut blackened winter-damaged shoots back to healthy, green tissue.

Old

Weak, crossing

BEFORE

AFTER

In late winter or early spring, remove old, weak, or damaged shoots; stems that are crossing or crowded; and stems that stick out too far and look asymmetric. Don't be afraid to cut a lot away.

REMOVING FLOWERS

Five-leaflet leaf

Roses can look messy as they fade. Cut off by pruning the stem back to the first healthy five-leaflet leaf.

Shaping young trees

As a tree grows, you can affect its shape by pruning once a year, usually in winter. Take it easy, though. Don't prune just for the sake of pruning; that does more harm than good. If you don't have a good reason for making a cut, don't do it. Follow these guidelines:

- **Use sharp pruning shears, loppers, or saws,** which make clean cuts without tearing the wood or bark.
- **Cut branches back** to a healthy shoot, leaf, or bud, or cut back to the branch collar at the base of the branch, as shown far right. Don't leave any stubs; they're ugly and prone to decay.
- **Remove any dead or damaged branches** and any twigs or limbs that are very spindly or weak.
- **Where two limbs cross over or rub** against each other, save one limb—usually the thicker, stronger one—and prune off the other one.
- **Prune or widen narrow crotches.** Places where a branch and trunk or two branches form a narrow V are weak spots, liable to split apart as the tree grows. Where the trunk of a young tree exhibits such a crotch or where either of two shoots could continue the growth of a branch, prune off the weaker of the two. Where you wish to keep the branch, insert a piece of wood as a spacer to widen the angle, as shown in the drawings below. Leave the spacer in place for a year or so.

One trunk or several?

If you want a young tree to have a single trunk, identify the leader or central shoot and let it grow straight up, unpruned. The trunk will grow thicker faster if you leave the lower limbs in place for the first few years, but if they're in

WHERE TO CUT

When removing the end of a branch, cut back to a healthy leaf, bud, or side shoot. Don't leave a stub. Use sharp pruning shears to make a neat cut that slices the stem rather than tears it.

When removing an entire branch, cut just outside the slightly thickened area, called the branch collar, where the branch grows into the trunk.

the way, you can remove them. At whatever height you choose, select the shoots that will become the main limbs of the tree. Be sure they are evenly spaced around the trunk, pointing outward at wide angles. Remove any lower or weaker shoots. As the tree matures, the only further pruning required will be an annual checkup to remove dead, damaged, or crossing shoots.

Several of the trees in this book, including crapemyrtle, redbud, chaste tree, and Texas mountain laurel, are often grown with multiple trunks, for a graceful, clumplike appearance. When buying a multiple-trunk tree, choose one with trunks that diverge at the base. The more space between them, the better. Prune multiple-trunk trees as previously described for single-trunk trees. Remove some of the branches growing toward the center of the clump, so that it doesn't get too dense and tangled, reducing ventilation.

AVOIDING NARROW CROTCHES

A tree's limbs should spread wide, like outstretched arms. If limbs angle too close to the trunk or to each other, there isn't room for them to grow properly and they may split apart after a few years, ruining the tree.

SINGLE-TRUNK TREES: Correct narrow crotches on a young tree by removing the less desirable limb or by widening the angle with a wooden spacer block. Choose well-spaced shoots to become the main limbs of a shade tree.

MULTIPLE-TRUNK TREES: Whether the stems of a multiple-trunk tree emerge from the ground or from a single trunk near the ground, widen angles if necessary to keep the trunks from touching.

Pruning shrubs

Shrubs are generally carefree plants, but they almost always look better if you do some pruning at least every other year. As a minimum, remove dead twigs from time to time, and if any branches are broken by storms or accidents, remove them as soon as convenient, cutting back to a healthy bud or branch or to the plant's crown. Also, unless the shrub produces attractive seedpods or berries, it's a good idea to trim off the flowers after they fade.

Beyond this routine pruning, some shrubs require more attention. (The entries in Plant Profiles, pp. 116–151, give more information on when and how to prune particular shrubs.) Basically, shrub pruning falls into three categories: selective pruning, severe pruning, and shearing.

Selective pruning means using pruning shears to head back or thin individual shoots in order to refine the shape of the bush and maintain its vigor, as well as limit its size. (See the drawing at right.) This job takes time but produces a very graceful and natural-looking bush. Cut away weak or spindly twigs and any limbs that cross or rub against each other, and head all the longest shoots back to a healthy, outward-facing bud or to a pair of buds. You can do selective pruning on any shrub, deciduous or evergreen, at any time of year.

Severe pruning means using pruning shears or loppers to cut away most of a shrub's top growth, leaving just short stubs or a gnarly trunk. This kind of cutting back is usually done once a year in late winter or early spring. Although it seems drastic, severe pruning is appropriate in several situations.

It makes certain fast-growing shrubs, such as vitex and butterfly bush, flower more profusely. It keeps others, such as salvia, artemisia, and verbena, compact and bushy.

One or two severe prunings done when a shrub is young can make it branch out at the base, producing a bushier specimen or a fuller hedge plant. Nurseries often do this pruning as part of producing a good plant, and if you buy a shrub that's already bushy, you don't need to cut it back yourself. Older shrubs that have gotten tall and straggly sometimes respond to a severe pruning by sprouting out with renewed vigor, sending up lots of new shoots that bear plenty of foliage and flowers. This strategy doesn't work for all shrubs, though—sometimes severe pruning kills a plant. Don't try it unless you know it will work. Check with a pruning specialist, such as an arborist, or a knowledgeable person at a nursery.

Shearing means using hedge shears or an electric hedge trimmer to trim the surface of a shrub, hedge, or tree to a neat, uniform profile, producing a solid mass of greenery. Both deciduous and evergreen shrubs and trees can be sheared; those with small, closely spaced leaves and a naturally compact growth habit usually look best. A good time for shearing most shrubs is late spring, after the new shoots have elongated but before the wood has hardened, but you can shear at other times of year. You may have to shear some plants more than once a year.

If you're planning to shear a plant, start when it is young and establish the shape—cone, pyramid, flat-topped hedge, or whatever. Looking at the profile, always make the shrub wider at the bottom than on top; otherwise the lower limbs will be shaded and won't be as leafy. Shear off as little as needed to maintain the shape. Once it gets as big as you want it, shear to maintain its size.

SELECTIVE PRUNING. Remove weak, spindly, bent, or broken shoots (red). Where two branches rub on each other, remove the weakest or the one that's pointing inward (orange). Cut back long shoots to a healthy, outward-facing bud (blue).

SEVERE PRUNING. In late winter or early spring, before new growth starts, cut back all the stems close to the ground.

SHEARING. Trim with hedge clippers to a neat profile.

Making a hedge

To make a hedge that's dense enough that you can't see through it, choose shrubs that have many shoots at the base. If you can find only skinny shrubs, prune them severely the first spring after planting to stimulate bushier growth.

Hedge plants are set in the ground as described on pp. 201–202 but are spaced closer together than they would be if planted as individual specimens. We took that into account in creating the designs and plant lists for this book; just follow the spacings recommended in the designs. If you're impatient for the hedge to fill in, you can space the plants closer together.

A hedge can be sheared, pruned selectively, or left alone, depending on how you want it to look. Slow-growing, small-leaved plants, such as boxwood and dwarf yaupon holly, make rounded but natural-looking hedges with no pruning at all, or you can shear them into any profile you choose and make them neat. Choose one style and stick with it. Once a hedge is established, you cannot start or stop shearing it without creating an awkward transition phase that may last a few years before the hedge looks good again.

Getting a vine off to a good start

Nurseries often sell climbing vines as young plants attached to stakes or trellises. To plant the vine, simply tie the plant and stake with string or twine to the base of a permanent support they are to climb ❶. The original stake can be removed after the plant becomes attached to its new home ❷.

Once they're started, twining vines, such as wisteria and Carolina jasmine, can scramble up a lattice trellis, although it helps if you tuck in any stray ends. The plants can't climb a smooth surface, however. To help them cover a fence with wide vertical slats or a porch post, you have to provide something the vine can encircle. Screw a few eyebolts to the top and bottom of such a support and stretch wire, nylon cord, or polypropylene rope between them. (The wires or cords should be a few inches out from the fence, not flush against it.) Clinging vines, such as trumpet creeper and cross vine, can climb any surface by means of their adhesive rootlets and need no further assistance or care.

So-called "climbing roses" don't really climb at all by themselves—you have to fasten them to a support. Loosely fixed twist-ties or twine are handy for this job. Roses grow fast, so you'll have to tie-in the new shoots every few weeks from spring to fall.

After the first year, most vines need annual spring pruning to remove any dead, damaged, or straggly stems. If vines grow too long, you can cut them back anytime and they will branch out from below the cut.

STARTING A VINE

❶ At planting, loosely tie stem and shoots to a stake.

❷ When the vine is established on its permanent support, you can remove the planting stake.

Caring for Perennials

Perennials are simply plants that send up new growth year after year. A large group, perennials include flowering plants, such as daylilies and purple coneflower, as well as grasses, ferns, and hardy bulbs. Although some perennials need special conditions and care, most of those in this book are adaptable and easy to grow. Get them off to a good start by planting them in well-prepared soil, adding a layer of mulch, watering as often as needed throughout the first year, and keeping away weeds. After that, keeping perennials attractive and healthy typically requires just a few minutes per plant each month.

Routine annual care

Some of the perennials that are used as ground covers, such as lilyturf, mondo grass, and vinca, need virtually no care. On a suitable site, they'll thrive for decades even if you pay them almost no attention at all.

Most garden perennials, though, look and grow better if you clean away the old leaves and stems at least once a year. When to do this depends on the type of plant. Perennials such as firebush, cigar plant, and Turk's cap have leaves and stalks that turn tan or brown after they're frosted in fall. Cut these down to the ground in late fall or early spring; either time is okay.

Some perennials, such as oxeye daisy, columbine, yarrow, verbena, and dianthus, have foliage that is more or less evergreen, depending on the severity of the winter. For those plants, wait until after they've bloomed or until the fall; then cut back leaves or stems that are discolored or shabby looking. Don't leave cuttings lying on the soil, because they may contain disease spores. To avoid contaminating your compost, send diseased stems or leaves to the dump.

Right after you've cleared away the dead material is a good time to renew the mulch on the bed. Use a fork, rake, or cultivator to loosen the existing mulch, and add some fresh mulch if needed. Also, if you want to sprinkle some granular fertilizer on the bed, do that now, when it's easy to avoid getting any on the plants' leaves. Fertilizing perennials is optional, but it does make them grow bigger and bloom more than they would otherwise.

Remove faded flowers

Removing flowers as they fade (called "deadheading") makes a garden bed look neater, prevents unwanted self-sown seedlings, and often stimulates a plant to continue blooming longer than it would if you left it alone, or to bloom a second time later in the season. (The same is true for shrubs and annuals as well as for perennials.)

Pick large flowers, such as daisies, daylilies, irises, and hibiscus, one at a time, snapping them off by hand. Use pruning shears on perennials such as salvia, gaura, phlox, and yarrow that produce tall stalks crowded with lots of small flowers, cutting the stalks back to the height of the foliage. Use hedge shears on bushy plants that are covered with lots of small flowers on short stalks, such as lantana, Turk's cap, and verbena, cutting the stems back by about one-half their length.

Instead of removing them in the late fall, you may want to let the faded flowers remain on black-eyed Susans, 'Autumn Joy' sedum, and the various ornamental grasses. These plants all bear conspicuous seedpods or seed heads that are on stiff stalks, which remain standing and look interesting throughout the fall and winter months.

Pruning and shearing perennials

Some perennials that bloom in summer or fall respond well to being pruned earlier in the growing season. Aster, chrysanthemum, Mexican sage, garden phlox, and 'Autumn Joy' sedum all form tall clumps of stems topped with lots of little flowers. Unfortunately, tall stems are liable to flop over in stormy weather, and even if they don't, too-tall clumps can look leggy or top-heavy. To prevent floppiness, prune these plants when the stems are about 1 ft. tall. Remove the weakest stems from each clump by cutting them off at the ground; then cut all the remaining, strong stems back by about one-third. Pruning in this way keeps these plants shorter, stronger, and bushier, so you don't have to bother with stakes to keep them upright.

Purple heart and 'Powis Castle' artemisia are grown more for their foliage than for their flowers. You can use hedge shears to keep them neat, compact, and bushy, shearing off the tops of the stems once or twice in spring and summer.

PRUNING A PERENNIAL

Prune to create neater, bushier clumps of some summer- and fall-blooming perennials such as garden phlox, chrysanthemums, and 'Autumn Joy' sedum. When the stalks are about 1 ft. tall, cut them all back by one-third. Remove the weakest stalks at ground level.

Dividing perennials

Most perennials send up more stems each year, forming denser clumps or wider patches. Dividing is the process of cutting or breaking apart these clumps or patches. This is an easy way to make more plants to expand your garden, to control a plant that might otherwise spread out of bounds, or to renew an old specimen that doesn't look good or bloom well anymore.

Most perennials can be divided as often as every year or two if you're in a hurry to make more plants, or they can go for years if you don't have any reason to disturb them. Fall is the best time to divide most summer- and fall-blooming perennials, but you can also do it in early spring.

There are two main approaches to dividing a perennial, as shown in the drawings at right. You can leave the plant in the ground and use a sharp spade to cut it apart, and then lift out one chunk at a time. Or you can dig around and underneath the plant and lift it out all at once; shake off the extra soil; and lay the plant on the ground or a tarp where you can work with it.

Some plants, such as yarrow and some ferns, are easy to divide. They almost fall apart when you dig them up. Others, such as daylilies and most grasses, have very tough or tangled roots and you'll have to wrestle with them, chop them with a sharp butcher knife, pry them apart with a sharp spade, or even cut through the roots with a hatchet or pruning saw. However you approach the job, before you insert any tool, take a close look at the plant at ground level, and be careful to divide between, not through, the biggest and healthiest buds or shoots. Using a hose to wash away loose mulch and soil will also make it easier to see what you're doing.

Don't make the divisions too small; they should be the size of a plant that you'd want to buy, not just little scraps. If you have more than you need or want, choose the best-looking ones to replant and discard or give away the others. Replant new divisions as soon as possible in freshly prepared soil. Water them right away, and water again whenever the soil dries out over the next few weeks or months, until the plants are growing again.

Hardy bulbs, such as narcissus and snowflakes, can be divided every few years. Dig clumps after bloom when the foliage turns yellow. Shake the soil off the roots; pull the bulbs apart; and replant them promptly, setting them as deep in the soil as they were buried before.

DIVIDING PERENNIALS

You can divide a clump or patch of perennials by cutting down into the patch with a sharp spade, then lifting out the separate chunks.

Or you can dig up the whole clump, shake the extra soil off the roots, and then pull or pry it apart into separate plantlets.

Problem Solving

Some plants are much more susceptible than others to damage by severe weather, pests, or diseases. In this book, we've recommended plants that are generally trouble free, especially after they have had a few years to get established in your garden. But even these plants are subject to various mishaps and problems. The challenge is learning how to distinguish the problems that are really serious from those that are merely cosmetic, and then deciding how to solve—or, better yet, prevent—the problems that are serious from occuring.

Pests, large and small

Deer and rabbits are liable to be a problem if your property is surrounded by or adjacent to fields or woods. You may not see them, but you can't miss the damage they do—they bite off the tops or eat whole plants of cannas, daylilies, and many other perennials. Deer also eat the leaves and stems of roses, azaleas, and many other trees and shrubs. Commercial or homemade repellents that you spray on the foliage may be helpful if the animals aren't too hungry and you use them often. (See the box, below right, for thoughts on

deer-proof plants.) But in the long run, the only solution is to fence out deer and to trap and remove smaller animals.

Squirrels are cute but naughty. They normally don't eat much foliage, but they do eat some kinds of flowers and several kinds of bulbs. They also dig up new transplants, and they plant nuts in your flower beds and lawns. Field mice can kill trees and shrubs by stripping the bark off the trunk, usually near the ground. Gophers eat the roots of shrubs, trees, and perennials. Moles don't eat plants, but their digging makes a mess of a lawn or flower bed. Persistent trapping is the most effective way to control these little critters. (You can protect the roots of some plants from gophers by planting the plants in wire cages sold at many nurseries.)

Aphids, beetles, caterpillars, grubs, grasshoppers, spider mites, white flies, scale insects, slugs, snails, and countless other pests can cause minor or devastating damage in a home landscape. Most plants can afford to lose part of their foliage or sap without suffering much of a setback, so don't panic if you see a few holes chewed in a leaf. However, whenever you suspect that insects or related pests are attacking one of your plants, try to catch one of them in a glass jar and have it identified, so you can decide what to do about it.

Identify, then treat

Don't jump to conclusions and start spraying chemicals on a supposedly sick plant before you know what (if anything) is actually wrong with it. That's wasteful and irresponsible, and you're likely to do the plant as much harm as good. Pinpointing the exact cause of a problem is difficult even for experienced gardeners, so save yourself frustration and seek out expert help from the beginning.

If it seems that there's something wrong with one of your plants—for example, if the leaves are discolored, have holes in them, or have spots or marks on them—cut off a sample branch, wrap it in damp paper towels, and put it in a plastic bag (so it won't wilt). Take the sample to the nursery or garden center where you bought the plant, and ask for help. If the nursery can't help, contact the nearest office of the state's Cooperative Extension Service or a public garden in your area and ask if they have a staff member who can diagnose plant problems.

Meanwhile, look around your property and around the neighborhood, too, to see if any other plants (of the same or different kinds) show similar symptoms. If a problem is widespread, you shouldn't have much trouble finding someone who can identify it and tell you what, if anything, to do. If only one plant is affected, it's often harder to diagnose the problem, and you may just need to wait and see what happens to it. Keep an eye on the plant, continue with watering and other regular maintenance, and see whether the problem gets worse or goes away. If nothing more has happened after a few weeks, stop worrying. If the problem continues, intensify your search for expert advice.

Plant problems stem from a number of causes: insect and animal pests, diseases, and poor care, particularly in winter. Remember that plant problems are often caused by a combination of these; all the more reason to consult with experts about their diagnosis and treatment.

Deer-proof plants?

Planting from lists of deer-proof plants often results in disappointment. What's deer-proof in one area may not be in another. And if deer are really hungry, they'll eat almost anything. If you live in an area where deer are common, check with local nurseries, public gardens in your region, or the nearest Cooperative Extension Service office for advice and planting solutions.

DEER-CONTROL FENCING
If your property borders a woodland, deer can be a real problem. Deer have been known to jump very tall fences. Experience shows that a wide midheight fence is one of the best ways to keep out deer. This fence is suitable for a larger property. It is about 6 ft. wide and 5 ft. high and consists of angled poles fixed to posts spaced about 10 ft. apart. Attach wires at 12-in. intervals to the poles. For advice on deer fences that work best in your area, consult your Cooperative Extension Service.

There are several new kinds of insecticides that are quite effective but much safer to use than the older products. For example, insecticidal soap, a special kind of detergent, quickly kills aphids and other soft-bodied insects, but it's nontoxic to mammals and birds and it breaks down quickly, leaving no harmful residue. Horticultural oil, a highly refined mineral oil, is a good control for scale insects, which frequently infest gardenias, camellias, and other broad-leaved evergreens. Most garden centers stock these and other relatively safe insecticides.

Before using any insecticide, study the fine print on the label to make sure that the product is registered to control your particular pest. Carefully follow the directions for how to apply the product, or it may not work.

Diseases

Several types of fungal, bacterial, and viral diseases can attack garden plants, causing a wide range of symptoms such as disfigured or discolored leaves or petals, powdery or moldy-looking films or spots, mushy or rotten stems or roots, and overall wilting. If you suspect that a plant is infected with a disease, treat it as you would an insect problem. Gather a sample of the plant and show it to someone who can identify the problem before you do any spraying.

In general, plant diseases are hard to treat, so it's important to prevent problems. Choose plants adapted to your area and are disease-resistant plants. Space plants far enough apart so

that air can circulate between them, and remove dead stems.

Perennials that would otherwise be healthy are prone to fungal infections during humid weather, especially if plants are crowded or if they have flopped over and are lying on top of each other or on the ground. If your garden has turned into a jungle, look closely for moldy foliage and if you find any, prune it off and discard (don't compost) it. It's better to cut the plants back severely than to let the disease spread. After each pruning cut, dip the blades into a 1:10 solution of bleach and water to avoid spreading the disease. Avoid repeated problems by dividing the perennials, replanting them farther apart, and pruning them early in the season so they don't grow tall and floppy again. Crowded shrubs are also subject to fungal problems in the summer and should be pruned so that air can flow around them.

Winter damage

Even though much of Texas enjoys relatively mild winters, occasional cold spells can damage normally hardy plants. After a particularly hard winter, wait until at least midspring to assess the severity of the freeze damage. At that time, new growth will tell you just how far back a plant has been killed. You can then prune out limbs that are brown and dead.

Glossary

Amendments. Organic materials or minerals used to improve the soil. Peat moss, pinebark, and compost are commonly used.

Annual. A plant that grows from seed, flowers, produces new seeds, and dies during a single growing season; a tropical plant treated as an annual in that it is grown for only a single season's display and then removed after it freezes.

Balled-and-burlapped. Describes a tree or shrub dug out of the ground with a ball of soil intact around the roots; the ball is then wrapped in burlap and tied for transport.

Balled-and-
burlapped

Bare-root

Bare-root. Describes a plant dug out of the ground and then shaken or washed to remove the soil from the roots.

Chlorosis. Yellowing of the foliage usually due to a lack of iron uptake in alkaline soils.

Compound leaf. A leaf consisting of two or more leaflets branching from the same stalk.

Container grown. Describes a plant raised in a pot that is removed before planting.

Crown. The part of a plant where the roots and stem meet, usually at soil level.

Cultivar. A cultivated variety of a plant, often bred or selected for some special trait such as double flowers, compact growth, cold hardiness, or disease resistance.

Deadheading. Removing spent flowers during the growing season to improve a plant's appearance, prevent seed formation, and stimulate the development of new flowers.

Deciduous. Describes a tree, shrub, or vine that drops all its leaves in winter.

Division. Propagation of a plant by separating it into two or more pieces, each piece possessing at least one bud and some roots. Plants commonly divided include perennials, bulbs, grasses, and ferns.

Division

Drainage. Movement of water through soil. If water poured into a foot-deep hole drains completely in a few hours, the drainage is good.

Drip line. An imaginary line beneath a tree that marks the perimeter of the tree's canopy. This area benefits from direct rainfall and "drip" from leaves. Because many of the tree's feeder roots are found along the drip line and beyond, this area is the best for fertilizing and watering.

Dry-laid. Describes a masonry path or wall that is installed without mortar.

Edging. A barrier that serves as the border between lawn and a planting bed. Edgings may be shallow trenches or barriers of plastic, brick, or metal.

Exposure. The characterization of a site according to the sun, wind, and temperature acting upon it.

Formal. Describes a style of landscaping that features symmetrical layouts, with beds and walks related to adjacent buildings, and often with plants sheared to geometric or other shapes.

Foundation planting. Traditionally, a narrow border of evergreen shrubs planted around the foundation of a house. Contemporary foundation plantings often include deciduous shrubs, grasses, perennials, and other plants as well.

Full shade. Describes a site that receives no direct sun during the growing season.

Full sun. Describes a site that receives at least eight hours of direct sun each day during the growing season.

Garden soil. Soil specially prepared for planting to make it loose enough for roots and water to penetrate easily. Usually requires digging or tilling and the addition of some organic matter.

Grade. The angle and direction of the ground's slope in a given area.

Ground cover. A plant providing continuous cover for an area of soil. Commonly a low, spreading foliage plant such as Asian jasmine, vinca, or lilyturf.

Habit. The characteristic shape of a plant, such as upright, mounded, columnar, or vase-shaped.

Hardiness. A plant's ability to survive the winter temperatures in a given region without protection.

Hardscape. Parts of a landscape, such as walks, walls, and trellises, made of wood, stone, or other materials.

Herbicide. A chemical used to kill plants. Preemergent herbicides are used to kill weed seeds as they sprout, and thus to prevent weed growth. Postemergent herbicides kill plants that are already growing.

Hybrid. A plant with two parents that belong to different species or genera.

Interplant. To use plants with different bloom times or growth habits in the same bed to increase the variety and appeal of the planting.

Invasive. Describes a plant that spreads quickly, usually by runners or seeds, and mixes with or dominates the adjacent plantings.

Landscape fabric. A synthetic fabric, sometimes water permeable, spread under paths or mulch to serve as a weed barrier.

Loam. Soil rich in organic matter and with mineral particles in a range of sizes. Excellent for many garden plants.

Microclimate. A small-scale system of factors affecting plant growth on a particular site, including shade, temperature, rainfall, and so on.

Mowing strip. A row of bricks or paving stones set flush with the soil around the edge of a bed, and wide enough to support one wheel of the lawn mower.

Brick mowing strip

Mulch. A layer of organic or other materials spread several inches thick around the base of plants and over open soil in a bed. Mulch conserves soil moisture, smothers weeds, and moderates soil temperatures. Where winters are cold, mulches help protect plants from freezing. Common mulches include compost, shredded leaves, pine straw, lawn clippings, gravel, cotton-seed hulls, and landscape fabric.

Native. Describes a plant that is or once was found in the wild in a particular region and was not imported from another area.

Nutrients. Elements needed by plants. Found in the soil and supplied by organic matter and fertilizers, nutrients include nitrogen, phosphorus, potassium, calcium, magnesium, sulfur, iron, and other elements, in various forms and compounds.

Organic matter. Partially or fully decomposed plant and animal matter. Includes leaves, trimmings, and manure.

Peat moss. Partially decomposed mosses and sedges. Dug from boggy areas, peat moss is often used as an organic amendment for garden soil.

Perennial. An herbaceous plant with a life span of more than two years, usually much longer. Cool-season perennials usually go dormant during the summer. Warm-season perennials go dormant during the winter.

Pressure-treated lumber. Softwood lumber treated with chemicals that protect it from decay.

Propagate. To produce new plants from seeds or by vegetative means such as dividing plant parts, taking cuttings, and grafting stems onto other plants.

Retaining wall. A wall built to stabilize a slope and keep soil from sliding or eroding downhill.

Rhizome. A horizontal underground stem from which roots and shoots emerge. Some swell to store food. Branched rhizomes (those of iris, for instance) can be divided to produce new plants.

Root-ball. The mass of soil and roots dug with a plant when it is removed from the ground; the soil and roots of a plant grown in a container.

Selective pruning. Using pruning shears to remove or cut back individual shoots in order to refine the shape of a shrub, maintain its vigor, or limit its size.

Selective pruning

Severe pruning

Severe pruning. Using pruning shears or loppers to cut away most of a shrub's top growth, leaving just short stubs or a trunk.

Shearing. Using hedge shears or an electric hedge trimmer to shape the surface of a shrub or hedge, or to deadhead annuals or perennials.

Soil pH. The alkalinity or acidity of the soil, which affects plant growth and nutrient uptake. Alkaline soils in the western two thirds of Texas are often amended with sulfur and iron products.

Specimen plant. A striking plant, often providing year-round interest, placed for individual display.

Spike. An elongated flower cluster on which individual flowers are attached directly to the main stem or are on very short stalks attached to the main stem.

Tender. Describes a plant that is damaged by cold weather in a particular region.

Underplanting. Growing short plants, such as ground covers, under a taller plant, such as a shrub.

Variegated. Describes foliage with color patterns in stripes, specks, or blotches.

Index

NOTE: Page numbers in **bold italic** refer to illustrations.

Photo Credits

Front Cover: *(main image)* Charles Mann, Antique Rose Emporium; *top left & top right* Richard Shiell; *top middle* Charles Mann

Back Cover: *left* Richard Shiell; *right* Saxon Holt

page 1: Charles Mann

page 7: Richard Shiell

page 8: Jrtmedia/Dreamstime.com

pages 18–19: Le-thuy Do/Dreamstime.com

page 23: *top left, top right & middle left* Jerry Pavia; *middle right* Saxon Holt; *bottom right* Greg Grant; *bottom left* Richard Shiell

page 26: *top left & middle right* Karen Bussolini; *top right* David McDonald; *bottom right* Rita Buchanan; *bottom left* Greg Grant

page 32: *top* Lauren Springer Ogden; *middle* Greg Grant; *bottom right* Rita Buchanan; *bottom left* Saxon Holt

page 38: *top left, top right & bottom right* Richard Shiell; *middle left* Rick Mastelli; *middle right* Saxon Holt; *bottom left* Greg Grant

page 43: *top* Richard Shiell; *middle left & middle right* Greg Grant; *bottom right* Ruth Rogers Clausen; *bottom left* Jerry Pavia

page 47: *top left* Richard Shiell; *top right & bottom right* Greg Grant; *middle left* Rita Buchanan; *middle right* Karen Bussolini; *bottom middle* Charles Mann; *bottom left* Galen Gates

page 50: *top left* Galen Gates; *top right* Rita Buchanan; *middle left* Jerry Pavia; *middle center* Charles Mann; *bottom right* Carole Ottesen; *bottom left* Greg Grant

page 54: *top left & top right* Charles Mann; *middle* Greg Grant; *bottom* Jerry Pavia

page 59: *top* Saxon Holt; *middle & bottom* Charles Mann

page 62: *top left* Jerry Pavia; *top right & bottom left* Richard Shiell; *middle right* Saxon Holt; *bottom right* Greg Grant

page 69: *top left & bottom left* Greg Grant; *top right* Charles Mann; *bottom right* Galen Gates

page 73: *top left* Jerry Pavia; *top right* Thomas Eltzroth; *middle left* Galen Gates; *middle right* Greg Grant; *bottom right* Saxon Holt; *bottom left* Charles Mann

page 77: *top & middle right* Greg Grant; *middle left* Rita Buchanan; *bottom* Charles Mann

page 83: *top* Richard Shiell; *middle* Jerry Pavia; *bottom* Greg Grant

page 86: *top* Thomas Eltzroth; *middle left, middle right & bottom* Greg Grant

page 90: *top left* Jerry Pavia; *top right* Richard Shiell; *middle right* Greg Grant; *bottom right* Charles Mann; *bottom left* Thomas Eltzroth

page 97: *top left & bottom left* Jerry Pavia; *top right & middle right* Rita Buchanan; *bottom right* Richard Shiell

page 103: *top left* Charles Mann; *top right & bottom left* Jerry Pavia; *bottom right* Saxon Holt

page 109: *top left* Karen Bussolini; *top right* Greg Grant; *middle right* Jerry Pavia; *bottom* Saxon Holt

page 115: *top left & bottom right* Jerry Pavia; *top right* Greg Grant; *middle right* Carole Ottesen; *bottom left* Galen Gates

pages 116–117: Zhou Minyun/Dreamstime.com

page 118: *left* Photos Horticultural/Michael and Lois Warner; *right* Saxon Holt

page 119: Charles Mann

page 120: *top* Charles Mann; *middle* Rita Buchanan; *bottom* Greg Grant

page 121: *top* Galen Gates; *bottom* Charles Mann

page 122: *top middle & bottom right* Jerry Pavia; *bottom left* Greg Grant

page 123: *top* Thomas Eltzroth; *middle* Greg Grant; *bottom* Charles Mann

page 124: Saxon Holt

page 125: *top* Jerry Pavia; *middle* Charles Mann; *bottom* Karen Bussolini

page 126: *top left* Charles Mann; *top right & bottom* Saxon Holt

page 127: *top left* Saxon Holt; *top right* Galen Gates; *bottom right* Richard Shiell

page 128: *top left* Jerry Pavia; *bottom left* Greg Grant; *bottom right* Charles Mann

page 129: *both* Jerry Pavia

page 130: *all* Charles Mann

page 131: *top* Carole Ottesen; *middle* Galen Gates; *bottom* Saxon Holt

page 132: *top* Rita Buchanan; *bottom* John Elsley

page 133: *left* Cheryl Richter; *right* Jerry Pavia

page 134: *bottom left* Richard Shiell; *bottom middle & middle right* Jerry Pavia; *top right & bottom right* Greg Grant

page 135: *top left & bottom right* Richard Shiell; *top right* Ruth Rogers Clausen

page 136: *top left* Charles Mann; *middle left* Karen Bussolini; *bottom left* Saxon Holt; *right* Richard Shiell

page 137: *top left* Galen Gates; *top right* Jerry Pavia

page 138: *top left & top right* Charles Mann; *bottom left* Greg Grant

page 139: *top* Charles Mann; *middle* Greg Grant; *bottom* Richard Shiell

page 140: *top* Thomas Eltzroth; *bottom* Richard Shiell

page 141: *both* Greg Grant

page 142: *top middle & bottom left* Richard Shiell; *bottom right* Greg Grant

page 143: *top right & bottom left* Charles Mann; *middle* Greg Grant; *bottom right* Saxon Holt

page 144: *top left* Greg Grant; *top right* Richard Shiell; *bottom* Charles Mann

page 145: *top left & bottom right* Charles Mann; *top right* Jerry Pavia; *bottom left* Richard Shiell

page 146: *left* Charles Mann; *right* Jerry Pavia

page 147: *top* Charles Mann; *bottom* Saxon Holt

page 148: *top & bottom left* Greg Grant; *bottom right* Jerry Pavia

page 149: *top left* Richard Shiell; *top right* Greg Grant; *middle* Jerry Pavia; *bottom* Charles Mann

page 150: *left* Jerry Pavia; *right* Saxon Holt

page 151: Brian Vanden Brink

pages 152–153: Nytumbleweeds/Dreamstime.com

page 221: Saxon Holt

page 222: Ruth Rogers Clausen

If you like *Texas Home Landscaping*,

check out these and other fine Creative Homeowner books

wherever books are sold.

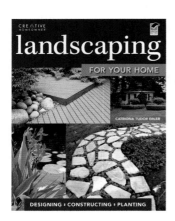

LANDSCAPING FOR YOUR HOME

Complete guide for all aspects of home landscaping.

Over 900 photographs and illustrations.
352 pp.
8½" × 10⅞"
$21.95 (US)
BOOK #: CH274600

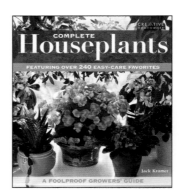

COMPLETE HOUSEPLANTS

Secrets to growing the most popular types of houseplants.

Over 480 photographs and illustrations.
224 pp.
9" × 10"
$19.95 (US)
BOOK #: CH274820

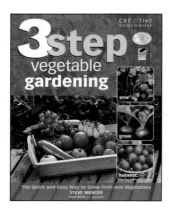

3 STEP VEGETABLE GARDENING

A quick and easy guide for growing your own fruit and vegetables.

Over 300 photographs.
224 pp.
8½" × 10⅞"
$19.95 (US)
BOOK #: CH274557

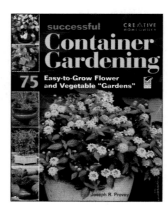

SUCCESSFUL CONTAINER GARDENING

Information to grow your own flower, fruit, and vegetable "gardens."

Over 240 photographs.
160 pp.
8½" × 10⅞"
$14.95 (US)
BOOK #: CH274857

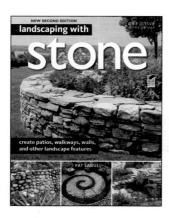

LANDSCAPING WITH STONE

Ideas for incorporating stone into the landscape.

Over 335 photographs.
224 pp.
8½" × 10⅞"
$19.95 (US)
BOOK #: CH274179

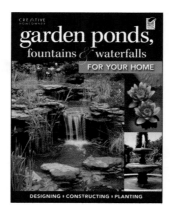

GARDEN PONDS, FOUNTAINS & WATERFALLS FOR YOUR HOME

Secrets to creating garden water features.

Over 490 photographs and illustrations.
256 pp.
8½" × 10⅞"
$19.95 (US)
BOOK #: CH274450

For more information and to order direct, go to **www.creativehomeowner.com**